Transgressive Readings

Transgressive Readings

The Texts of
Franz Kafka and Max Planck

Valerie D. Greenberg

THE UNIVERSITY OF MICHIGAN PRESS

Ann Arbor

1993 1992 1991 1990   4 3 2 1

Library of Congress Cataloging-in-Publication Data

Greenberg, Valerie D.
    Transgressive readings : the texts of Franz Kafka and Max Planck
Valerie D. Greenberg.
        p.   cm.
    Includes bibliographical references and index.
    ISBN 0-472-10158-7 (alk. paper)
    1. Discourse analysis. 2. Literature and science. 3. Kafka,
Franz, 1883–1924—Criticism and interpretation. 4. Planck, Max,
1858–1947. I. Title.
P302.G69 1990
401'.41—dc20   90-45985

For B. T.
on behalf of the animals
and their friends

Acknowledgments

Reversing the usual sequence, I want to first thank my husband, Robert A. Greenberg, M.D., for support and assistance far beyond the call of duty. He cheerfully and competently assumed the duties of a research assistant, combing the library, ordering out-of-the-way publications, photocopying, running errands, and generally saving me much precious time. Meanwhile, in spite of the many other heavy demands on him, he also managed the household and kept all of us well fed.

Among colleagues, my gratitude is extended especially to Sander Gilman, whose kindness, generosity, and creative genius have been of great help to me and to many others in the field. Sander is one of the truly interdisciplinary thinkers and scholars.

For some years now, I have been the fortunate recipient of eloquent support and critical inspiration from my former colleague at Duke University, James Rolleston. Since I have never properly thanked him, I shall do so here where his writings on Kafka have played a signal role.

I could not begin to know how to adequately thank my friends and colleagues Teresa and Chris Soufas for their good advice and for Chris's early, encouraging review of the manuscript.

I am indebted to Kate Hayles for her expert and helpful criticism of the manuscript. My appreciation is also extended to anonymous readers.

A Mellon Foundation grant for the program in literary theory at Tulane University financed my participation in a summer seminar led by J. Hillis Miller. Hillis's lectures and discussions stimulated my thinking in areas that proved productive for this study.

My interest in relations between science and literature was deepened by the poetry and person of Fred Chappell, in particular by his long poem *Midquest*. I have also learned a great deal from scientists—both from personal acquaintance and from their writings—whose interdisciplinary interests include the humanities. Years ago when I was teaching at Duke, I noticed that some of the best students in my literature classes were science majors. That piqued my curiosity sufficiently to wonder how those students related their intellectual efforts in disparate areas. Once an honors student majoring in chemistry who took my seminar on women in German literature left me with the cryptic comment that she had taken the literature course because it was "intellectual" in contrast to her science courses that were "analytical." She graduated, so I never had a chance to question her further, and I have been wondering ever since what she meant.

Contents

Introduction

Transgressing disciplinary boundaries means new questions can be posed and new insights gained about the nature of disciplinary models, conventions, and rhetoric. While cross-disciplinary inquiry provides an opportunity to examine knowledge in a revised context, it is at the same time a subversive undertaking since it is likely to violate the sanctuaries of accepted ways of perceiving. Among the most fortified boundaries have been those between the natural sciences and the humanities. Nonetheless, it can be argued that each requires consideration of the methods, language, and modes of thought of the other if it is to make optimally informed contributions not only to scholarship, but to understanding the most pressing challenges that face society and humanity in general, even life on earth. Each discourse can supply new critical perspectives on the other, suggesting alternative connections and reassessments of the shape, location, and ramifications of knowledge. Unyielding separation between the arts and the sciences is itself a historical construct and will, no doubt in the manner of all disciplinary divisions, change its character over time.

These are some of the imperatives that inform this study of literature and science. How does one define and practice interdisciplinarity? It seems to me that one of the most supportable approaches, in practice, is in terms of what the two otherwise apparently disparate disciplines share: language and textuality. While I do not offer definitions, in fact they are studiously avoided, I hope that my practice suggests an interdisciplinary model, at least for reading. As exemplary texts I have chosen the writings of two thinkers whose legacy helped determine the intellectual history of this century. Franz Kafka and Max Planck are no doubt a peculiar, but also, I believe, a legitimate, pair whose very incongruity enhances the notion of an intertextual dialogue of literature and science between texts as well as within texts and across history. Additional familiar figures who appear in the dialogue format are Friedrich Nietzsche, Sherlock Holmes, and John H. Watson, M.D.

Central to such a study is the problematizing of language on several levels. The view of language upon which my arguments depend encompasses a sense of the dubiousness and the limits of human language, albeit also of its immeasurable power. I agree with a statement by Paul M. Churchland: "The hole in this rationale is the claim that language is the primary canvass of representation. I suggest that it is quite obviously the *physical brain* that constitutes the primary canvass or instrument of world-representation, and that language is merely a device which permits distinct brains to engage in a collective rather than an individual process of improving their representations of reality. . . . And that it can do so *without* language is . . . patent."[1] We always seem to be searching — as if insecure of identity and needing affirmation — for marks that irrevocably distinguish the human from other species. Many of these distinguishing marks have been revealed as unsupportable constructs. Language, a primary one, may well be as complex, or more complex, among other species (including language in all its signing manifestations) than in its human versions; it is just that we can neither learn to "speak" nor comprehend the other. What we are left with is the ambivalent distinction of our texts — our language in its written form, ambivalent because it is the root of the trouble we have caused the living planet, yet it is also the source, repository, progenitor, and propagator of culture. If we have come to or are coming to the end of written texts, then we are coming — for better or for worse — to the end of a culture, including its most brilliant forms.

One era whose culture is judged by most standards to have been brilliantly productive is that of pre–World War I central Europe — the time when Kafka and Planck wrote the texts exam-

---

1. "Karl Popper's Philosophy of Science," *Canadian Journal of Philosophy* 5 (September 1975): 155.

ined here. This circumstance raises a second problem of language—that of the possible relationship between a national language and a way of viewing the world. To what extent, in other words, has an entire branch of science—one whose influence on this century can hardly be overestimated—been determined by the peculiarities of a national language? Did theoretical physics evolve, in the main, as it did because its first proponents wrote and thought in German? It is a knotty issue I do not address since I can see no justifiable way to investigate it or arrive at any supportable conclusions. While I freely use Whorf's writings in this study, I do differ from his interpretation of the discernible closeness of this connection. Suffice it to add that beyond its own realm and consequences, theoretical physics also established the models and the discourse of that second branch of science whose ramifications we can as yet neither grasp nor measure—modern molecular biology and genetics. The reason for this connection is the disillusionment of some of the leading physicists with their own science once it had led to the production of the atomic bomb, and their determination in the post–World War II period to devote themselves to what they saw as a science of life. Thus the vocabulary, the concepts, and the manner of investigation—dominated by reduction to the smallest constituent parts and by the impulse to manipulate and alter—was assumed from physics into the new field.[2]

In such a sequence, translation in the broadest sense shows its power. Translation in such a study as this one—which relies heavily upon the workings of grammar and syntax—is a central issue. Generally, I have done my own translating. The reason is that most other translations distort the very aspects of the text I need to examine, in their laudable attempt to produce an elegant

---

2. For this discussion I am indebted to Evelyn Fox Keller's lecture "Fractured Images of Science, Language, and Power: A Postmodern Optic, or Just Bad Eyesight?" presented at the seventh annual meeting of the Group for Research into the Institutionalization and Professionalization of Literary Studies, GRIP, Minneapolis, Minn., April, 1989, and to her book *A Feeling for the Organism. The Life and Work of Barbara McClintock* (New York: Freeman, 1983).

or at least normal-sounding English version. I have completely disregarded these two goals. Consequently, though I am a native speaker of English, my translations will often give the impression of having been worked out by someone in a lower- level language class. My sole interest was to be as accurate as possible in rendering the features of the text with which this study is most concerned.

One additional issue of "language" that must be addressed when one is examining scientific texts is mathematics. I use quotation marks because one of my arguing points is that mathematics is not a language but a rhetoric in relation to the text of natural language in which it is embedded. Mathematical *concepts* permeate this study and are absolutely essential to its arguments, but I do not examine the equations themselves, for the reason that it is, generally speaking, not equations, but the pattern of their connection to language that is of interest here.

Oddly enough, theorists such as Harold Bloom, Jacques Derrida, and Hayden White, whose works have influenced this study, themselves bracket scientific language from their intertextual, deconstructive, and tropological readings. Nevertheless, I have felt free to work their approaches into my readings of Planck's papers on theoretical physics. Without Derrida's thought, including the versions of his interpreters and commentators, I would not have been likely to break through old habits of reading. I also depend upon Bloom's notion of misreading and intertextuality, and upon White's conviction that logic itself follows tropological moves. White provides an evocative metaphor for this study with the etymology of the word *discourse*: suggesting "a movement 'back and forth' or a 'running to and fro.' This movement," he maintains, "may be as much prelogical or antilogical as it is dialectical."[3] Two of the goals of this study are to interrogate standard

3. Hayden White, *Tropics of Discourse: Essays in Cultural Criticism* (Baltimore: Johns Hopkins University Press, 1978), 3; Harold Bloom, *A Map of Misreading* (New York: Oxford University Press, 1975); and among Derrida's works, the two that play a special role in this study are "White Mythology: Metaphor in the Text of Philosophy," trans. F. C. T. Moore, *New Literary History* 6 (Autumn 1974): 5–74, and the essay on Kafka "Devant la Loi," trans. Avital Ronell, in *Kafka and the Con-*

logic, and to realize in itself the interdisciplinary principles it is investigating. For example, "oscillation" is both examined in the text and followed by the text in a self-conscious procedure.

My closest associates in the literature/science (or science/literature) project, however, are scholars who in their individual ways are creating interdisciplinary scholarship. Of the many who could be mentioned, I refer only to several whose work, because it integrates the sciences, is particularly congenial to this study: Michael A. Arbib and Mary B. Hesse's *The Construction of Reality*, Douglas R. Hofstadter's *Gödel, Escher, Bach: An Eternal Golden Braid*, and recent writings by N. Katherine Hayles. Another is Robert M. Markley who, in a recent paper, provides an apt description of this study in the course of characterizing his concept "interphysics": it "does not provide a metanarrative but a dynamic model of contested territories . . . ."[4]

Kafka scholars, including Walter Benjamin, have long recognized affinities to science and mathematics in Kafka's texts. A particularly insightful essay that implies such connections in *The Trial* is James Rolleston's Introduction to the volume of essays on *The Trial* that he edited. Other references can be found in the important recent collection *Kafka and the Contemporary Critical Performance*, edited by Alan Udoff whose introduction connects Kafka's work to physics. One of Stanley Corngold's excellent essays deals with patterns arguably scientific and mathematical: the double helix and recursion.[5] My reworking of the math/science connection in Kafka's texts is, however, different from all of these.

temporary Critical Performance: Centenary Readings, ed. Alan Udoff (Bloomington: Indiana University Press, 1987), 128–49.

4. "From Kant to Chaos: Physics, Metaphysics, and the Institutionalization of Knowledge," paper presented at the seventh annual meeting of GRIP, Minneapolis, Minn., April, 1989.

5. See especially Walter Benjamin's "Max Brod's Book on Kafka. And Some of My Own Reflections," in *Illuminations*, ed. Hannah Arendt, trans. Harry Zohn (New York: Harcourt, Brace and World, 1968), 141–48; James Rolleston, ed., *Twentieth Century Interpretations of* The Trial (Englewood Cliffs, N.J.: Prentice-Hall, 1976); Stanley Corngold, "Kafka's Double Helix," in *Franz Kafka: The Necessity of Form* (Ithaca, N.Y.: Cornell University Press, 1988), 105–36.

On the one hand it might seem that I have privileged Max Planck, since his texts are accorded more pages than Kafka's. This reflects less the greater volume of Planck's writings than my assumptions about the potential readership of this book. I presume that most readers will be more familiar with Kafka's texts than Planck's, and that it is therefore necessary to provide a larger chunk of Planck's writings and more explanatory material on early twentieth-century physics. I have also assumed that it is not necessary to provide evidence of the countless interpretations of Kafka's works. They continue to appear each year, including this one, so that one could constitute an entire private library made up only of Kafka criticism. Planck also has many interpreters, but, as far as I know, all are philosophers of science, historians of science, or physicists, and none has read Planck's work in terms of literary or linguistic features (other than to praise his style, as Einstein did on several occasions).

On the other hand, it is actually Kafka who plays a privileged role as a kind of *McGuffey's Reader*, a guide to reading, partly because Kafka has written a good deal about different kinds of reading.[6] We can get a sense of what kind of reader Kafka was from examining the reading strategies presented in his diaries. They send mixed messages. From his reading of Dostoyevski's *The Brothers Karamazov*, for example, we can tell that he is a strong misreader who inclines to a reading that subverts the narrator's.[7] From his reading of a passage in the daily newspaper we can tell that his perception of a text can function on two mutually exclusive levels. On one day he can read the text—which has to do with the question of Swedish neutrality in the war—unproblem-

---

6. In his recent excellent study, *Kafka's Rhetoric: The Passion of Reading*, Clayton Koelb finds that Kafka proposes and illustrates in his texts two fundamentally different kinds of reading—one that exercises a painful, wounding power over the reader, and one that requires less engagement and provides more pleasure (Ithaca, N.Y. : Cornell University Press, 1989). See especially chapter 4, "Two Readings of Reading."

7. *Tagebücher 1910–1923*, ed. Max Brod (Frankfurt am Main: S. Fischer, 1986), entry for 20 December 1914, 328. Translations mine.

atically, accepting it "as it is intended." Had he read it "three days earlier," however, he would have had the profound feeling ("bis in den Grund gefühlt") that it had been written by "a Stockholm ghost," and that its standard journalistic phrases were "creations of air" ("Gebilde aus Luft") that are accessible only to the eye, but not to the sense of touch ("die man nur mit dem Auge genießen, niemals aber mit dem Finger ertasten kann").[8] I take his metaphors to mean that there is a second kind of reading that breaks through to a level where language appears to be literal, where its nonreferentiality, its metaphorical nature is felt with such force that it is no longer possible to read anything "as it is intended." Kafka's reading of the news from Sweden demonstrates how language itself can construct meaning irrespective of subject matter, which is one of the main theses of my investigation of Kafka's and Planck's texts. Kafka turns the tables again, however, when he recounts his reading of the "legend" "Before the Law" together with his sometime fiancée, Felice Bauer. Felice was very attentive and made a "good observation." As a result, Kafka writes, "For the first time I realized the meaning of the story, . . . " ("Mir ging die Bedeutung der Geschichte erst auf, . . . ").[9] This suggests that there is one meaning and it can be discerned by one interpreter. He undercuts our conviction—gleaned from his own texts—of the instability and revisability of interpretation. In these brief selections—written at the time of the composition of *The Trial*—we see a spectrum from a confident, positivist reading to a reading that suggests that language can never be reliable. We will latch on to his coattails as a reader who can transport us from the scientific to the literary and back again.

A postscript: I hope that the brevity of this volume serves to compensate for the fact that it is designed to be read sequentially and in entirety. It is structured in recursive fashion so that each chapter grows out of and depends upon what precedes it.

---

8. *Tagebücher 1910–1923*, entry for 19 January 1915, 333.
9. *Tagebücher 1910–1923*, entry for 24 January 1915, 335.

CHAPTER I

Claret with Kafka and Planck, Watson and Holmes

He shook his head sadly.

"I glanced over it," said he. "Honestly, I cannot congratulate you upon it. Detection is, or ought to be, an exact science, and should be treated in the same cold and unemotional manner. You have attempted to tinge it with romanticism, which produces much the same effect as if you worked a love-story or an elopement into the fifth proposition of Euclid."

"But the romance was there," I remonstrated. "I could not tamper with the facts."

"Some facts should be suppressed, or, at least, a just sense of proportion should be observed in treating them."

— Arthur Conan Doyle, "The Sign of the Four"

I thought it was the first time in my life that I had so easily observed from the window an incident down in the street that concerned me so closely. In and of itself, this kind of observation is familiar to me from Sherlock Holmes.

— Franz Kafka, diary entry, January 5, 1912

The famous opening scene of "The Sign of the Four" shows the great detective about to slip into a cocaine-induced torpor when the above rather testy exchange with Watson occurs. It can be taken as a prototype of an old-fashioned dialogue between the literary and the scientific points of view. Old-fashioned because, at first glance, it seems to exemplify the cliché of "cold and un-emotional" "exact science," and geometry on the one hand, and the literary art or "romance" on the other. We have come a long way from those rigid categories on which C. P. Snow depended for his "Two Cultures" lecture in 1959. More characteristic for the

---

Epigraphs from *The Annotated Sherlock Holmes*, ed. William S. Baring-Gould (New York: Clarkson N. Potter, 1967), 1:611; and *Tagebücher 1910–1923*, ed. Max Brod (Frankfurt am Main: S. Fischer, 1986), 171. Translations mine.

present time is the title *One Culture: Essays in Science and Literature.*[1] It is understood today that science is embedded in culture just as literature is and therefore is subject to historical, ideological, and linguistic determinants, as are any other projects of the human intellect. At second glance, the brief excerpt from a Holmes-Watson dialogue suggests those very possibilities. Read against the grain of the obvious, it offers a model that subverts the notion of the straightforward division between the literary type and the logician-scientist, transposing them in a chiasmatic switch.

We are abetted in our sighting of subversion by Franz Kafka, who might well have read "The Sign of the Four." Kafka is identifying himself in the above quotation not with the "romance" writer Watson, but with the scrupulous observer and reader of signs, Holmes; that is, with the "science" of "detection"—a position suggesting the possibility of a reading of Kafka's texts that considers literature and science. By exploring the Holmes/Watson connection and Kafka's involvement, we are setting up a model for a dialogue between the scientific and the literary and ways of reading that dialogue. The dialogue is a classical one that ranges over history and implicates many texts. Detecting the dialogue and reading it require willingness to transgress "a consistently and heavily policed border"[2] between the disciplines. In this extralegal, transdisciplinary mission we enlist texts by Kafka and by Max Planck, founder of quantum physics. What has been written of Kafka's texts—"that the meaning of our century's entire history is compressed within them"[3]—could be maintained of the

---

1. C. P. Snow, *The Two Cultures and the Scientific Revolution* (Cambridge: Cambridge University Press, 1959); George Levine, ed., *One Culture: Essays in Science and Literature* (Madison: University of Wisconsin Press, 1987). A recent statement of these issues is Stephen Toulmin's "The Construal of Reality: Criticism in Modern and Postmodern Science," in *The Politics of Interpretation*, ed. W. J. T. Mitchell (Chicago: University of Chicago Press, 1983), 99–117.

2. John R. R. Christie, "Introduction: Rhetoric and Writing in Early Modern Philosophy and Science," in *The Figural and the Literal: Problems of Language in the History of Science and Philosophy, 1630–1800*, ed. Andrew E. Benjamin, Geoffrey N. Cantor, and John R. R. Christie (Manchester: Manchester University Press, 1987), 4.

3. James Rolleston, "Kafka-Criticism: A Typological Perspective in the Cen-

corpus of Planck's writings as well. Of Planck, it has been written that "[i]n December 1900 the German physicist Max Planck ushered in the twentieth century. . . . "[4] Kafka and Planck are among the most influential figures in the history of twentieth-century thought.

Looking once again at the excerpt from "The Sign of the Four," a Holmes fan might note, first of all, that the portrait of the two men is not accurate in the context of the story itself and of the other Holmes stories. Context, whether the language is that of cells in a living organism, or that of a text, supplies meaning. Holmes, after all, is the ultimate artistic personality—temperamental, musical (almost a virtuoso violinist), moody, unconventional, messy in his habits, a night owl, and a cocaine addict. Watson is the prosaic medical man. Thus we have a first transposition from the text above. The "scientific" Holmes suggests suppression of facts; the writer of romances, injecting interdisciplinarity and ethics, maintains that the facts encompass the romance *and* the geometry and cannot be tampered with. Holmes's remarks represent a venture into literary criticism, a trade for which he is clearly unsuited. The work he "cannot congratulate" Watson for is Watson's (and Conan Doyle's) first effort at writing up a Holmes adventure, the novel "A Study in Scarlet" (1887). As a literary critic, Holmes is hopelessly unaware, offering as a referential text only one of Euclid's propositions. Whereas by contrast, the Holmes stories themselves are examples of the self-conscious, self-reflexive mode—referring to themselves, whether to a real (such as "A Study in Scarlet") or an invented title, in many of the adventures. How does Watson perform as a reader of Holmes? The "literary" Watson as composer and narrator of the tales has control over the figure of Holmes. The reader gets to know Watson himself from the inside, through his descriptions of his own re-

---

tenary Year," in *Kafka's Contextuality*, ed. Alan Udoff (Baltimore: Gordian Press and Baltimore Hebrew College, 1986), 20.

4. Bruce Gregory, *Inventing Reality: Physics as Language* (New York: Wiley, 1988), 74.

actions and feelings, whereas Holmes we know through Watson's interpretation of Holmes.

Conan Doyle has apparently given the literary control over the scientific, "romanticism" over logic. The fatal flaw in this assertion is that, in fact, Holmes's practices illustrate neither logic nor anything that could reasonably be called a "science of deduction" (Holmes's appellation). The naming of Holmes's methods has no foundation in the methods themselves. Here we have another example of self-undermining, for by calling his methods "deductive," or "logical," Holmes is deconstructing the foundation of science and logical operations—the referentiality of naming. The only thing logical or scientific about Holmes's methods is his calling them that. "The Sign of the Four" is unusual in that it provides plenty of evidence that contradicts the self-namings of the Holmes stories. First of all, it is unique in presenting the reader with a resentful, truculent Watson, who not only asserts his own contrary interpretation of events, but also reviews and questions Holmes's methods:

Could there be, I wondered, some radical flaw in my companion's reasoning? Might he not be suffering from some huge self-deception? Was it not possible that his nimble and speculative mind had built up this wild theory upon faulty premises? I had never known him to be wrong, and yet the keenest reasoner may occasionally be deceived. He was likely, I thought, to fall into error through the over-refinement of his logic—his preference for a subtle and bizarre explanation when a plainer and more commonplace one lay ready to his hand. Yet, on the other hand, I had myself seen the evidence, and I had heard the reasons for his deductions. When I looked back on the long chain of curious circumstances, many of them trivial in themselves, but all tending in the same direction, I could not disguise from myself that even if Holmes's explanation were incorrect the true theory must be equally outré and startling. (658–59)

Watson's dialectical argument does not close with a synthesis. A subjunctive "if"-clause keeps the door open to the possibility of failed logic and the isomorphism of "true theory" with incorrect explanation. The partners do agree on cause-and-effect sequentiality — "chains" of events — but Watson suggests the possibility that Holmes's confidence could be grounded in "self-deception" or "faulty premises," options capable of undermining any logical argument. Thus we find the writer of "romance" engaging in metalogical analysis of the supposedly analytical half of the partnership. More than that, it is Holmes, not Watson, who peppers his conversation with quotations from Goethe and his eighteenth-century colleague, the prolific novelist Jean Paul — references that mark Holmes as the *homme des lettres*. Holmes, on the other hand, provides Watson with a disquisition on statistical probability, an abiding concern not only of Max Planck and other physicists, but of any contemporary branch of the sciences. One of Conan Doyle's presumptuous, bumbling detectives from Scotland Yard snidely calls Holmes "Mr. Theorist," asserting that "facts are better than theories, after all" (641). Conan Doyle's ironic choice of this "brusque and masterful professor of common sense" (659) to express such an opinion indicates that a contrary view of the relationship between "facts" and "theories" is intended. Thus we find ourselves allied with Holmes as advocate of the theoretical nature of interpretation, including interpretation that relies on "causes and inferences and effects" (640). This view accords with those philosophers of science who believe that the discovery of facts depends upon the theory set up to catch them.[5]

An additional noteworthy feature of "The Sign of the Four" is a connection to the natural world: one main character is a dog named Toby who leads Holmes and Watson on a scent, first heading in the wrong direction (through no fault of the dog's), then resuming an accurate pursuit. In the story, much is made of the Toby character (though critical commentary sorely neglects him) who comes home with Watson and Holmes and shares their breakfast. Closer to our concerns are remarks by Holmes and

---

5. For an overview of main directions in the philosophy of science, see Harold I. Brown, *Perception, Theory and Commitment: The New Philosophy of Science* (Chicago: University of Chicago Press, 1979). Toulmin's discussion is also pertinent.

Watson—"I am close on the track" and "he has evidently picked up the scent again" (659)—that merge Holmes with Toby. The analogy puts us "on the track" of the biological foundations of all pursuits, even of the "science of deduction." For sociobiologist E.O. Wilson "the binding force [between art and science] lies in our biology and in our relationship to other organisms."[6]

Why do I find a model in a mystery? Because the mystery in any Holmes/Watson story is not the mystery but the mystery of the relationship between the partners. Their stories are classics, the figures have become icons, their relationship an archetype. What would Watson be without Holmes, and Holmes without Watson? Each without the other would be only partial, a poor amputated remnant. They have been elevated to classics by the complex of crossings and partings and mutual interdependence that makes them partners and opponents in a dialogue and debate in which it would be inappropriate and unproductive to choose sides. "Perhaps, it suggests a new form of cultural analysis in which science and art should be understood as interrelated elements of a unique linguistic systematization that cannot be dissociated."[7]

Clearly, one must proceed with caution. The distinctions between the enterprises called "science" and "literature" are obvious, not to speak of the imprecision of those terms. There is, after all, no such thing as "science," which is in truth a complex of disparate endeavors, each operating within different discourses, nor is there a monolith called "literature." The sciences consist of many stages and processes amenable to different types of investigation. From those many stages I have culled the stage of the text—the communication of science in written language. A case can be made for science being primarily textual discourse; scien-

---

6. E.O. Wilson, *Biophilia* (Cambridge, Mass.: Harvard University Press, 1984), 63.

7. Edouard Morot-Sir, review of Wilda C. Anderson's *Between the Library and the Laboratory: The Language of Chemistry in Eighteenth-Century France*, in *South Atlantic Review* 51 (May 1986): 126.

tific facts and theories only become legitimate when they have been "put into texts and offered for the consumption of other readers—i.e., other scientists," at which time they can be "subject to further commentary and attempts at verification."[8] Richard Rorty suggests "another way of looking at physics": "What makes them physicists is that their writings are commentaries on the writings of earlier interpreters of Nature, not that they all are somehow 'talking about the same thing'. . . . "[9] Rorty also argues for the equal legitimacy of the various disciplinary discourses, the descriptions of the sciences being "on a par with the various alternative descriptions offered by poets, novelists, depth psychologists, sculptors, anthropologists, and mystics. The former are not privileged representations in virtue of the fact that (at the moment) there is more consensus in the sciences than in the arts."[10] I take these judgments as foundational for the examination of texts as a dialogue between the literary and the scientific. "The literary" and "the scientific" are notions that skirt the need to define literature or science, yet encompass the intersections between literary and scientific texts. Among the goals of this study is not to provide definitions, but to examine instead how different kinds of definitions operate.

Focusing on texts requires focusing on language and demands a set of descriptive tools that are themselves language and again implicated in the language under study. There can be no true metalanguage. We must reckon at the outset with questions Stephen Toulmin raises: "In what respects, and to what extent, are our choices of interpretation imposed on us by the exigencies of our subject matter? In what respects, and to what extent, are

8. William Frawley, "Science, Discourse, and Knowledge Representation: Toward a Computational Model of Science and Scientific Innovation," in *The Languages of Creativity: Models, Problem-Solving, Discourse*, Studies in Science and Culture, vol. 2, ed. Mark Amsler (Newark: University of Delaware Press, 1986), 69.

9. Richard Rorty, "Philosophy as a Kind of Writing: An Essay on Derrida," *New Literary History* 10 (Autumn 1978): 142.

10. Richard Rorty, *Philosophy and the Mirror of Nature* (Princeton: Princeton University Press, 1979), 362.

we free to make those choices on some other basis, or for reasons of other kinds?"[11] When we bring terms like symbol, allegory, and parable, for example, to the texts of Kafka, we are determining the outcome of the investigation by our choice of a *literary* metalanguage. When we bring terms like facts, logic, and objectivity to bear on the scientific texts of Max Planck we also predetermine the outcome of our reading. According to Gillian Beer, "the nature of discovery may be predetermined by the conditions for its description."[12] The disciplinary terms set parameters and limits. In that sense our language does the thinking for us, creating interpretation, in the end constructing what we call reality. Given the constraints of language, and the fact that *any* name imposes limitation and distortion, I attempt to circumvent the borders of disciplinarity by providing the rudiments of an overarching, transdisciplinary terminology. Beer suggests such a possiblity: "symmetry . . . simplicity, development, hierarchy, chance, . . . provide models, ideals, and implied narratives in science as much as literature."[13]

Within our framework of reading, models, text, and dialogue, there operates a set of terms with varying characteristics—from philosophical constructs to patterns to processes—that connect the texts of Kafka and Planck to each other and to other texts as well, and provide an interlocking support system for the notion of interdisciplinarity of texts. They are self-reflexive, in that they describe my procedures, but they also play a role in directing my readings of the texts. For example, my reading *oscillated* between Holmes and Watson in order to piece together a multidimensional picture. The term is borrowed from Max Planck's "oscillators," projected as a heuristic device to arrive at an explanation for anomalies in the measurements of radiation frequencies. The fact

---

11. Toulmin, "Construal of Reality," 113.

12. Gillian Beer, "Problems of Description in the Language of Discovery," in George Levine, ed., *One Culture*, 52 and 46.

13. Beer, "Problems of Description," 46. Wilson attributes the development of such desiderata of science and scientific discovery to the evolutionary requirements of the brain (*Biophilia*, 60).

that the oscillators were imagined to be something like electrons had little to do with the value of the concept, which depended upon its role in the context of the experimental vocabulary of turn-of-the-century theoretical physics. *Oscillation* describes behavior in electric currents, and occurs in biological, mathematical, and engineering descriptions. It is a quintessential transdisciplinary description and process. "The ideas of oscillation and vibration are essential to the study of the dynamics of nonmonotonic evolution, characterized by to and fro motion, regular or irregular. . . . [P]eriodic phenomena are ubiquitous in the inanimate world as well as in living organisms, which makes the study of periodic phenomena intrinsically important."[14] "Oscillatory phenomena" (3) can arise spontaneously in inanimate processes. "Periodic behavior" is as common in "biological systems" as in chemical systems and "inert matter" (7). Examples of biological rhythms are "respiration, cardiac muscle contraction, alternation of watchfulness and sleep, reproduction cycles in plants," "protein synthesis or metabolic activities," and "central nervous systems (EEG), as well as . . . the action potential of neurons responsible for the transmission of nerve signals" (7). James Gleick, in his review of the reorientations in mathematics and the sciences that are subsumed under the name *chaos theory*, uses the term *oscillation* in descriptions that encompass the new developments in all the scientific disciplines.[15]

One of Kafka's favored rhetorical and structural devices is the chiasmus that also plays a role in Planck's texts, and as figure, pattern, and idea in this investigation.[16] In rhetorical or literary terms

---

14. Pierre Berge, Yves Pomeau, and Christian Vidal, *Order within Chaos: Towards a Deterministic Approach to Turbulence* (New York: Wiley, 1984), 3.

15. *Chaos: Making a New Science* (New York: Viking, 1987).

16. For a different, but related discussion of the chiasmus and Kafka, see Stanley Corngold, "Metaphor and Chiasmus in Kafka," *Newsletter of the Kafka Society of America*, no.2 (December 1981): 23–31. A revised version appears in the volume *Franz Kafka: The Necessity of Form* (Ithaca, N. Y.: Cornell University Press, 1988), 90–104. The chiasmus is a central concern of Corngold's Kafka studies. It belongs to Corngold's agenda of affirmation, whereas I associate it with an agenda of subversion.

the chiasmus is a logically structured trope consisting of "the inversion of the order of syntactical elements in the second of two
juxtaposed and syntactically parallel phrases or clauses."[17] The
chiasmus is a preeminent example of the interdisciplinary term,
structure, and concept. There is evidence that, like hierarchy that
it appears to subvert, chiasmus is a pattern with roots deep in the
mind or experience. A study of children's first drawings showed
that a diagonal cross is one of the six basic diagrams they use.[18]
In genetics the chiasmata are sites on a chromosome where genes
are transposed, producing a "recombinant (crossover) chromosome which contains a combination of the alleles originally present on the two parental chromosomes"; it entails, in other words,
exchange and fusion. "Crossing-over is a reciprocal recombina-
tion event" that is less likely to occur, the closer, or more closely
linked two genes are on a chromosome.[19] It is a process on which
the genetic diversity of life forms depends. Not only our very
genetic makeup, but our vision, and thus our perception of the
world, depend upon the chiasmus. The optic chiasm is the site
where the optic nerve fibers from half of each retina cross, "the
left side of the visual field is thus 'seen' by the right side of the
brain." At the chiasm "the visual representation has . . . been
transformed from bilateral to unilateral," combining the two
fields of vision and therefore making perception of whole objects
possible.[20] On the level of simple engineering, the chiasm supplies structural support for scaffolding. It plays a related role in
this study. Since chiasm or chiasmus does not have a verb form,
it lacks the dynamic connotations of oscillation. The verb trans-

---

17. *Webster's Third New International Dictionary*, unabridged ed. (Springfield,
Mass.: Merriam-Webster, 1961).

18. Desmond Morris, *The Biology of Art: A Study of the Picture-Making Behaviour
of the Great Apes and its Relationship to Human Art* (New York: Knopf, 1962). The
"picture-making behaviour" of chimpanzees showed comparable basic structures.

19. C.B. Gillies, "Crossing-over (genetics)," in *McGraw-Hill Encyclopedia of
Science and Technology*, 6th ed., vol.4 (New York: McGraw-Hill, 1987), 523-24.

20. William D. Willis, Jr., and Robert G. Grossman, *Medical Neurobiology: Neuroanatomical and Neurophysiological Principles Basic to Clinical Neuroscience*, 3d ed. (St.
Louis: Mosby, 1981), 328-29.

pose, however, imparts the idea of an event to the crossover, making it applicable to processes.

A concept nearly universal in its disciplinary applications is "hierarchy." Hierarchy crosses not only all scientific disciplines, but also applies to sociology, politics, and religion. Language itself is hierarchical, its grammatical and syntactical forms organized according to strict ranking, with its main and subordinate clauses, for example, its nouns and verbs in the top ranks, and connectives in the lower. A description of hierarchy in ecosystems applies to language as well: "we normally adopt hierarchical explanations when dealing with complex systems. We look to higher levels for significance and to lower levels for mechanisms."[21] Species that live in groups organize themselves hierarchically. The brain, individual muscles, and genes are organized hierarchically. It is nearly impossible to avoid speaking of "levels," much as one might like to resist the authoritarian implications. Yet the notion of ordered grades is more complex than it appears at first glance. There are multiple interactions among vertical orders and subsystems that intersect many orders and each other.

One volume on hierarchical structures divides its contents into four basic categories: "Hierarchy in Concept," "Inorganic Hierarchical Structures," "Organic Hierarchical Structures," and "Hierarchy in Artifact," and includes the consideration of hierarchy in biology, epistemology and metaphysics, cosmology, and computer languages.[22] One of the topics most relevant to this study is that of boundaries in hierarchical systems. Implicit in our deliberations is the question of where the boundaries are between

21. R. V. O'Neill, D. L. DeAngelis, J. B. Waide, and T. F. H. Allen, *A Hierarchical Concept of Ecosystems* (Princeton: Princeton University Press, 1986), 56. The reference is to H. H. Pattee's article that connects hierarchy theory to Niels Bohr's interpretation of quantum mechanics (see my chap. 2): "The Complementarity Principle in Biological and Social Structures," *Journal of Social and Biological Structures* 1 (April 1978): 191–200.

22. Lancelot Law Whyte, Albert G. Wilson, and Donna Wilson, eds., *Hierarchical Structures* (New York: American Elsevier, 1969).

the systems called disciplines, within the systems called texts, and among language structures; and how do we manage their violation. Lancelot Law Whyte, "finds that the concept of 'a sequence of higher and lower levels' has been important in western thought since Plato."[23] Defining it in a uniform way is another matter, and the diversity in *Hierarchical Structures* alone shows that to be impossible. One mathematical version of hierarchy, however, has particular applicability to Kafka's texts:

... in 1907 the Irish-born physicist, Fournier d'Albe, published a diagram and a numerical description of an infinite hierarchical universe, designed to meet the Olbers radiative and Seeliger gravitational conditions, built on an octahedral principle from the smallest to infinitely large units. The six parts at each level are at the vertices of a regular octahedron, itself repeated six times at the next level, and so on, generating in this case a hierarchy of empty centres.[24]

We shall see that the notion of a "hierarchy of empty centres" organized by mathematical logic is applicable to Kafka's texts. Categories related to hierarchy that have central applications in this study are exclusion, mastery, order/disorder, and law—all of which are also descriptions of language.

Another pattern or system that operates in mathematics, logic, computer functions, and biological systems is *recursion*. Recursion depends upon and produces hierarchical orders, and like hierarchy, has many definitions according to context. A simple one is "a process that operates on the product of its own operation."[25] Recursion, however, is more fundamental and pervasive than that

23. Reported by Donna Wilson, "Forms of Hierarchy: A Selected Bibliography," in *Hierarchical Structures*, 288.

24. Lancelot Law Whyte, "Structural Hierarchies: A Challenging Class of Physical and Biological Problems," in *Hierarchical Structures*, 10. On Fornier d'Albe (1868–1933) see also the mixed assessment by mathematician Benoit B. Mandelbrot, inventor of fractal geometry which is important to my study (chap. 3), in Benoit B. Mandelbrot, *The Fractal Geometry of Nature*, rev. ed. (San Francisco: W.H. Freeman, 1983), 396.

25. Humberto R. Maturana and Francisco J. Varela, *The Tree of Knowledge: The*

brief definition indicates. The procedure it describes is a universal one, ranging from its role in the transmission of genetic information, to language, the solution of equations, computer functions, music, brain function, and thought processes themselves. Life itself emerged from autocatalytic systems "where each molecular entity plays a part in catalyzing the production of the next entity."[26]

The discussion of recursion, its forms, and its implications that is most influential in this study is found in Douglas R. Hofstadter's *Gödel, Escher, Bach: An Eternal Golden Braid.*[27] Hofstadter's book is exemplary because of its true interdisciplinarity, its exemplification of "trans-" in the many possibilities that prefix offers, such as transgression, transposition, translation, transaction, or transference. I test these terms on selected texts; Hofstadter more boldly exercises the "trans-" on categories such as music and visual art, number theory, physics, theoretical biology, and artificial intelligence. Recursivity is apparent in the composition of his text, as it is at some points in this one. Recursion can also be called back-reference or nesting, and entails moving from one level to the next smaller, lower, or simpler level in the same operation by means of duplication or repetition of an element or elements. Hofstadter illustrates the idea as stories inside stories, paintings inside paintings, parenthetical comments inside parenthetical comments. All language is recursive, involving the nesting of structures within structures, but the German language is particularly so since grammatical units can be framed by parts of verbs or verb forms. After exploring recursion in several contexts, Hofstadter also finds it in particle physics:

We have seen recursion in the grammars of languages, we have seen recursive geometrical trees which grow upwards forever, and we have

---

Biological Roots of Human Understanding, trans. Robert Paolucci (Boston: New Science Library, 1988), 253.

26. O'Neill, et al., *Hierarchical Concept*, 108.

27. New York: Vintage, 1980. See also William Poundstone's interesting study of a computer game, *The Recursive Universe: Cosmic Complexity and the Limits of Scientific Knowledge* (Chicago: Contemporary Books, 1985).

seen one way in which recursion enters the theory of solid state physics. Now we are going to see yet another way in which the whole world is built out of recursions. This has to do with the structure of elementary particles: electrons, protons, neutrons, and the tiny quanta of electromagnetic radiation called "photons." We are going to see that particles are—in a certain sense which can only be defined rigorously in relativistic quantum mechanics—nested inside each other in a way which can be described recursively, perhaps even by some sort of "grammar."

. . . What happens is that no particle can even be defined without referring to all other particles, whose definitions in turn depend on the first particles, etc. (142). . . . The grammar is a result of basic laws of physics, such as conservation of energy, conservation of electric charge, and so on. And, like the grammar of human languages,[28] this grammar has a recursive structure, in that it allows deep nestings of structures inside each other. (145)

A pattern as fundamental to language as recursion must have implications for the process known as reading. Mathematician Mitchell Feigenbaum's phrase "things work on themselves again and again" (Gleick, *Chaos*, 185) in discussing the conceptual operations that led to his calculation of the mathematical order in nonlinear systems also tells us the story of the imposition of order that goes on in the course of reading a text. Reading continually "operates on the product of its own operation," producing, like an autocatalytic system, the next stage by incorporating new information into an open, unstable system.

I have designated oscillation, chiasmus, hierarchy, and other features variously as *systems, constructs, terms, words, concepts, ideas, structures,* and *features.* The lack of uniformity is intended. This group of terms defies categorization, some falling into one or the other or all of the above categories. If they defy categorization, do they also escape the inevitable self-implication of language, transcending to metalanguage? I would contend, instead, that

---

28. I need to stipulate here that from the perspective of this text, particles as described are also a "grammar of human language" (as opposed to being *Nature, Reality, Truth,* or *Essence*).

collectively such a group of designations can take us further toward transdisciplinary readings than can purely literary or purely scientific terminology. They suggest not a metanarrative, but a dynamic model of relations between literary and scientific language that not only discerns transpositions within texts but also encompasses its own transpositions by reading literature in a scientific way and science in a literary way.

Although in each disciplinary context connotations and applications of transgressive terminology will be different, a unifying character remains.[29] In the cases of *oscillation, chiasmus, hierarchy,* and *recursion*, that character may depend upon pattern recognition. These and other patterning operations interact to reveal textual meanings beyond the ostensible ones. Margolis writes:

That pattern-recognition is central to thinking is a familiar idea. . . . So it is essentially universal to concede an essential role to the cuing of patterns and patterned responses; but the articulation of just what is happening when a pattern is recognized is an unsolved problem. Because so little can be said, the dominant tendency (until very recently, at least) has been to move as quickly as possible from pattern-recognition to some algorithmic, rule-following procedure which can be articulated in a discussion and perhaps instantiated on a computer program.[30]

Margolis disagrees that a "viable cognitive theory must be implementable as a computer program," and denies the privileging of logic as the true story of reasoning. He maintains, on the con-

29. William Paulson provides a useful comment on what I call transgressive terminology: "a concept such as redundancy that is not inherently limited to the theory of information becomes at once more specific and more complex as a result of its articulation within that theory, and can retain something of this meaning when returned to its original field or imported into yet another territory. This process may in turn lead to new kinds of conceptual thought concerning the literary text, . . ." *The Noise of Culture: Literary Texts in a World of Information* (Ithaca, N.Y.: Cornell University Press, 1988), 65–66. From my perspective, however, "can retain something of this meaning" understates the power of a term such as *chiasmus*, for example, to remain fundamentally intact in changing fields.

30. Howard Margolis, *Patterns, Thinking, and Cognition: A Theory of Judgment* (Chicago: University of Chicago Press, 1987), 3.

trary, that "[p]attern-recognition is all there is to cognition" (3), and that "rule-following processes, including logic, must be reduced to pattern-recognition, and not the reverse" (4), even though "no one can say much yet about what the brain is doing when it recognizes a pattern" (3). Our examination of Kafka's and Planck's texts will generally accord with the argument made by Margolis that "reasoning is a specialization of pattern-recognition applied to language," and that logic "is a by-product of the capacity for informal reasoning (pattern-recognition applied to patterns of language)" (61). That is, I am privileging the category "patterns" over the category "logic," although those patterns can demonstrate a rigor, particularly in Kafka's texts, that lead me to refer to them as a peculiar kind of logic, or "antilogic," thus, once again, dislodging and mixing nicely defined categories.

Pattern recognition is itself a queasy concept. On the one hand there is "the human imagination which leads us to discover in the universe the patterns that our minds have put there. The utmost resourcefulness and probity of language are needed, both by scientists and poets, to outwit the tendency of description to stabilize a foreknown world and to curtail discovery."[31] Kafka's and Planck's texts, in their disparate ways, incorporate this cautionary note that extends as well to their readers. Caution is in order. On the other hand, according to the results of recent research on the dynamic structures of proteins—on which all life processes depend—they "show signs of what paleontologists call convergent evolution. Nature seems to favor certain kinds of shapes, which appear again and again with slight variations. . . ."[32] We discover or apply everywhere patterns that require interpre-

---

31. Beer, "Problems of Description," 56.

32. James Gleick, "Secret of Proteins is Hidden in Their Folded Shapes," *New York Times*, June 14, 1988. Rudolf Arnheim offers an interdisciplinary exploration of the perception of shapes and pattern in the visual arts in connection with mathematical and physical concepts in *The Power of the Center* (Berkeley: University of California Press, 1982); further stimulating explorations can be found in Gyorgy Kepes, ed., *Structure in Art and Science* (New York: George Braziller, 1965) and in Cyril Stanley Smith, *A Search for Structure: Selected Essays on Science, Art, and History* (Cambridge, Mass.: MIT Press, 1981).

tation. Does it matter whether we are recognizing patterns or imputing them based on our neurological makeup? Since we have no way of finding out the "truth," we must operate as if we were recognizing patterns and bracket the other option pending further news.

The concept of language that this study presumes is elaborated in Michael A. Arbib and Mary B. Hesse's *The Construction of Reality*,[33] a work that integrates the philosophy of science, epistemology, language theory, and neurobiology. The authors challenge positivistic, or "verificationist," views with a model of cognition that consists of networks of "schemas." They propose a recursive process of acquisition and formation of knowledge: "we 'construct' the natural world in a complex feedback process in which theoretical models and sensory input are assimilated and accommodated in a self-modifying sequence of prediction and test" (176). Their view of language is that all language is metaphorical. There can be no language that is literally referential, "assimilated to an ideal logic," or purified of tropes (150). They are opposing the "literalist view of language" (148) that has been "bound up since the seventeenth century with . . . scientific method" (154). "In the seventeenth century, the rise of science was accompanied by the conception of an 'ideal language' that would enable us to read off from the 'book of nature' the true science that exactly expresses reality. . . . Human ideal language for purposes of science will be language that has exactly one name for each distinct essence, and its grammar will reproduce the real causal relations among essences in the world" (149). The metaphor of reading the language of the book of nature is still prevalent in some scientific circles. This view of language is rejected, of course, not only by Arbib and Hesse, but by many contemporary thinkers. Lakoff and Johnson show how metaphor, no longer apparent as such, pervades and directs even our most ordinary everyday usage.[34] For these writers, as for Arbib and Hesse, "meaning

---

33. (Cambridge: Cambridge University Press, 1986).

34. George Lakoff and Mark Johnson, *Metaphors We Live By* (Chicago: University of Chicago Press, 1980).

changes, or tropes, of various kinds are, in fact, pervasive in language."[35] Arbib and Hesse's views are particularly congenial to this study because of the deep familiarity with the sciences and history and philosophy of science on which their conclusions are based. Their reasoning provides support for reading Max Planck's texts for their metaphorical content:

> It may be thought that these considerations apply only to "literary" uses of metaphor and that scientific use of language must necessarily abstract from vague meaning associations and evaluations. But if we look at the implications of recent discussions of the theory ladenness of observation, of realism and the use of scientific models, we find that use of language in scientific theory conforms closely to the metaphoric model. Scientific revolutions are, in fact, metaphoric revolutions, and theoretical explanations should be seen as metaphoric redescriptions of the domain of phenomena.[36]

It is important to add their proviso: "[this] does not mean, however, that the metaphoric view entails abandonment of logic and deduction in science" (157). They make a distinction between the types of metaphoric usage in literature and in science, where metaphors "are extended and developed by logic as well as by analogy" (157) — a distinction that I dispute in my readings of Kafka's and Planck's texts.

Although Arbib and Hesse make no reference to Nietzsche, there are close correspondences between their views on language and metaphor and those expressed by Nietzsche in his essay "On Truth and Lie in an Extramoral Sense" (1873). Since I have taken

---

35. Arbib and Hesse, *Construction of Reality*, 150.

36. Arbib and Hesse, *Construction of Reality*, 156. There is an enormous body of literature on metaphor in science. See, for example, Mary Hesse's *Revolutions and Reconstructions in the Philosophy of Science* (Bloomington: Indiana University Press, 1980), and the writings of Max Black. Selected related examples are Thomas S. Kuhn, "Metaphor in Science," in *Metaphor and Thought*, ed. Andrew Ortony (Cambridge: Cambridge University Press, 1979), 409–19; and Nancy Leys Stepan, "Race and Gender: The Role of Analogy in Science," *ISIS* 77 (June 1986): 261–77, which shows how metaphors charged with powerful ideologies can control and shape science.

that essay as a model for the literary-scientific dialogue (chap. 2), its relationship with the Arbib and Hesse thesis on language is particularly relevant. Nietzsche shares the notion of the inescapable metaphorical nature of language. He does not, however, make the distinction that Arbib and Hesse make between scientific and literary uses of metaphor. Nietzsche would subscribe to their assessment: "that the historical sequence of fundamental theories do [sic] not exhibit convergence toward universal truth in any ideal language. Perhaps there is no such language, in which case there are no strictly universal laws of nature, only discoverable regularities in our local (though large) regions of space and time" (158). If we leave out "perhaps" and "(though large)," these ideas could have come directly from Nietzsche's text. The question of "universal laws of nature" is one we will pursue in Max Planck's texts in conjunction with Nietzsche's. Like Nietzsche, Arbib and Hesse associate science with the disenchantment of the world, with its "objectification" (160) and its resultant manipulation for the sake of mastery. And they believe, as Nietzsche does, that metaphor "entails some loss of information about the world," since "no two particular objects or events share *exactly* the same properties" (151). "[I]n practice . . . language works by capturing *approximate* meanings . . ." (152). For Nietzsche, metaphor and language itself depend upon erasing the fine distinctions inherent in the "essence of things."

While metaphor is a rhetorical structure and linguistic process as fundamentally descriptive of scientific as it is of literary texts, it differs from transgressive terminology in that it is not in use in the scientific disciplines. The distinction between literary-rhetorical concept and universal pattern is analogous to the dialogue between story telling and logic *within* Kafka's and Planck's texts as well as *between* them. The "law" of this study is dialogue—the dialogue of a text with itself as well as with other texts.[37] That dialogue may go by several related names; I have

---

37. This is not related to the dialogics of Bakhtin. Suffice it to mention only his insistence upon the separateness of artistic discourse, the overriding impor-

chosen to call it a dialogue between the literary and the scientific. Am I suggesting conjunctions as strange as the one Holmes thinks up to shock Watson? That is, do I propose to "work a love story or elopement into the fifth proposition of Euclid"? In a word, yes—more or less. The challenge is to determine, if possible, whether Kafka or Planck is the love story or the geometry, or both.

Planck's discovery of the unit of energy he called the *quantum* led to a revolution in twentieth-century thought. He is, like Kafka, a figure whose work has stood for the questioning, undermining, and ultimate displacement of secure worldviews. Kafka and Planck have each provided a metaphor that spans the century. One can hardly avoid coming across a term used in all Western languages and cultures: *Kafkaesque*.[38] Although the term has developed its own diffuse connotations, quite apart from any connection with Kafka or his works, it can be associated, generally speaking, with uncertainty, in particular uncertainty in the face of unpredictable and often labyrinthian workings of an inaccessible entity that determines the fate of helpless individuals.

Planck's investigations in theoretical physics resulted in another powerfully connotative term: *Planck's constant*. What it represents and initiated—quantum physics—is foundational for the modern world. A *constant* is a measurement in physics that is true and unchanging under all imaginable conditions; for example, the speed of light is a constant. Planck's constant—represented by a very small number (6.6×10^{-27}) and the letter h—is a unit by which a quantum of energy is calculated. The formula is: e (energy) =

---

tance of genre, the stylistic uniqueness of the novel, the "social tone," and the "combining of languages and styles into a higher unity." See especially the essay "Discourse in the Novel," in *The Dialogic Imagination: Four Essays by M. M. Bakhtin*, ed. Michael Holquist, trans. Caryl Emerson and Michael Holquist (Austin: University of Texas Press, 1981).

38. For a review of the history and current usage of Kafkaesque, see Kurt Neff, "Kafkas Schatten. Eine Dokumentation zur Breitenwirkung" in Hartmut Binder, ed., *Kafka-Handbuch* (Stuttgart: Kröner, 1979), 2:881–88.

h (Planck's constant) times *v* (frequency of radiation). The discovery that this constant represents was the discovery that energy is not continuous, but moves instead as separate or discrete units or jumps (quanta). Up to Planck's time, one of the axioms of physics was that nature never makes jumps; energy, and thus motion and matter, are all continuous. "Logically, this assumption is tantamount to the strict determination of the future. Quantum theory, on the other hand, asserts a restriction on the extent to which we can determine physical quantities. It thus also implies a limited determination of the future."[39] Planck's proof of discontinuity therefore gave rise to uncertainty that shook the foundations not only of physics, but by implication also of metaphysics, including the notion of causality. It led eventually, through the work of Albert Einstein, Niels Bohr, Werner Heisenberg, and others, to the deciphering of the atom and all of the momentous consequences of that knowledge. Max Born, fellow theoretical physicist and Nobel laureate who had worked with Planck, wrote of the discovery of the quantum:

There is no doubt that it was an event of the first order, comparable with the scientific revolutions brought about by Galileo and Newton, Faraday and Maxwell. Like these it has changed the whole aspect of physics and deeply influenced all neighbouring sciences, from chemistry to biology. Its philosophical implications reach far beyond the epistemology of science itself into the deepest roots of metaphysics.[40]

Planck did not foresee these results when he worked out the equations that led to them and when he first presented his work in 1900; most physicists did not accept the implications until over a decade later. Planck, in fact, resisted for many years the notion that his discovery could not be encompassed by classical physics

---

39. Friedrich Hund, *The History of Quantum Theory*, trans. Gordon Reece (New York: Harper and Row, 1974), 16.

40. Max Born, "Max Karl Ernst Ludwig Planck," *Obituary Notices of Fellows of the Royal Society* 6 (1948): 161–80, reprinted in *The World of the Atom*, eds. Henry A. Boorse and Lloyd Motz (New York: Basic Books, 1966), 1:462.

and did everything he could think of to disprove that revolution-ary consequence. Kafka, of course, resisted the consequences of his work in a different manner, attempting to erase its traces. Nei-ther succeeded in his efforts. These two reluctant mothers[41] of metaphor brought forth concepts so powerful that they are still effective after all that has intervened since their time.

The first objection that might be raised to calling Planck's con-stant a metaphor is the scientific one: over and over again the measurement has proved that it describes how things really work. "[I]t appears in all atomic, nuclear, and high energy processes." It is responsible for the stability of life processes: "[i]f action were not quantized, even small environmental changes would change the genetic structure, but the existence of a quantum of action means that genes retain their structures unless enough energy, let us say in the form of a high-energy photon, is absorbed to disrupt this structure. Thus genes can only change their structure discon-tinuously and not gradually."[42]

I would respond that Kafkaesque also tells a reliable story of how things really work, down to the level of life functions. The difference between them has to do with the location of the ob-server. It also has to do with whether the observer has tools, in the form of sophisticated measuring instruments. Planck's con-stant is not discernible on the macroscopic level. "That h is a very small number indicates that the discontinuities in nature are very minute. To the unaided eye, therefore, action, . . . energy, radi-ation, all appear continuous. Only to the physicist who peers deeply into matter and observes the behavior of the tiny individ-ual components of matter (electrons, atoms, protons, neutrons) are the discontinuities apparent, and the need for a finite h and a quantum theory obvious."[43] To the unaided eye, the reader of

---

41. A strange idea suggested by Kafka's diaries in which there are several refer-ences to pregnancy and birth in connection with Kafka's person and with the process of writing.

42. Boorse and Motz, eds., *The World of the Atom*, 1:490.

43. Boorse and Motz, eds., *The World of the Atom*, 1:490.

history books and newspapers, the victim of political terror, tor-
ture, repression, arbitrary bureaucracy, organized crime, or just
a frighteningly unexplainable and uncontrollable situation, the
need for the term and concept *Kafkaesque* is also obvious. Distance
radically changes configuration and character. The laws and logic
that prevail on the level of atomic and subatomic particles are not
the laws and logic of the world of the unaided eye. And yet there
is a transgressive term that crosses that boundary between the
everyday large and the unimaginably small. The term is *uncertainty*. It is the overarching creation and consequence of both
metaphors. *Kafkaesque* is a term for *not* knowing. *Planck's constant*,
however, is a term for ultimate knowing; a constant is the permanently and irrevocably true. For Planck, constants "must of
necessity retain their meaning for all time and for all cultures,
even extra-terrestrial and extra-human ones."[44] We have the
paradox that metaphysical uncertainty was introduced by that
which is most certain.

Prigogine and Stengers put the paradox in different terms:

Universal constants not only destroy the homogeneity of the universe
by introducing physical scales in terms of which various behaviors become qualitatively different, they also lead to a new conception of objectivity. No observer can transmit signals at a velocity higher than that of
light in a vacuum. Hence Einstein's remarkable conclusion: we can no
longer define the absolute simultaneity of two distant events; simultaneity can be defined only in terms of a given reference frame.[45]

However, relativity, to which Prigogine and Stengers refer here,
did not fundamentally break with classical physics. The true
revolution and most disturbing paradoxes resulted from the earlier discovery by Planck.

---

44. Max Planck, "The Unity of the Physical World-Picture," trans. Ann Toulmin, in *Physical Reality: Philosophical Essays on Twentieth-Century Physics*, ed. Stephen
Toulmin (New York: Harper and Row, 1970), 19.

45. Ilya Prigogine and Isabelle Stengers, *Order Out of Chaos: Man's New Dialogue
with Nature* (New York: Bantam, 1984), 217–18.

It is important to note just what Planck did as a theoretical physicist, for it does not accord with the usual image of the working scientist struggling over results in his laboratory. Once his student days were over, Planck never touched a laboratory experiment. What he did is known as *Gedankenexperimente*—"thought experiments." (The original German term is frequently used in English-language texts on theoretical physics.) That is, using equations, and taking into consideration known physical results, he worked out problems in his head, then presented his hypotheses in lectures or articles.

Planck's papers, like *The Trial*, are founded on and conjure up a restricted fictional world within which a drama is enacted in language. It is obvious that the "world" of a text called, for example, "On the Theory of the Energy Distribution Law of the Normal Spectrum" will be one within limited parameters. Less obvious is a relationship between a scientific text and drama or fiction. On December 14, 1900, Planck read before the German Physical Society in Berlin a lecture that can be said (though no one realized it at the time) to have ushered in the atomic age. It was the first public presentation of the equations upon which the quantum of action depends. The first sentence of the theoretical exposition reads as follows: "In a diathermic medium with a light velocity c and surrounded by reflecting walls are found, in appropriate separation from each other, a large number of linear, monochromatically vibrating resonators . . . ."[46] In a 1911 paper entitled "On the Hypothesis of Quantum Emission," the opening sentence of the theoretical exposition reads: "Let us imagine, in the familiar

---

46. Max Planck, "Zur Theorie des Gesetzes der Energieverteilung im Normalspektrum," 1st pub. in *Verhandlungen der Deutschen Physikalischen Gesellschaft* 2 (1900): 237–45, in Max Planck, *Physikalische Abhandlungen und Vorträge* (Braunschweig: Vieweg, 1958), 1:700. This three-volume set, the most accessible collection of Max Planck's scientific publications and lectures, will be referred to in future notes as *PAV*. Translations are mine. English translations of the paper are available in the following volumes: *Planck's Original Papers in Quantum Physics*, German and English ed., ed. Hans Kangro, trans. D. ter Haar and Stephen G. Brush (London: Taylor and Francis, 1972), 38–45; D. ter Haar, *The Old Quantum Theory* (Oxford: Pergamon, 1967), 82–90.

manner, a spatially wide-expanded vacuum, filled with stationary black radiation and bordered by reflecting walls, and resting in that vacuum, at appropriate distances from each other, a large number N of linear, homogeneous oscillators absorbing and emitting radiation with the frequency v. . . . "[47] The question treated in these papers is the nature of black-body radiation, which refers to the behavior of radiation inside an imagined hollow enclosure that is heated to different temperatures. The radiation is transmitted by imaginary, microscopic elements called "oscillators" (Planck originally called them "resonators") that emit the same energy as a perfectly black body does. In Planck's papers, "let us imagine" is a recurring phrase — similar to "let's pretend" or "once upon a time" — that introduces the premises of a fairy tale-like world, more fanciful and thrilling than the following matter-of-fact premise: "Someone must have slandered Joseph K., for one morning, without having done anything bad he was arrested."[48] Both, however, invite creation and imposition of new fictions to complete and extend their narratives — the inevitable response of the reader/interpreter.

If papers on theoretical physics can have a story-telling quality, it is not surprising to discover that the entity called *the court* in *The Trial* shares some features with the black-body radiation thought experiment. It is an organic unity, called (by Josef K.'s lawyer) a great "court organism" [*Gerichtsorganismus*, 104] that remains eternally in suspension [*ewig in der Schwebe*, 104]. When subjected to a disturbance it compensates for the disturbing factor and restores its own equilibrium. The file in an active case proceeds as does radiation in the imaginary, heated enclosure: it "remains in circulation, as required for uninterrupted office traffic, is directed to the higher courts, returns to the lower ones, and thus swings up and down with larger and smaller oscillations, with larger and smaller delays" (136). The isomorphism apparent

---

47. *PAV*, 2:261.
48. Franz Kafka, *Der Prozeß*, ed. Max Brod (Frankfurt am Main: S. Fischer, 1986), 7.

between the experimental and the literary patterns could, perhaps, be described as metaphorical in nature. But to what single metaphor could such a complex pattern be reduced? A different kind of transdisciplinarity seems to be at work that cannot be reduced to a rhetorical trope. It appears we are dealing with what Gleick (with reference to Goethe's theory of color) calls "boundary conditions and singularities" (165). The most important difference between the processes described as isomorphic patterns is expressed in the sentence in Kafka's text that immediately follows the above quotation: "These paths are incalculable" (136). By contrast, Max Planck calculated the frequencies of the energy emitted by the entities he imagined oscillating in the enclosure. What he came up with was calculable but unbelievable and unacceptable, just as outré to Planck and his fellow physicists as are the workings of Kafka's court that trace a pattern like a swinging pendulum which, if disturbed, for example, by a mathematical entity called a strange attractor, will result in chaos whose pattern emerges again only on a different level of calculation.

Rhetoric can lead to literary discoveries in Planck's scientific texts. Hyperbole is common, such as the term *ungeheuer* which can mean enormous, immense, huge, vast, colossal, tremendous, or terrific. Striking Planckian hyperboles are "enormous simplification"[49] and the paradoxical "relatively enormous."[50] Planck shows a preference for certain metaphors. Physics, in particular its canonical theories, is equated with an edifice with strong foundations that can only be shaken by heavy artillery (meaning powerful new hypotheses).[51] Anthropomorphic relations are expressed in such terms as "satisfactory," which is the primary criterion for the acceptability of a hypothesis or theory. (This is despite the fact that in his essays Planck asserted that scientific progress depends upon the emancipation of science

---

49. *PAV*, 2:275.
50. *PAV*, 2:253.
51. Even today you can hardly find a work on any aspect of science that does not uncritically assume the metaphor of the building (plus foundation) or edifice of science.

from anthropomorphisms. Apparently he was not thinking of his own scientific rhetoric.) Related to these are personifications, for example the language used to describe the action of the oscillator: it is "capable of accomplishing" something; it can be "hindered"; it "needs" something; it "takes possession" of something.[52] Among the terms that are laden with value by their repetition in contexts that assume the reader's complicity and support are *meaning, knowledge, unity* and *simplicity* (referring to hypotheses or theories, or the physical world-picture in general), *future*, and *further development*. Of such terms one that bears a particularly heavy burden of meaning is *experience*—an existentially fluid category that in Kafka's texts is reduced to meaninglessness. Paul K. Feyerabend writes about the tradition of experience in physics:

. . . a never examined, mystical and stable entity. . . . All that is known about experience is that it is something that springs to the eye, that it is a "divine illumination" this time not by God, and not through the mind, but by Nature, and through the senses; and which guarantees success. . . . Nor are we able to determine what experience *tells us*. Experience taken by itself is mute. It does not provide any means of establishing a connection with language. . . . [53]

Many of these features of Planck's writing are inherent in the nature of scientific language itself. In scientific and mathematical papers today it is common to find hypotheses, theories, or proofs characterized as "rich," "powerful," or "elegant," making them hardly distinguishable from a late model sports car or investment broker. Language replete with aesthetic, metaphysical, or "subjective" implications supports a value-charged text; we must acknowledge that a scientific text is loaded with extrascientific meaning.

---

52. *PAV*, 2:253.

53. "On the Improvement of the Sciences and the Arts, and the Possible Identity of the Two," *Boston Studies in the Philosophy of Science*, eds. Robert S. Cohen and Marx W. Wartofsky (Dordrecht, Holland: Reidel, 1967), 3:405, 3:398, and 3:395.

In his papers, Planck would occasionally mention that he had applied "successive recursion" to get from one equation to the next. That is, each new mathematical step resulted from an operation on the terms of the previous step. Kafka was a master of recursive structures that extend and elaborate the inherent recursivity of language itself.[54] Moreover, Kafka's text not only exemplifies, but also points to its own recursivity, drawing attention to it by describing the core of the narrative as recursive, for example: "If he [Josef K.] were alone in the world he could easily have disregarded the trial, though it was also certain, of course, that then the trial would never have arisen at all" (108). Gleick's definition applies to this self-designation in *The Trial* and to Planck's recursive operations on equations: recursive is *"self-referential,* the behavior of one guided by the behavior of another hidden inside it."[55] Planck's recursive process, however, is a linear and predictable one that need only be followed along its inevitable path. Kafka's version contests that linear logic, opening recursion to continual self-undermining instead of self-affirmation, and denying the closure that a "satisfactory" recursive equation achieves.

Planck believed, as he wrote in a 1908 essay, that to ascertain the state of development of any science one needs to check "how the science defines its basic concepts and how it classifies its various areas. Since even the final, most mature results of research are frequently already contained implicitly . . . in the precision and serviceability of the definitions and in the manner of classifying the material."[56] With "classification" and "definition" he is describing the procedures of science and of mathematics, as well

---

54. Stanley Corngold provides a subtle and complex discussion of recursion in Kafka's writings, to the end of showing how it enacts affirmation. His examination encompasses Kafka's selfhood which separates it from my use of recursion. We also part on matters of language, referentiality, and the metaphysical. See "Kafka's Double Helix," *The Literary Review* 26 (Summer 1983): 521–36, and its much revised version in *Franz Kafka: The Necessity of Form,* 105–36.

55. Gleick, *Chaos,* 179.

56. "Die Einheit des physikalischen Weltbildes," lecture delivered December 9, 1908, at the University of Leiden, in Max Planck, *Vorträge und Erinnerungen* (Darmstadt: Wissenschaftliche Buchgesellschaft, 1965), 29–30; also in *PAV,*

as a basic method of organizing and acquiring knowledge. The text of *The Trial* raises the question of whether the results of such a procedure are the only version of "what it means to *know* something." These words are a quotation from Feigenbaum's discussion of the failure of linear equations, of standard mathematics, to provide "an understanding of global, long-term behavior." Standard mathematics and physics—the physics of isolating "mechanisms"—were not relevant to calculating the transitions of orderly systems to chaos. Feigenbaum discovered the mathematical order in chaos, but in doing so became aware that the problem "completely changes what it means to *know* something."[57] In working out the denial of the values evident in Planck's text—the validity of experience, the possibility of dependable knowledge, and so on—*The Trial* may be proposing another kind of knowing. Whenever it is indicated that Josef K. "has no doubts" about something, he is wrong (according to evidence elsewhere in the text). The protagonist never gets hold of portions of information or definitions that reliably lead to knowledge. One of the most commonly used verbs is *appeared*, which serves to undermine the many statements it prefaces.[58] Nothing is proposed in *The Trial* that is not taken away again or denied, including the possibility of naming—a basic function of the human intellect, God's initial assignment to Adam, and a means of asserting mastery or control.[59] For example, after Josef K.'s arrest, he discusses the matter

---

3:6–29; orig. pub. in *Physikalische Zeitschrift* 10 (1909): 62–75; trans. in Stephen Toulmin, ed., *Physical Reality: Philosophical Essays on Twentieth-Century Physics*, trans. Ann Toulmin (New York: Harper and Row, 1970), 1–27; and in Max Planck, *A Survey of Physical Theory*, trans. R. Jones and D. H. Williams (New York: Dover, 1960), 1–26. Translation of this quotation is mine.

57. All quotations from Gleick, *Chaos*, 174–75.

58. Walter Speidel, *A Complete Contextual Concordance to Franz Kafka "Der Prozess"* (Leeds: W. S. Maney and Son, 1978).

59. Derrida, in his essay on Kafka's "Before the Law," associates naming with literature itself: "or, indeed, that this name of literature is destined to remain improper, without an assured concept or reference, so that 'literature' has something to do with the drama of naming, the law of the name and the name of the law" ("Devant La Loi," trans. Avital Ronell, in *Kafka and the Contemporary Critical Performance*, ed. Alan Udoff [Bloomington: Indiana University Press, 1987], 131).

later that evening with his landlady. In the course of the long discussion, continuing over several pages, K. variously designates the morning's events as: "it," "the whole thing," "not something scholarly," "nothing," "everything," "something like that," and "such a thing" (22). Within the recursive organization of this particular section of text, the protagonist never names the central topic. The geographic center of this section is the sentence: "But one is so unprepared." At the core of a logical structure is a refusal to name and a state of unreadiness. We face the paradox that in a text constituted in part by devices of a logical type, we are left without a final meaning of the workings of these devices — a "hierarchy of empty centres" like the one generated by mathematician Fournier d'Albe's octahedral principle.

Why compare the words of Franz Kafka and Max Planck, of all people? They are as odd a couple as Watson and Holmes, and as unlikely as those two contemporaries to be insightful readers of each other's texts. Why — as my whimsical title implies — share a bottle of claret with them? As any Holmes fan will know, claret was a favorite beverage of the detecting pair. The outré notion that Kafka and Planck could also have drunk wine together occurred to me because during Kafka's years as a student in Prague, and for some years thereafter, he occasionally attended get-togethers at the home of an acquaintance, a woman named Berta Fanta. She arranged the evening socials so that her Prague circle could meet distinguished guests and talk about important issues of the day. (Kafka's friend, Max Brod, attended these regularly and would have been a source of reports to Kafka about the sessions Kafka did not attend.) The guests included one Albert Einstein who, while he was a professor at the University of Prague in 1911–12, dropped by to talk about relativity. Other guests lectured on psychoanalysis and on other current topics, and one physicist, a friend of Einstein's named Freundlich ("friendly" in German), talked about Planck's quantum theory.[60] Planck him-

---

60. Sources for the biographical information are: Hartmut Binder, ed., *Kafka-*

self, who lived in Berlin, never attended, nor is there any reason to believe that Kafka attended when quantum theory was discussed, let alone that anyone drank claret. The title refers to the mixing of culture in central Europe in the brilliant decade and a half that preceded World War I. In a time and a place that were the source of many of the determining ideas of the twentieth century, physicists and poets, and other leading German-speaking intellectuals of the day, circulated from city to city—Einstein is exemplary in his moves from Zurich to Prague to Berlin—and new ideas, theories, and styles moved with them. There would be no avoiding contagion among culturally aware, intellectually active readers infected by language and history. Kafka and Planck were both part of this world—Kafka more as a wide-ranging, voracious reader and lively participant in the Prague cultural scene, Planck as the first German specialist in theoretical physics and preeminent leader in the scientific establishment.

If Kafka may have had contact with Einstein, why not write about Kafka and Einstein instead of Kafka and Planck? Primarily because Einstein was a maverick; he stood outside society and rejected it in many ways, even as a young man. Planck, a leader in institutionalized science, held the highest offices available to a scientist. He was, among other things, rector of the University of Berlin, secretary of the Mathematical-Physical Section of the Prussian Academy of Sciences, president of the Kaiser Wilhelm Society, and profoundly influential teacher, administrator, lecturer, and writer. Planck was, it can be argued, the most representative scientist of his day; thus his writings and his style stand for mainstream science of the early twentieth century. Secondly, the

---

Handbuch, vol. 1 (Stuttgart: Kröner, 1979); Max Brod, *Über Franz Kafka* (Frankfurt am Main: Fischer Bücherei, 1966); Christa Jungnickel and Russell McCormmach, *Intellectual Mastery of Nature: Theoretical Physics from Ohm to Einstein*, vol. 2 (Chicago: University of Chicago Press, 1986) (on Einstein and Freundlich); Philipp Frank, *Einstein: His Life and Times*, trans. George Rosen (New York: Knopf, 1957); Ernst Pawel, *The Nightmare of Reason: A Life of Franz Kafka* (New York: Farrar Straus Giroux, 1984); Klaus Wagenbach, *Franz Kafka: Eine Biographie seiner Jugend 1883–1912* (Bern: Francke, 1958).

fact that Kafka and Planck are unlikely to have known of each other's existence enhances the notion of a distinctly textual dialogue between the scientific and the literary.

Planck's life span encompassed Kafka's. Planck was born in 1858. Kafka was born in 1883 — the next generation after Planck's — and died early, in 1924 at the age of 40. Planck survived to beyond World War II, dying in 1947 at the age of 89, having experienced the two world wars and the loss of his first wife and their four children, the last a son executed by the Nazis.[61] Planck was a patrician, the distinguished scion of a distinguished line of academicians, Protestant theologians and jurists, a pillar of society and of his church, a German patriot and monarchist who, like most of his colleagues, supported his country fully in its entry into World War I. He enjoyed a level of prestige and public influence unimaginable in Kafka's life. Kafka, on the other hand, could not be identified with any establishment. His political views tended to be Socialist and assume the perspective of the outcast and the disadvantaged. Kafka's ancestors had been Jews confined to ghettos in towns or, in the case of his father, in a dirt-poor village in Bohemia. His father worked his way up from the most extreme poverty and deprivation to prosperous middle-class citizenship in Prague. The differences between Kafka and Planck are legion, yet they also shared some important qualities. They shared the central European cultural heritage, with both, for example, being graduates of a German-language humanistic *Gymnasium*, or secondary school. They were still of a time and an education immersed in the classical heritage (absorbed with enthusiasm in Planck's case, resisted in Kafka's). Over the course of their lifetimes and the history they inherited, they could not help being determined by processes, structures, and institutions of — despite all local differences — a common culture of ideas.

---

61. Biographical information on Planck comes primarily from the following sources: Max Born, *Obituary* (n. 40); Barbara Lovett Cline, *Men Who Made a New Physics* (Chicago: University of Chicago Press, 1987); J. L. Heilbron, *The Dilemmas of an Upright Man: Max Planck as Spokesman for German Science* (Berkeley: Univer-

Kafka and Planck were both compulsive about their work, modest and self-critical to a fault, seeking to create with absolute rigor and precision. Commentators refer to their almost religious approach to their work: for Planck physics and for Kafka writing played a role comparable to the sacred in their lives. In the case of Kafka, however, he was committed to language in spite of knowing that it is a deceptive, imperfect, unreliable deity. Kafka and Planck were craftsmen of language in the service of clarity, even purity of style.[62] Their written language, however, was also determined by the strictures and limits of a technical style—the scientific format with equations in Planck's case, legal or bureaucratic style in Kafka's. Kafka had earned a doctorate in law from the University of Prague (a prerequisite for government service rather than a serious course of study) and was employed as a claims officer and accident prevention specialist at the Workers Accident Insurance Institute for the Kingdom of Bohemia in Prague.[63] In the case of both Kafka and Planck there is a dialectical relationship between their technical and nontechnical writings. Planck's philosophical essays can be interpreted as undermining the rhetoric of his scientific papers (an example is the case of anthropomorphism mentioned above). Kafka wrote a report for the insurance company on safety measures in stone quarries around the same time he was writing *The Trial*. This technical report is a text whose linguistic isomorphism with *The Trial* suggests a synthesis distinct from subject matter.[64] (See chap. 3 in this volume.)

sity of California Press, 1986); and Armin Hermann, *Max Planck in Selbstzeugnissen und Bilddokumenten* (Reinbek bei Hamburg: Rowohlt, 1973).

62. Einstein singled out Planck's "unpretentious [*schlicht*], genuinely artistic" writing style for praise in a tribute on the occasion of Planck's inauguration as Rector of the University of Berlin. Albert Einstein, "Max Planck als Forscher," *Die Naturwissenschaften*, November 7, 1913, 1077–79.

63. See Klaus Hermsdorf's thorough review of Kafka's technical education, his working conditions, and technical writings in "Arbeit und Amt als Erfahrung und Gestaltung," in Franz Kafka, *Amtliche Schriften*, ed. Klaus Hermsdorf (Berlin: Akademie, 1984), 9–87.

64. On this point Clayton Koelb correctly remarks about Kafka: "It was not

Kafka's and Planck's texts can be regarded singly and collectively as explorations of the idea of law. The law that plays a role in Kafka's text is written law, and treated as if it were absolute, but at the same time it is also arbitrary and inaccessible, and subject to all kinds of interpretation that may or may not be reliable. Kafka's is a text where all authority within reach is proven corrupt or meaningless and thus undermined. Planck's texts, on the other hand, harken to authorities, such as the foundational theories of predecessors, and, above all, to the notion of the constant, as a universal law of nature. Yet Planck, with his introduction of the quantum, undermined accepted laws and introduced indeterminacy. The texts of Kafka and Planck are simultaneously lawful and unlawful, as their language is characterized by order and subversive disorder.

Derrida maintains of Kafka's parable or brief "legend" (Kafka's appellation) "Before the Law" (which also appears in *The Trial*) that it "does not tell us what kind of law manifests itself in its non-manifestation: natural, moral, juridical, political?" "We know neither what nor who this is, nor where: is it a thing, person, discourse, voice, document, or simply a nothing that incessantly defers access to itself . . . ?" "This," he suggests, "perhaps, is where literature begins. A text of philosophy, science, or history, conveying knowledge or information, would not give up a name to a state of not-knowing. . . . "[65] Derrida is setting up an opposition that is not tenable. His list of three types of texts that "would not give up a name to a state of not-knowing" rests on the premise that scientific, philosophical, and historical textual discourses exist in a realm of certainty that distinguishes them from literary discourse. In this view those three categories must have dispensed with rhetoric, with multiple meanings and con-

---

enough for him to know what a given discourse intended to say in a given context: he was (as a writer) more often concerned with meanings that such a discourse would have if its context-determined intention were ignored." *Kafka's Rhetoric: The Passion of Reading* (Ithaca, N.Y.: Cornell University Press, 1989), 16.

65. Derrida, "Devant La Loi," 142, 143, 142.

notations, with the impossibility of direct referentiality and become something that is no longer language but reality itself. Surely Derrida would not really subscribe to that view. Yet he seems to assume, unquestioned, the view of scientific language rooted in the seventeenth century and discussed by Arbib and Hesse as "the literalist view of language." On the contrary, there is no privileged language, and thus no privileged text that can be literally referential or dispense with the "meaning changes, or tropes, of various kinds. . ." that are "pervasive in language" (Arbib and Hesse). We shall find in representative scientific texts by Planck, which are only one example of the many that could be proposed, that there are "names" "given up" "to a state of not-knowing." In his essays Planck seems to be wrestling, Jacob-like, with an absent Law of Nature, an ultimate and foundational Law behind the individual laws discoverable by physicists. There is no more certainty of "knowledge or information" being conveyed by a text of science than by a text of literature. One could justifiably discuss distinctions between different *kinds* of knowledge or information. Derrida seems sure, in this passage, that there can be only one kind of "knowledge or information." Derrida's assertion would imply, in contrast to Rorty's argument for equality of discourses, that the texts of science, philosophy, and history have an inside track to reality, one that somehow circumvents the pitfalls of language.

Derrida's own characteristic deconstructive maneuver sets up a drama of progressive exclusion—a kind of musical chairs. As in mathematical set theory, each step turns on positing yet another outside(er) that must be excluded because it names itself and thus cannot be included in the set continually being deconstructed. Two brief, self-descriptive samples from Derrida's "Devant La Loi" are: "The place from which it tells us about the laws of literature, the law without which no literary specificity would take shape, this place cannot be simply *in* literature"; "the text also points obliquely to literature, speaking of itself as a literary effect—and thereby exceeding the literature of which it speaks" (147). When viewed as a process, the method is isomorphic to

Gödel's refutation of the notion of logical completeness in number theory, indicating that there is reason to view Derrida's method as grounded in mathematical logic.[66]

I should like to propose another option: that is, positing a train of steps in the *other* direction—toward the *inside*—always positing yet another *in*clusion, yet another inside(er). The ultimate inside of life (as far as we presently know) is the genetic codes—the logic of biology (just as the ultimate inside of matter is sought in terms of the logic of physics). Though we may learn more and more about DNA and the other genetic message carriers we share with all living organisms (with the exception of some primitive viruses), we will never be able to gain entry to the "Law" of the laws that governs our selves.[67] There we arrive at an unknown and unknowable (by the conscious mind) Law, that is, "what remains concealed and invisible in each law," "the law itself, that

---

66. In "White Mythology" one of Derrida's arguments depends on metaphors from geometry: "This self-destruction may always follow two lines, which are almost tangents but yet are different: They repeat each other, copy each other, and diverge from each other according to certain laws" (71). More importantly, his central argument deconstructing the notion of " 'founding' tropes" (18) follows the logic of sets in number theory, with the addition of Russell's paradox, that is that most sets are not members of themselves, with the exception of some "self-swallowing" sets that do contain themselves as members (see Hofstadter, *Gödel, Escher, Bach*, 20). "If we wanted to conceive and classify all the metaphorical possibilities of philosophy, there would always be at least one metaphor which would be excluded and remain outside the system: that one, at least, which was needed to construct the concept of metaphor, or, to cut the argument short, the metaphor of metaphor. This extra metaphor, remaining outside the field which it enables us to circumscribe, also extracts or abstracts this field for itself, and therefore removes itself from that field as one metaphor less" (18). ("White Mythology: Metaphor in the Text of Philosophy," trans. F. C. T. Moore, *New Literary History* 6, no.1 [Autumn 1974]: 5–74.) This unacknowledged mathematical-logical referentiality indicates that even in deconstruction there may be no escaping the persuasive and powerful legitimacy of the mathematical.

67. H. H. Pattee raises a question that is also related to the mystery of the Law in Kafka's "Before the Law": "Why is it that a complete description of the informational sequence of DNA along with all the details of the coding give no clue to the laws under which all these structures and mechanisms operate?" ("The Complementarity Principle in Biological and Social Structures," *Journal of Social and Biological Structures* 1 [April 1978]: 195.)

which makes laws of these laws, the being-law of these laws";
"the place and origin of law"; "the law which says 'you must' and
'you must not' " (Derrida, "Devant La Loi," 134). This is the Law
that is always present and always absent — commanding and pro-
hibiting without ever itself being known to those who have no
choice but to obey the Law. From insect societies to mammals to
hubristic Homo sapiens, all must follow some scheme, some set
of behaviors[68] determined by a Law that is equally inaccessible to
all (meaning that it is not justifiable to believe there are final answers in the human brain and nervous system).[69] The text of that
Law is both readable (in the laboratory sense) and unreadable.
"Reading a text might indeed reveal that it is untouchable,
properly intangible *precisely because it can be read*, and for the same
reason unreadable to the extent to which the presence within it
of a clear and graspable sense remains as hidden as its origin. Un-
readability thus no longer opposes itself to readability" (Derrida,
"Devant La Loi," 137). Derrida takes us, then, with appropriate
undecidability, on our path as readers of the readable/unreadable,
pursuing "the paradoxical logic of boundaries" (146).

---

68. This is apparent when one reads about the overarching schemes of social
behavior having to do with such matters as hierarchies, communication, learning,
socialization, parenting, aggression, and social spacing (Edward O. Wilson, *Sociobiology*, abridged ed. [Cambridge, Mass.: Belknap, 1980]). Another relevant text
is Gunther S. Stent, ed., *Morality as a Biological Phenomenon* (Berkeley: University
of California Press, 1980).

69. In *Philosophy and the Mirror of Nature* (chap. 2) Rorty fancifully suggests con-
versations with beings from outer space whose difference from humans is that
they are sensible of their own brain chemistry and communication consists in
describing it while thinking.

CHAPTER 2

Planck as Reader (Nietzsche)

We cut up and organize the spread and flow of events as we do, largely because, through our mother tongue, we are parties to an agreement to do so, not because nature itself is segmented in exactly that way for all to see. . . . The real question is: What do different languages do, not with these artificially isolated objects but with the flowing face of nature in its motion, color, and changing form; with clouds, beaches, and yonder flight of birds? For, as goes our segmentation of the face of nature, so goes our physics of the Cosmos.

—Benjamin Lee Whorf, "Languages and Logic"

Undoubtedly, the need for this new articulation speaks in the work of Nietzsche. Undoubtedly, also, it would give rise to a displacement and a rewriting of the meaning of science, of knowledge, of truth, which is to say, of some other terms also.

—Jacques Derrida, "White Mythology"

Close associations between Kafka and Nietzsche are generally accepted and have been widely explored.[1] By contrast, the notion of connecting Nietzsche's thought, commonly classified as "antiscientific," with Planck's would seem outré and hardly justifiable. Not only as a representative of scientific reason and the academic

---

Epigraphs from *Language, Thought, and Reality: Selected Writings of Benjamin Lee Whorf*, ed. John B. Carroll (Cambridge, Mass.: MIT Press, 1956), 240–41; and "White Mythology: Metaphor in the Text of Philosophy," trans. F. C. T. Moore, *New Literary History* 6, no. 1 (Autumn 1974), 65.

1. Stimulating explorations of the Kafka-Nietzsche relationship can be found, for example, in Stanley Corngold's "Kafka's Other Metamorphosis," and Alan Udoff's "Before the Question of the Laws: Kafkan Reflections," both in *Kafka and the Contemporary Critical Performance*, ed. Alan Udoff (Bloomington: Indiana University Press, 1987), 41–57 and 178–213. Also in Peter Heller, "Kafka and Nietzsche," *Proceedings of Comparative Literature Symposium*, ed. W. T. Zyla (Lubbock: Texas Tech Press, 1971), 71–95; Ralf R. Nicolai, "Nietzschean Thought in Kafka's 'A Report to an Academy,'" *The Literary Review* 26 (Summer 1983): 551–64; and Margot Norris, *Beasts of the Modern Imagination: Darwin, Nietzsche, Kafka, Ernst, and Lawrence* (Baltimore, Md.: Johns Hopkins University Press, 1985).

establishment, but also as a conservative nationalist and church-goer, Planck would likely have found Nietzsche's writings alien and offensive.[2] The two might have in common only their relatively close birthdates—Nietzsche in 1844 and Planck in 1858—and their love of Alpine landscapes.

In this chapter I propose that, contrary to accepted views, a scientist looking for affirmation of science might well find it in a text by Nietzsche. That scientist, however, will also find an uncovering of limits to logic and mathematics and his attention will be directed to the grounding of his assumptions in language—a perspective generally not found among mainstream practitioners of science. In an essay by Nietzsche we find not only Nietzsche's powerfully argued case in support of the literary side of a debate between the literary and the scientific, but another sphere of meaning that contradicts his apparent message. In addition, by designating Planck the scientist-reader we are led by Nietzsche's text to find in Planck a deconstructor of his own scientific texts. For that text by Nietzsche we turn to one that has been the object of much attention in recent years (particularly by theorists of rhetorical strategies such as de Man and Derrida), the brief posthumous fragment "On Truth and Lie in an Extramoral Sense."[3] It can be argued that this little text has now become canonical and, in a sense, originary in the Western debate of ideas, one reason being that Nietzsche is seen as an original "deconstructor" and acknowledged precursor of Derrida. "On Truth and Lie" is central to that assessment. Derrida's discussion of the essay in his "White Mythology" anticipates our reading with its observation that Nietzsche is "risking a continuity between metaphor and concept, as between man and animal, knowledge and instinct" (although his use of the term "risking" betrays his collusion in the very an-

---

2. We have no record of whether Planck read Nietzsche. Planck's papers, diaries, and library were destroyed in an allied bombing raid on Berlin in 1944.

3. "Über Wahrheit und Lüge im aussermoralischen Sinne," Friedrich Nietzsche, *Sämtliche Werke*, Kritische Studienausgabe in 15 Bänden, ed. Giorgio Colli and Mazzino Montinari (Munich: Deutscher Taschenbuch, 1980), 1:875–90. The Colli/Montinari is the authoritative Nietzsche edition. Translations are mine.

thropocentrism that Nietzsche sets out to undermine), and that Nietzsche's work pronounces "the need for" a "new articulation" "between metaphor and concept" that "would give rise to" "a rewriting of the meaning of science."[4]

In his "Rhetoric of Tropes (Nietzsche)" de Man provides a suggestive reading of "On Truth and Lie in an Extramoral Sense."[5] De Man's observations on Nietzsche's self-undermining rhetoric must be the point of departure for any rereading of the essay. In our case it is the point of departure in both senses, that is, we presume it and depart from it. In a later essay de Man provides another connection for our reading: he calls Nietzsche's essay a "late Kantian text."[6] To place Nietzsche in the Kantian tradition places him closer than expected to his fellow scaler of mountain heights (like Zarathustra), Max Planck. Of Planck's famous 1908 lecture "The Unity of the Physical World-Picture," Stephen Toulmin writes: "Max Planck's Leiden lecture . . . shows how far, in Germany also, contemporary theoretical physics was developing within the framework of a philosophical tradition. The problem of physical reality . . . is clearly presented here as a problem in post-Kantian philosophy."[7] Indeed, Planck himself

4 All quotations are from Jacques Derrida, "White Mythology," 64–65. For Derrida and Nietzsche see, for example, Gayatri Chakravorty Spivak, "Translator's Preface," in Jacques Derrida, *Of Grammatology* (Baltimore, Md.: Johns Hopkins University Press, 1976), xxi–xxxii.

5. Paul de Man, *Allegories of Reading: Figural Language in Rousseau, Nietzsche, Rilke, and Proust* (New Haven, Conn.: Yale University Press, 1979).

6. "Anthropomorphism and Trope in the Lyric," in *The Rhetoric of Romanticism* (New York: Columbia University Press, 1984), 239.

7. *Physical Reality: Philosophical Essays on Twentieth-Century Physics*, ed. Stephen Toulmin (New York: Harper and Row, 1970), 1. This collection of essays on theoretical physics includes the English translation by Ann Toulmin of Planck's lecture quoted above. I use this translation for all quotations from this lecture; translations from other Planck lectures are mine. Planck's Leiden lecture was also published in translation with seven additional lectures in *A Survey of Physical Theory*, trans. R. Jones and D. H. Williams (New York: Dover, 1960). The Leiden lecture–"Die Einheit des Physikalischen Weltbildes"—was originally published in 1909 in *Physikalische Zeitschrift* 10:62–75, and can also be found in Max Planck, *Physikalische Abhandlungen und Vorträge*, 3 vols. (Braunschweig: Vieweg, 1958), 3:6–29, as well as the collection *Vorträge und Erinnerungen* (Darmstadt: Wissenschaftliche

writes in the conclusion of his lecture: "Those great men [Copernicus, Kepler, Newton, and others] did not speak about their 'world-picture'; they spoke about 'the world' or about 'Nature' itself. Now, is there any recognizable difference between their 'world' and our 'world-picture of the future'? Surely not! For the fact that no method exists for proving such a difference was made the common property of all thinkers by Immanuel Kant" (26–27). It is important to note, however, that in other lectures Planck also distanced himself from Kant's theories as they affected physics; for example, Kant's ranking of causality and Euclidean geometry among the a priori categories.[8]

We take this lecture by Planck as a close, though contentious, relative of Nietzsche's essay "On Truth and Lie." Like Nietzsche's, it too is a polemic addressed to a specific adversary. In Nietzsche's case the adversaries were certain groups — academic philosophers, for example. In Planck's case the adversary was physicist-philosopher Ernst Mach, with whom this lecture inaugurated a "classical" (Toulmin) polemical exchange that lasted several years. In a similar vein to Nietzsche's (but with different content), Planck attacked his opponent's views as a threat to the integrity of the intellectual foundations of physics. Our reading places this and other essays by Planck in the position of sparring partners — to use a metaphor from Socrates — with Nietzsche's essay in a debate on science, language, and by implication, on literature.

Planck's assessment of the lesson learned from Kant is not contradicted by Nietzsche's essay. For Nietzsche there is an "inaccessible and undefinable X" (880) at the essence of things that our necessarily metaphorical language prevents us from ever knowing. Language arbitrarily assigns qualities to things — "hard" to

---

Buchgesellschaft, 1965), 28–51. This last collection is my source for all quotations from lectures (except for the Toulmin translation).

8. See Planck, "Die Kausalität in der Natur," *Vorträge*, 250. There is a lucid discussion of the relationship of Kant's theories to postclassical physics in Werner Heisenberg, *Physics and Philosophy: The Revolution in Modern Science* (New York: Harper and Row, 1958), 86–92.

rocks, for example, as if the idea of "hard" were known to us outside of its association with rock that stimulates in us a sensation
we call *hard*. There is no logic at the origin of language, and "the
whole material in which and with which the man of truth, the
researcher, the philosopher later works and builds originates, if
not in cloud–cuckoo land, then at least not in the essence of
things" (879). Nietzsche's deconstructive arguments cease, however, at a term, an idea, a concept that is a foundational premise:
the *essence of things*. It is the premise his essay requires in order to
move at all from one assertion to the next. He joins Max Planck
who wrote, toward the conclusion of a long career (the consequence of which was the undermining of the classical physical interpretation of the world): "[T]he real outside world basically
stands not at the beginning but at the destination of physical research; it is a destination that will never be completely reached,
but which must continuously be kept in sight if one wants to
make progress."[9] Planck's "real outside world" is the equivalent of
Nietzsche's "essence of things"; they are ultimately unknowable
but must be assumed. Beyond that grounding they share the term
picture, which for both is a secondary but nevertheless a valid,
privileged, and necessary stage of thought. For Nietzsche, picture
is the second in his hierarchical triad of the origins of concepts:
nerve stimuli are the "grandmothers," pictures the "mothers" (882)
of concepts (which thus must represent the children). The further
away from "pictures" and "first impressions," the closer to the ar-
tificiality of "schemata" or concepts that are responsible for building a "pyramidal order based on castes and ranks, a new world of
laws, privileges, and subordination" in opposition to the vivid
(*anschaulich*), intuitive world of first impressions (881–82). We
must note that with his ordering of "nerve stimuli," "pictures,"
(sometimes "sounds"), and "concepts," Nietzsche himself has
created a scheme based on a hierarchical ordering of "concepts,"
the very notion he most strenuously condemns.

Max Planck proposes a story of development from a more

---

9. "Foreword," *Vorträge*, vi.

authentic time that is almost identical to Nietzsche's with the difference that Planck is telling the story of the history of physics. The future "world-picture" of physics is "pale and prosaic," having lost its direct connection to life, compared to "the brilliant pageant of the original world-picture which grew from the manifold needs of human life and to which all the specific sense impressions made their contribution" (Toulmin, *Physical Reality*, 21). It is an evaluation equivalent to Nietzsche's "rule of abstractions," loss of the power of "vivid first impressions," in favor of "paler, cooler concepts" (881). To the foundational theses Planck and Nietzsche share, then, we must add that there was a past golden age when human beings (and physics) were more authentic, richer, closer to the life of the senses. Inherent in such views is a hierarchy, whether organized diachronically or synchronically. Nietzsche's ranking of nerve stimulus-picture-sound-concept, or from lesser abstraction at the top to greater at the lower end tells both a diachronic and synchronic story. While Planck's view of *historical* development overlaps with Nietzsche's interpretation, their synchronic ranking is diametrically opposite. Planck writes of the second law of thermodynamics as having "the rank of a principle" (39). For Planck—as we would expect of a scientist— the greater the abstraction and generalization, the higher the rank.

For both Planck and Nietzsche, an entity called *Nature* is their dialogue partner. *Nature* is a ubiquitous term among physicists and scientists in general. They, like Nietzsche, presume the term is descriptive in a manner generally agreed upon: *Nature* is female (in German, its grammatical gender as well; Nietzsche quarrels with the "arbitrary" (878) assignment of grammatical genders); *she* is mysterious and has secrets; *her* secrets are expressed in a language that men can read; *she* can be mastered and conquered. A recently published history of German theoretical physics is titled *Intellectual Mastery of Nature*, after a quotation from Planck's prominent predecessor and the leading light in German science of his day, Hermann von Helmholtz.[10] Even today, these terms re-

---

10. Christa Jungnickel and Russell McCormmach, *Intellectual Mastery of Nature:*

main part of scientific investigators' discourse about something they call *Nature*.[11] In Nietzsche's essay we find a fundamental critique of the idea that Nature's "language" can be read by the human being trapped in the anthropomorphic imposition of names and qualities on things to whose "essence" he or she can have no access: "Overlooking the individual and the real gives us the concept, as it also gives us the form, whereas Nature knows no forms and concepts, therefore also no types, but only an X that is undefinable and inaccessible to us" (880). For different reasons, Nietzsche shares with the scientists the view of Nature that hides its secrets, though for Nietzsche it means an ultimate ineffability. How is such a condition expressed?—by the ineffable chiasmus X, "the cross-shaped reversal of properties" that, according to de Man (*Allegories*, 113), characterizes the rhetorical structure of "On Truth and Lie." The chiasmus also diagrams the successive transpositions that characterize the relationship between Planck's essay

---

Theoretical Physics from Ohm to Einstein, 2 vols. (Chicago: University of Chicago Press, 1986). The authors of this seminal study record the statements of Helmholtz without associating themselves with them: "It had been his desire to gain an 'intellectual mastery over nature,' which an understanding of the laws of nature offered its possessor. His colleagues often used this same expression when speaking of the results of physical research and of the specific contribution of physics to the ascendancy of culture over nature. Through a certain kind of inquiry and with a certain body of ideas, they said, physical nature could be mastered. The mastery they spoke of was in the first instance intellectual. . . . The intellectual mastery of nature was followed by the material mastery, which was carried out by practical men: 'by means of such preliminary knowledge of the laws, we are in a position to let natural forces work for us, after our will and wishes.' As evidence for this, Helmholtz said: 'The whole development of industry in recent times, and the whole change in the form of human life and activity connected with it, depend in an essential way on our mastery over the forces of nature' " (1:xxiii). On the subject of mastery over nature, also see Evelyn Fox Keller, *Reflections on Gender and Science* (New Haven, Conn.: Yale University Press, 1985).

11. Keller studies such terms in *Reflections on Gender*. The *New York Times* obituary for theoretical physicist and Nobel laureate Richard P. Feynman quotes him as having said: "If you want to learn about nature, to appreciate nature, it is necessary to understand the language that she speaks in. . . . She offers her information only in one form; we are not so unhumble as to demand that she change before we pay any attention" (*New York Times*, February 17, 1988).

and the Nietzsche text. They come together at fundamental points, then they part again in opposite directions.

Nietzsche the cosmologist/astronomer, Nietzsche the evolutionary biologist, Nietzsche the geologist—unlikely appellations to say the least. Yet it is indeed the perspective of these and other sciences that Nietzsche's text assumes at the outset and this perspective prevails in the essay as a whole. It begins as follows:

In some remote corner of universe emptied into countless shimmering solar systems there was once a star on which clever animals invented cognition. It was the most arrogant, dishonest minute in "world history": but it was only a minute. After nature had taken a few breaths, the star froze, and the clever animals had to die. — Someone could invent a fable like this, yet would still not have sufficiently illustrated how miserable, shadowy, and fleeting, how futile and arbitrary the human intellect appears in nature. There were eternities in which the intellect did not exist, and when it has passed away again, nothing will have changed. (875)

The passage follows a dialectical path: first an account according to cosmology. Cosmology is the branch of astronomy "dealing with the origin, structure, and space-time relationships of the universe."[12] Space in this passage ranges from the small "corner" and individual star to solar systems to the vastness of the entire universe; time oscillates between the briefest moment and eternity. The perspective of the narrator is astronomical or geological time — the perspective from which the span of human existence, or the existence of any "intelligent animal," on earth is equivalent to only a "few breaths of nature." A sense of the ultimate mortality — extinction — dominates the passage. According to the narrator's moral judgment, however, the extinction is deserved.

The suggestion (in the subjunctive mood) that such a story

---

12. *Webster's Third New International Dictionary*, unabridged ed. (Springfield, Mass.: Merriam-Webster, 1961).

could be invented introduces the second part of the dialectical proposition. That is, if such a story could be invented, then perhaps the one we just read *was* invented, a reader might think in response to the narrator's programming. As in Kafka's texts, however, that subjunctive forces open the antithesis that in a true dialectic would prefer to be closed. We cannot know whether the story is a fable or a scientifically sound account. The outcome of the literature/science debate is suspended in the openness of the subjunctive mood. Nor does the next turnabout resolve the debate, for it adds yet another layer of uncertainty for the reader and refuses to provide answers: *if* someone *had* invented such a fable, the invention would still be insufficient to describe the true conditions. In rides the knight-narrator with a synthesis to rescue the reader in distress: the subjunctive is dropped for the narrator *knows* "how miserable, how shadowy, . . ." the human intellect is in the context of nature, and the narrator is confidently certain of the cosmological ratio of "eternities" to the fleeting moment of human history. What appears with the notion of a "fable" to have been a momentary, possible assumption of a literary point of view, proceeds, in other words, to the affirmation of a grounding of the story in epistemological certainty. We are forewarned that we ought read the essay *against* its ostensible attack on intellect and undermining of science, or at least be sure to avoid accepting an initial impression at face value. We will find that we must read the much-revised Nietzsche once again in a revisionary manner.

The notion of the insignificance of the human intellect within the context of nature obviously valorizes a larger and dominant entity, "nature," which for Nietzsche is the standard by which he measures humanity and finds it paltry and wanting.

Reason tells us . . . that the individual human being, we human creatures, all of us including our world of the senses, yes even including our entire planet, signify only a miniscule nothing in the great, incomprehensibly sublime Nature whose laws do not conform to what goes on in a little human brain, but have existed since before there was any life on earth and will continue to exist when the last physicist has disappeared from the face of the earth.[13]

No, we have not just read a continuation of Nietzsche's opening passage. This passage was written by Max Planck for a lecture he delivered at the University of Leiden in 1929. The title is "The World-picture of the New Physics"; it was meant to be a further development, twenty years later, of the thoughts he presented at Leiden in his first lecture on the same topic. During those intervening years there had been revolutionary developments in the world of theoretical physics. Quantum mechanics had arrived on the scene, and with it the final undermining of the worldview of classical physics and a serious blow to the philosophical foundations of causality. Like Nietzsche, Max Planck, the physicist-philosopher, reviews developments from a cosmological perspective and takes his stand on the issues with the insignificance of *all* human projects in mind. This is only one example of a number of noteworthy transgressions into each other's territory by two thinkers who would seem to be least likely to share ideas.

Nietzsche's essay continues with an exclusively biocentric perspective as it makes connections between humans and other species, beginning on the first page with the reference to the mosquito that also feels itself the center of the world. In a Darwinian story of origins, Nietzsche explains the intellect in biological terms as the only means of survival for the weak human species that lacks "horns or a sharp predator's bite" (876). Human beings require a way of arranging themselves peacefully with others since to exist they require a "herd." His examples of grammatical gender, of metaphor, and the arbitrariness of linguistic reference are from nature and biology. "What is a word? The representation of a nerve-stimulus in sound" (878). What was the first metaphor? "A nerve-stimulus first translated to a picture" (879). The name "leaf" that cannot encompass the manifold forms of the leaf is a

---

13. *Vorträge*, 207.

further central example of anthropomorphic generalization where, in nature, individuation is the case. The spider and the bee provide important descriptive references for Nietzsche. He refutes syllogistic logic with the example of defining the mammal and pointing to a camel as an example thereof. He offers the thesis that what are called the "laws of nature" depend upon individual perception and would not be called "laws" at all if we had the option of perceiving in the different ways a bird, a worm, or a plant perceives. His metaphor for the original and "primitive" world of metaphors is a geological one, comparing that original world to the lava mass of a volcano (883). His references oscillate from the "height of the telescopic" "to the depth of the microscopic world," (885) and from the "orbit of the stars" to "chemical processes" (886). In sum, his critique of science is grounded in scientific reference, that is, among others, in a biological view that reapportions the weights of the species, reassigning significance *away* from Homo sapiens, and condemning the error of human species-centeredness. The only capacity that separates human beings from the other animals is the capacity for abstraction, and this capacity leads to the pale schemata at the root of the "pyramidal order" of castes, laws, and subordination. It is not a capacity that justifies claims of superiority, rather the contrary. And who can know whose perceptions—human or those of the insects or the birds—are the "right" ones? They perceive a completely different world and it is pointless to ask whether their perceptions or ours are correct, for no standard exists by which such a judgment could be measured. A reading of Nietzsche's essay that ignores this extraspecies perspective falls into the very trap Nietzsche describes—the anthropomorphic trap, the confinement to abstractions, and the aggrandizement of language. We are obviously suggesting an alternative to de Man's reading of the Nietzsche essay. De Man's focus is on Nietzsche's definition of truth as a trope, but I would argue, with Norris, that "it is the violence representation does to life, rather than to truth, that Nietzsche most thoroughly excoriates"

(14).[14] Truth, indeed, is *not* the primary matter and is a term Nietzsche easily deconstructs.

The borders between specialities in the scientific disciplines have, in many cases, become blurred. There is biophysics, for example, or biochemistry, or geophysics, and so on, not to speak of the overarching concepts such as chaos theory, hierarchy, or recursion that implicate most disciplines, or particular areas of inquiry that require a multidisciplinary approach, such as the investigation of the first moments of the universe, involving the techniques and theories of particle physicists and cosmologists. Even a rhetorical trope—chiasmus—can partake of a transdisciplinary life with the sciences. Such interdisciplinarity is anticipated in Nietzsche's biologically oriented text by notions that anticipate discussions surrounding later physical theories. After remarking that there is no way to decide whether animal or human perception is more valid, Nietzsche continues with an assertion about causality and subject-object relations that dips into a discussion that has occupied theoretical physicists—among others—at least through Max Planck and the developers of quantum mechanics.

It seems to me that correct perception—that would mean the adequate expression of an object in the subject—is contradictory and an absurdity: for between two absolutely different spheres, as between subject and object, there is no causality, no correctness, no expression, but rather at the most an aesthetic attitude, I mean a suggestive transference, a stammering translation into a completely foreign language. For this, however, a freely composing and freely inventing intermediate sphere and intermediate force is in any case necessary. (884)

Nietzsche's argument consists of four main topics: (1) perception, (2) relation between subject and object, (3) causality, and (4) medi-

---

14. In Norris's powerfully argued *Beasts of the Modern Imagination*, I found a sympathetic discussion of the biocentric in Nietzsche. She makes her discoveries in a different context from mine, however, and takes them in different directions. I associate myself with her ethical stance as expressed on pp. 24–25.

ated translation. Because these topics are central to Planck's thinking and writing, we shall take their treatment by Nietzsche as a base from which to launch a "Planckian" reading of Nietzsche and a "Nietzschean" investigation of Planck's texts. For Nietzsche, the notion of causality is merely the result of a broad consensus on sequentiality.

Even the relationship between a nerve-stimulus and the image it produces is not a necessary one; however, if the same image is produced a million times and inherited through many generations, even in the end appears on the same occasion to all of humanity, it finally acquires the same significance it would have if it were the uniquely necessary image and as if that relationship of the original nerve-stimulus to the image it produced were a strict causal relationship. . . . (884)

Max Planck asks in a lecture: "How is it to be explained that in ordinary life we experience causal connection as something objective and independent of us, though we actually see no more of it than a regular series of personal sensations?" He first provides "the sceptic's" answer — that this impression is a purposeful one that depends upon habitual associations. Planck admits this interpretation, and that "by logic alone certainly nothing can be decided about the validity of the law of causality in the real world." There is no way of absolutely distinguishing between a causal connection between events and simple sequentiality. In fact, "whoever is unable occasionally also to imagine things that contradict causality will never be able to enrich his science with a new idea." Is there any point, Planck asks rhetorically, in talking about a specific causal relation when no one can truly understand it? His answer is yes: "because causality is . . . transcendental, is completely independent of the investigating mind, would even retain its significance in the complete absence of a knowing subject." Though not completely accessible to human understanding, it is valid under all circumstances. "Scientific thinking means causal thinking";[15] science depends upon causality and its ulti-

---

15. "Kausalgesetz und Willensfreiheit," *Vorträge*, 146, 142, 142, 161, 162.

mate goal is the full understanding of causal relations. There we have in a nutshell Planck's intellectual struggle with causality: for the sake of science he must save it at all cost, though his view will be modified toward greater subtlety and complexity when, a few years later, he must grapple with the full impact of quantum mechanics upon the notion of causality. A dialectical relationship with Nietzsche's text is apparent: on the one hand Planck's text shares the same perspective on causality as Nietzsche's; on the other hand it moves away and into the realm of the requirements of science whose lifeline, according to Planck, is the premise of an essential causality.

In addition to causality and the connection between sense-stimulus and conceptualization, Nietzsche's arguments cover the matter of the "laws of Nature" and their basis in human notions of time and space, mathematics and number. If we could share the perceptions of an animal, or if human beings each interpreted a stimulus differently, we would not talk about the laws of Nature, Nietsche argues.

What is for us, in general, a law of Nature; it is in itself not known to us, rather only its effects, i.e. its relations to other laws of Nature which, again, are only known as relations. Thus all these relations again and again refer only to each other and are in their essence completely incomprehensible to us; only whatever we ourselves bring to them, such as time, space, sequence, and number are really known to us.

"The mathematical rigor and the inviolability of the conceptions of time and space" are produced "in ourselves and with the same necessity with which the spider spins" (885).

Each of Nietzsche's main points — subject-object relations and causality, the connection between sense impressions and knowledge (a term foreign to Nietzsche's essay; in Planck's terms it is the "physical world-picture"), the meaning of laws of Nature and their expression in mathematical equations, the inviolability of conceptions of time and space — have been focuses of Max Planck's concerns as well as topics of heated debate in his time among physicists (and other scientists, philosophers, pundits, and anyone else who took an active role in the public discussion of ideas). Max Planck is a reliable guide to the terms of the debate in his time; those terms were fundamentally altered by the acceptance of relativity theories and, eventually, of quantum theory. By reading Max Planck's lectures on scientific topics, we can see how these developments gradually took hold and finally altered his perspective, moving him, over the years, closer to the stands we find in Nietzsche's essay. Let us read Nietzsche's and Planck's texts as if they were engaged in a dialogue with each other. Nietzsche gives the cue, for his essay ends with the personification (and reduction) of his ideas to two figures — "the man of reason" and the "intuitive man" (889) — who seem to personify the abstractions *science* and *art*. The earlier text also gives a cue by its hidden logic. Though Nietzsche denies the validity of logic, his text, in one of its many deconstructive gestures, follows a dialectical path. Max Planck's lectures, too, are structured dialectically — a form apparently congenial to sparring with intellectual opponents (in Planck's case they are, for example, "positivists," or "indeterminists") and to persuading an audience. Nietzsche's text that rejects the coldness and rigidity of logic, mathematics, and abstraction relies on its own logic, supplies the figure *8* instead of the word for it, and deals with the most abstract levels of conceptualization. A text that defines "truth" as a "mobile army of metaphors, metonomies, and anthropomorphisms" (880) is thereby defining itself as "truth," for Nietzsche's text is that very "army" in action to enhance proof of his concepts. A text whose project is a critique of science grounds itself on a "mobile army" of scientific metaphors. A text whose target is the inescapable anthropomorphism of all human thought, endeavor, imaginings, and namings concludes with the creation of human figures to personify the arguments it has presented.

We have reviewed the "literary-philosophical" text for its deconstructive rhetoric and its scientific features. Now we shall turn to the "scientific-philosophical" texts to see how they are implicated in the program of the earlier text. The nature of perception is of primary concern to both authors. For Nietzsche, perception can never be determined to be accurate or more than arbitrarily related to its object. The relationship functions by means of metaphors that, over the course of time, have become conventionally accepted as signifying the object. Planck is always sensible of, and in many ways always reacting to, the views of perception associated with Ernst Mach. Mach regarded the sense perceptions as the only reality and source of all knowledge in the sciences.[16] If such views were accepted as a basis of science, there would be a different physics for every physicist according to his or her individual perceptions, making scientific advance impossible. Planck joins Nietzsche in his distrust of sense perception as a (Planck means as the only) reliable source of information. Planck departs from Nietzsche on the matter of metaphor. Metaphor is foundational for Nietzsche; it is as unshakable in his essay as are the "essence of things" and "Nature." Metaphor is not mentioned in Planck's texts, making Planck's readings of his own text a process of "blindness and insight,"[17] for his texts depend upon metaphors, several of which (dice, edifice, dreams) curiously coincide with Nietzsche's. Neither does Planck show awareness of (or interest in) the question of the reliability of language, yet his own language in scientific articles is studded with the very anthropomorphisms he believes physics ought to leave, and has left, behind. The rhetorical development of his articles and the presentation of their scientific arguments depend upon agreement with readers on the meanings of terms such as *satisfactory* to assess a theorem, equation, or experiment. Planck does express doubts about the reliability of other interpretive devices, such as logic, measurement, and concepts. He writes that we form concepts in order

---

16. Mach's response to Planck's 1908 lecture was published in *Physikalische Zeitschrift* II (1910): 599–606; it is translated in Toulmin, *Physical Reality*, 28–43. An important discussion of the subject is Gerald Holton, "Mach, Einstein, and the Search for Reality," in *Thematic Origins of Scientific Thought: Kepler to Einstein* (Cambridge: Harvard University Press, 1973), 219–59.

17. From de Man's title, *Blindness and Insight: Essays in the Rhetoric of Contemporary Criticism* (Minneapolis: University of Minnesota Press, 1983).

to survive in the world, a necessarily uncertain and arbitrary process; even the basic concepts of mathematics are in dispute. Of logic he maintains "not everything that shows no logical contradiction is also reasonable," making logic only one of the possible procedures of thought.[18] Planck departs from Nietzsche with his requirement that there be agreed upon generalizations of perceptions in order for science to function. It is a purely practical requirement; Planck is committed to the progress of science. However, the connection is a complex one, for Nietzsche—who has no stake in the progress of science—also admits the practical need for agreed upon generalizations; they are necessary for survival. They are necessary, but based upon illusion.

The question is how to manage the "translation into the world of the senses and out of the world of the senses."[19] For Nietzsche there is no necessary correlation between the original nerve-stimulus and the image it conjures, between the perceiver and the perceived, or the "expression of an object in the subject." For Planck, on the other hand, subject can know object, but only if there is distance between them—the greater the distance, the greater the possiblity of knowledge. It becomes impossible, however, for the subject to know the object if that object is the subject itself, for it would be continuously altered by the examination; the knowing subject cannot be the known object.[20] "What does man actually know about himself? Can he even one time completely perceive himself, as if he were displayed in a lighted glass case? Does not Nature keep most everything secret from him, even about his own body, . . . the convolutions of the intestines, the rapid flow of the blood stream, the tremblings of tangled fibers . . ." (877). While the tone is more passionate and biological, the message is the same; the texts of the scientist and the "antiscience" philosopher continue to become entangled like un-

18. On concepts: "Die Kausalität in der Natur," 1932, *Vorträge*, 251; on logic: "Das Weltbild der neuen Physik," 1929, *Vorträge*, 207.
19. Planck, "Die Kausalität in der Natur," *Vorträge*, 257.
20. "Physikalische Gesetzlichkeit," 1926, *Vorträge*, 196.

ruly skeins of wool against the best efforts of disciplines to keep them separated.

Nietzsche's rule of absolute separation between subject and object also allows a halfhearted exception: "at the most an aesthetic attitude, I mean a suggestive transference, a stammering translation into a completely foreign language" between object and subject. "For this, however, a freely composing and freely inventing intermediate sphere and intermediate force is in any case necessary." By the back door, so to speak, Max Planck has entered Nietzsche's subject-object discussion. The equivalent for the physicist of an "intermediate sphere" are measurements that are themselves only comparable to a "stammering translation." For his lecture "Positivism and the Real External World" Planck wrote the following: "The physicist's ideal goal is knowledge of the real outside world; but his only research tool, his measurements, never tell him anything directly about the real world, but are always only a more or less uncertain message or . . . a sign that the real world transmits to him and from which he then tries to draw conclusions, similar to a linguist who must decode a document which comes from a culture completely unknown to him."[21] Planck's metaphor of mediation puts the physicist in the position of a reader, not just any reader, but one who has special training in language to try to ascertain the hidden message of a text. The text or document in the metaphor is analogous to the physicist's measurements—the "intermediate sphere" in Nietzsche's language, between object and subject. Both Planck and Nietzsche require the concept of translation from one language to another. For both the translation can only be "suggestive," "stammering," and "uncertain." The difference between them lies in Nietzsche's descriptive terms "freely composing and freely inventing" that inject a spontaneity that is not a desirable quality in measurements or decodable foreign texts. Nietzsche's adds to

21. "Positivismus und reale Außenwelt," 1930, *Vorträge*, 235. This essay has been translated as "Positivism and External Reality," in *The International Forum*, January 1, 1931, 12–16, and February 15, 1931, 14–19.

their joint interpretations the kind of thinking that goes into revolutionary science that breaks with accepted disciplinary models.[22]

According to Planck, science is based on the hypothesis of the existence of an outside world, direct knowledge of which can only be gotten via our senses "as if we could only perceive a foreign object through eyeglasses that have a different tint for every individual person."[23] That is, we are likely to be wearing glasses that exclude certain wave lengths, for example, and we would not know whether our vision was the correct one. Planck's "outside world" is like Nietzsche's "essence of things" that can never be known or even designated by names that, at most, refer to a single, isolated quality or aspect. They are joined in that belief and in their scepticism about (in Nietzsche's case, rejection of) human knowledge of that world. In 1933, in an introduction to a collection of his speeches and essays, Planck affirmed the inevitability of anthropomorphism, even in the project of science:

. . . physics, like every other science, contains an irrational core that one cannot define away without robbing research of its actual driving power, but which also, on the other hand, can never be completely explained.

As the development of the new physics is beginning to show more and more clearly, the inner reason for this irrationality lies in the circumstance that the human researcher is himself a piece of Nature, and therefore can never achieve the distance from Nature that would be necessary in order to reach a completely objective view of Nature. (*Vorträge*, vi)

---

22. The pathbreaking, now classic, but still controversial and to some extent refuted interpretation is from Thomas S. Kuhn, *The Structure of Scientific Revolutions*, 2d ed. (Chicago: University of Chicago Press, 1970). Its most powerful and lasting impact has been on researchers in the humanities and social sciences. There is a strong tendency for nonscientists writing on scientific matters to refer to Kuhn's text as uncritically as if they were literal readers citing the bible—an interesting example of the literary-scientific connection. Whereas philosophy of science has developed, expanded upon, and moved away from Kuhn's notion of the scientific "paradigm" in the more than a quarter of a century since his work was first published.

23. "Kausalgesetz und Willensfreiheit," *Vorträge*, 153.

At the same time, Planck remained a working scientist committed, above all, to the furthering and enhancement of the sciences in general and his science in particular. His commitment rests on faith in science, per se, in particular the future of a science that inevitably and continually progresses "upward," as knowledge and mastery of the world of the senses increases. Planck provides the researcher's answer to the problem of the distorting eyeglass lenses: take the tints caused by the glasses into consideration when judging an object. "Even the most ardent sceptic cannot dispute the fact that today we know how to see and hear into far greater distances, and command far more significant forces and speeds than a generation ago, and just as little can one doubt that this progress means a permanent increase of our knowledge that will not be considered erroneous or negated at a later time."[24] How can what appear to be opposite poles in Planck's thinking be reconciled? They need not be, just as one need not attempt to reconcile Nietzsche's "science" with his literary rhetoric. The oppositions make up the productive, if disputatious, dialogue within as well as between the texts—the oscillation between apparently irreconcilable opposites that are not opposites at all, but rather turns of the kaleidescope that rearrange human ideas to produce new associations and connections.

For Planck, in contrast to Nietzsche, "the outside world imposes itself upon us with elemental force."[25] Originally, according to Planck's account, interpretation of nature and the world were completely anthropocentric. Humans saw the forces of nature, animals, and plants only in relation to themselves. Science could only begin when man no longer saw himself and the planet he inhabited as the center of the universe, when he ignored his own immediate interests for the sake of "pure knowledge," "and withdrew to the more modest position of an attentively listening observer, who had to remain as quiet as possible in the background in order to influence as little as possible the features of the

---

24. "Das Weltbild der neuen Physik," *Vorträge*, 210.
25. "Vom Relativen zum Absoluten," 1924, *Vorträge*, 181.

objects he was investigating and the course of events being observed." At that point "the outside world began to unveil its secrets to him and in that way revealed the means by which he could force it into his service . . . ."[26] The diagnosis and story of origins is the opposite of Nietzsche's: in place of Nietzsche's moral excoriation of the arrogant, lying, inevitably ignorant species, ultimately and permanently dependent upon metaphor, we find the standard public relations for science — a confidently modest, ideal investigator who will eventually exercise appropriate mastery over the "object" being investigated without disturbing it. Let us compare Nietzsche's version of the same story.

The researcher of such [general] truths is basically searching only for the metamorphosis of the world in man; he is struggling for an understanding of the world as a human-like thing and the best he wrests for himself is a feeling of assimilation. Similar to the way the astrologist considers the stars in the service of mankind and in connection with its happiness and suffering, such a researcher views the entire world as connected to man . . . he starts from the error of believing that he has these things before him as pure objects. He therefore forgets that the original intuitive [or visual] metaphors [*Anschauungsmetaphern*] *are* metaphors and takes them for the things themselves. (883)

Which story is literary; which is scientific? Planck's story is one of progress to a superior condition; it can be interpreted as a story of hubris. Nietzsche's story is static — the human condition he describes is an unchanging one; his story is also a story of hubris. The difference is that Nietzsche designates it as such and Planck does not. They describe the same origin. To that origin Planck adds an open-ended process. What Nietzsche will add becomes apparent only toward the conclusion of his essay: it is a look to the past, to a better time when the world was imbued by man with myth and magic. In the imposition of that conclusion, Nietzsche departs from the arguments of the previous text, that is the rhetorical nature of "truth" and nonreferentiality of lan-

---

26. "Kausalgesetz und Willensfreiheit," *Vorträge*, 153.

guage, to tell a story of two people—"the rational man" and "the intuitive man"—and the qualities they represent. With his personifications of ideas—as the scientist and the artist—Nietzsche has created the very abstractions he so roundly condemns throughout the preceding text. By extension, the two types could also be aspects of one individual, or a characterization of the text itself—a didactic device of summary and guidance for the reader in the terms a reader understands best. All culture, artifacts, history, and events are subordinated to this typology in the concluding paragraph. And with the abandonment of his previous posture and turn toward the anthropocentrism he has exposed all along as inevitable, Nietzsche proves it *is* inevitable; with the dramatic portrait he deconstructs the shifting play of argument, counterargument, and metaphor he had set in dialectical motion and gives a round to his sparring partner Max Planck. For the scientist-figure (whose description suits the real-life Planck very well), noble and stoic, strides away with dignity, providing closure to the essay: "When a heavy thundercloud burst upon him, he wraps himself up in his cloak and with slow and measured steps walks away from beneath it" (890).[27] Nietzsche's description of the "man of reason" in contrast to the "man of intuition" comes very close to retelling Max Planck's story of the origin of the scientific viewpoint in contrast to the preceding anthropocentric interpretation of nature. Nietzsche, however, does not so clearly valorize the figure of the scientist as Planck does; Nietzsche's valorization is more subtle—portrayed as the bringer of closure in a two-character drama as spare and powerful as a drama by Beckett.

While Planck's certainty, as we have seen, is a qualified, tempered one, there *are* signs from the outside world, of which he is absolutely sure. They are the universal constants. These are the

---

27. I am using the felicitous translation of this sentence by Maximillian A. Mügge in Friedrich Nietzsche, *Early Greek Philosophy and Other Essays*, Vol. 2 of *The Complete Works of Friedrich Nietzsche*, ed. Oscar Levy (London: T.N. Foulis, 1911), 192.

"building blocks,"[28] of the physical world-picture, the absolute measurements — such as the speed of light or the mass and charge of an electron — that are independent of human qualities. Unlike units such as the centimeter or the gram, that are adapted to conditions on earth, the universal constants "must of necessity retain their meaning for all time and for all cultures, even extraterrestrial and extra-human ones" (Toulmin, *Physical Reality*, 19). "Building blocks" are also the ingredients of Planck's (literally) foundational and most frequently used metaphor: physics (or science itself) as an edifice, sometimes very specifically a building that has firm foundations (which may only be shaken by the "heavy artillery" of powerful new hypotheses) and rooms, and for which additions are built by scientists' efforts. Planck uses the metaphor so commonly that it becomes intrinsic to his rhetoric and his persona as scientist-narrator.

Nietzsche likes the building metaphor as well. He uses it twice in the brief essay, but to the effect of overturning Planck's imagery. Planck's has the heft and feel of Wilhelminian monumental classicistic architecture — the home of the Prussian Academy of Sciences in Berlin, for example. Nietzsche's edifice, constructed by "science" in the manner that bees construct their hives, is a considerably less dignified, less weighty structure. It is a burial vault for intuition [*Anschauungen*]:

As we saw, it is language that originally works on the construction of concepts, in later times it is science. Just as the bee builds the cells at the same time it fills them with honey, science works without stopping on that great columbarium of concepts, the burial place of intuitions, builds always newer and higher stories, supports, cleans, renews the old cells and endeavors above all to fill that monstrously towering framework and to arrange within it the entire empirical world, i.e. the anthropomorphic world. As the man of action binds his life to reason and its concepts, in order not to be washed away and not to lose himself, so the researcher builds his hut hard by the tower of science, in order to help

---

28. "Das Weltbild der neuen Physik," *Vorträge*, 213.

build it and to find protection under the already existing bastion. And he *needs* protection: for there are terrible powers that continually intrude upon him and confront the scientific truth with entirely different kinds of "truths" that bear the most heterogeneous labels. (886)

Would Max Planck recognize his project in Nietzsche's description? Certainly in its diachronic and synchronic procedures — its description of historical process and current state. Planck would also agree with the reference to outside, nonrational forces threatening the structure of science. Thus, on the level of concept there would be overlap. What he could *not* accept are the metaphors, the architecture of Nietzsche's construct. It is the pejorative tropes that would be alien and offensive — above all the association with death, but also of limits and confinement, of reduction and insignificant busy-ness. Planck's story is one of "emancipation" from anthropomorphism, from Nietzsche's "honey" that gets stuffed into rigid cells as into a Procrustean bed; the comparison of the task of science with the work of the bee is completely outside of Planck's ordinary discourse. And with this distinction we come to the heart of the textual dialogue: they meet in ideas; they share the same philosophical heritage; they separate in language. We can respond now to the central, rhetorical questions Nietzsche raised early in his essay: "Do names and things coincide? Is language the adequate expression of all realities?" (878). We already know his answer. Posing Planck as reader of the above paragraph suggests yet another dimension. Planck's reading provides proof that the answer to both of Nietzsche's questions is "no." For Planck and Nietzsche share, to a large extent, the same "realities"; what they do not share are the designations, the names of those realities. Both know of an "essence of things" beyond the grasp of human understanding except for isolated signs ("translations"), and of the human *Wissensdrang* ("urge to know" — Planck's term) or *Wahrheitstrieb* ("drive for truth" — Nietzsche's term) in spite or because of this coded essence. Yet for Planck, Nietzsche's metaphors, his namings, would overturn that reality, contradict and undermine it. According to that reading, in other words, Nietzsche's rhetorical tropes are distinguishable from another level of meaning in the text—a reading that contradicts Nietzsche's view of metaphor. If we posed Nietzsche reading Planck's lectures, we might find a transposed but equivalent response: he would probably find only cool, lifeless conceptualizing, what is missing is the "honey"—the metaphorical *Aufhebungen* (suspensions, annulments, nullifications, abrogations, repeals, rescissions).

There is a deep ambivalence about the notion of moving away from the intuitive [*Anschaulichkeit*], the original, or instinctive. For it is just as easy to argue that intuition is learned. Benoit Mandelbrot, founder of a new version of geometry called fractals that defies traditional thinking, reports: "When I came into this game, there was a total absence of intuition. One had to create an intuition from scratch. . . . Intuition is not something that is given. I've trained my intuition to accept as obvious shapes which were initially rejected as absurd, and I find everyone else can do the same."[29] Relativity and quantum mechanics also required, and eventually supplied, new intuitions. Each new science also requires a new language in order to understand and communicate it. "In other words, a great scientific invention implies a radical change in language for a given domain: methods, theories, experiments, all are parts of a totally determined, semantic, and closed system that depends on a philosophy of language."[30] Until that language is discovered, the new science will not cohere, nor will it be accepted. Without using the term metaphor, we are nevertheless very close to Nietzsche's views of the dependence of conceptualizing on language categories. Language sets terms and parameters, provides pictures, in a sense does the creative thinking for us. This is also a deeply ambivalent condition. In

29. As quoted in James Gleick, *Chaos: Making a New Science* (New York: Viking, 1987), 102.

30. Edouard Morot-Sir's excellent turn of phrase comes from his review of Wilda C. Anderson's *Between the Library and the Laboratory: The Language of Chemistry in Eighteenth-Century France, South Atlantic Review* 51 (May 1986): 127. See also Bruce Gregory, *Inventing Reality: Physics as Language* (New York: Wiley, 1988).

Nietzsche's essay the notion of developing *new* intuitions is missing. Therefore developments such as relativity and quantum mechanics cannot be encompassed by his descriptions of science.

In Planck's lectures there is no metalanguage, or reflection on the use and nature of language. Therefore interdisciplinarity, which requires admitting an alternative language, is also missing. These deficits suggest reading Nietzsche's and Planck's texts as the Danish cofounder of quantum theory Niels Bohr read — according to his principle of complementarity. That is to say, no single point of view can ever "read" or interpret a situation in its entirety. To "read" quantum mechanical events requires applying two mutually exclusive points of view, for one without the other is not explanatory. Bohr treated this notion as an epistemological one broadly applicable beyond the realm of atomic phenomena. These applications remain controversial, as does the "Copenhagen Interpretation" of quantum mechanics that originated at Bohr's institute (and is the interpretation I will present in the coming pages). Complementarity is a notion analogous to my procedures in this study. An essay by H. H. Pattee, "The Complementarity Principle in Biological and Social Structures," presents strong arguments for the cross-disciplinary applicability of Bohr's thesis:

. . . explanatory knowledge of biological and social systems — from cells to human societies — requires the simultaneous articulation of two, formally incompatible, modes of description. The source of this requirement lies in the subject-object duality, or the distinction between the image and the event, the knower and the known, the genotype and the phenotype, the program and the hardware, or the policy and the implementation, however one may choose to express this basic distinction. The essence of the concept of complementarity is not in the recognition of this subject-object distinction, which is common to almost all epistemologies, but in the apparently paradoxical articulation of the two modes of knowing.[31]

---

31. *Journal of Social and Biological Structures* 1 (April 1978): 192.

Pattee adds the important proviso that "this duality of descriptive modes and their incompatibility should not be thought of as a contradiction in any sense. In fact, there is none since the two modes of description are formally disjoint and contradiction can only occur within a single formal system" (193). The idea of "two modes of knowing" is a seminal one that connects complementarity with Kafka's texts in their suggestion of simultaneous, logically incompatible modes of comprehending. For Prigogine and Stengers, "[t]he real lesson to be learned from the principle of complementarity, a lesson that can perhaps be transferred to other fields of knowledge, consists in emphasizing the wealth of reality, which overflows any single language, any single logical structure."[32]

The necessity for the duality, or the complementary description of a phenomenon, originated with Einstein's research (1905) that applied Planck's quantum of action to the behavior of light in the photoelectric effect, showing that light, which according to the theories of classical physics consisted of waves, *also* followed the laws of behavior that govern particles. Light had to be regarded as *both* wave *and* particle, although the physical laws governing the behavior of waves and particles were mutually exclusive. Later, when Bohr developed his model of the structure of the atom in 1913,[33] and still later when Werner Heisenberg discovered in 1927 that an "Uncertainty Principle" governed the behavior of subatomic particles, an explanatory hypothesis was necessary and provided by Bohr with the notion of complementarity. The Uncertainty Principle arises from the impossibility of measuring with precision both the velocity and the position of a subatomic particle. The clearer the focus on one variable, the less clear the focus on the other. That mutual relationship is expressed in an equation that depends upon Planck's constant to express the

---

32. Ilya Prigogine and Isabelle Stengers, *Order Out of Chaos: Man's New Dialogue with Nature* (New York: Bantam, 1984), 225.

33. Developed, it has been argued, on the basis of Planck's publications from 1910 to 1912 on radiation theory. See Tetu Hirosige and Sigeo Nisio, "Formation of Bohr's Theory of Atomic Constitution," *Japanese Studies in the History of Science* 3 (1964): 6–28.

"minimum uncertainty."[34] The interference results from the wave/particle nature of light. Observation of particles (electrons, for example) requires bombardment with photons of light that, if it is of sufficient intensity (short wavelength) to permit an observer to see the particle clearly, will disturb its momentum, and if it is gentle enough (long wavelength) to avoid disturbing the particle, will not result in a clear enough picture to determine the particle's position. On the subatomic level, therefore, measurement itself interferes with the object being measured and thus the choice of experiment determines the outcome. The Uncertainty Principle applies not only to velocity and position, but to an entire class of "conjugal variables," including, for example, time and energy. These findings contradicted prevailing convictions about the nature of matter and energy and had important and wide epistemological repercussions. Heisenberg and Bohr saw the challenge to epistemology, logic, and language. Cline describes their dilemma when initially faced with their discoveries:

As physicists, they possessed a large vocabulary of technical words with which to describe the processes of nature, but their words referred back, in the end, to a fundamental distinction. A physical process could be analyzed in terms of moving particles or in terms of the propagation of a wave; language referred either to one case or the other. What is more, language implied that it was possible always to distinguish between the two cases. In back of words was the logical assumption that given two statements:

This is a particle.

This is not a particle.

one of the two must be correct. . . . That being the situation, it was

---

34. Heisenberg's principle "states that any measurement of position and momentum, any measurement of energy at a specified instant of time, must result in an uncertainty equal *at least* to Planck's Constant." Barbara Lovett Cline, *Men Who Made a New Physics*, (Chicago: University of Chicago Press, 1987) 207. "The classically complete description in space and time of causal connections between physical phenomena is replaced in quantum mechanics by the 'complementarity of space-time description and causality.' " Jungnickel and McCormmach, *Intellectual Mastery of Nature*, 2:369, quoting Heisenberg.

close to impossible *not* to ask loaded questions, questions which assumed that even though the electron displayed the character of both a wave and a particle, it "really" was one and not the other. Before progress could be made, Heisenberg and Bohr had to become distrustful not only of words but of intuition — "common" sense. (204)

Intuition, logic, causality, and therefore prediction in physics seemed no longer valid, nor did the language in which classical physics had been expressed, for it described a world of larger bodies in which different rules applied. "The real problem . . . was the fact that no language existed in which one could speak consistently about the new situation. The ordinary language was based upon the old concepts of space and time and this language offered the only unambiguous means of communication about the setting up and the results of the measurements. Yet the experiments showed that the old concepts could not be applied everywhere."[35] Bohr was the physicist who struggled most with the

---

35. Heisenberg, *Physics and Philosophy*, 174. There are many studies of the history and development of quantum physics in the context of its philosophical implications. Among them are: Milič Čapek, *The Philosophical Impact of Contemporary Physics* (Princeton: Van Nostrand, 1961); Paul Forman, "Weimar Culture, Causality, and Quantum Theory, 1918–1927: Adaptation by German Physicists and Mathematicians to a Hostile Intellectual Environment," *Historical Studies in the Physical Sciences* 3 (1971): 1–115; Gerald Holton, "The Roots of Complementarity," in his *Thematic Origins of Scientific Thought: Kepler to Einstein* (Cambridge: Harvard University Press, 1973), 115–61; Max Jammer, *The Conceptual Development of Quantum Mechanics* (New York: McGraw-Hill, 1966). A more strictly scientific presentation is Armin Hermann's *The Genesis of Quantum Theory (1899–1913)*, trans. Claude W. Nash (Cambridge, Mass.: MIT Press, 1971). Kurt Hübner, in his *Critique of Scientific Reason*, trans. Paul R. Dixon, Jr. and Hollis M. Dixon (Chicago: University of Chicago Press, 1983), presents a strong revisionist argument — that quantum mechanics did *not* have the purported effects on language, logic, and ideas of causality. Forman shows that major philosophical conclusions drawn by the founders of quantum mechanics had more to do with the pressure of contemporary ideologies than with the results of experiment. He presents this argument powerfully with regard to the ideas of causality, "Anschaulichkeit," and individuality in his article: "*Kausalität, Anschaulichkeit, and Individualität, or How Cultural Values Prescribed the Character and the Lessons Ascribed to Quantum Mechanics,*" in *Society and Knowledge: Contemporary Perspectives in the Sociology of Knowledge,* ed. Nico Stehr and Volker Meja (New Brunswick: Transaction Books, 1984),

problem of an adequate language for the new relations. Cline presents Bohr's thinking as follows: " . . . while man seeks to understand a reality which exists outside himself, the explanations which he finds for this reality are worded in human language, wholly man-made. As languages of words are invented by man, . . . so is the language of symbols, mathematics; it is more refined, less cumbersome than the other languages, but like them it reflects man's way of thought and not a pattern external to himself" (241). This description bears a close resemblance to Nietzsche's in "On Truth and Lie in an Extramoral Sense." We cannot expect Nietzsche to have raised the same issues as quantum mechanics fifty years before their time, but to a certain degree he did. That is, how valid are the a priori assumptions of logic? Are notions of causality, sequence in time and space, and inviolability of ideas of time and space themselves mere convention based on habit? Is the notion of the referentiality of language only a convention? The development and interpretation of quantum mechanics, as well as Einstein's theories of relativity, supported such questions. The answers affirmed Nietzsche, at least when it comes to events on the subatomic level and the language used to describe them, for the behavior of subatomic particles defied the worldview of classical physics and exposed its anthropomorphism. Laws of matter, energy, and motion that had been thought to be universal turned out to be conventions with limited applicability.

Special Relativity, proposed by Einstein in 1905, has to do with the invariance of the speed of light; it is "constant to all observers regardless of the motion of its source." Einstein's theory of General Relativity, published in 1915, proposed the warping of space-time by the pull of large bodies in space. Together they provided "a far-reaching revision of the physical world-picture" that Einstein regarded, in the case of general relativity, "as a step

333–47. The controversy over the interpretation of quantum mechanics continues to rage and the jury is still out on a final judgment. See also n. 38 on the Einstein/Bohr dispute.

in the direction of a physics describing a world existing independently of human convenience." Relativity defied the commonsense notions of time and space that Nietzsche saw as the inevitable product of the human imagination. Einstein, in a sense, responded to Nietzsche with a contradiction of Nietzsche's assertion of the "inviolability of ideas of time and space." Relativity meant that defiance of common sense, an overturning of habit and convention, was possible. The commonsense view sees space and time as separate; relativity proposes combined space-time as a fourth dimension. Common sense takes the mass of an object as independent of its motion; relativity determines that the mass of a body depends upon its speed. Common sense believes that two observers of an event, no matter what their respective positions, will clock that event as occurring at the same time; relativity proves that their clocks will show different times according to the position and motion of the observers. Thus, "the most far-reaching revision of the physical world picture before the creation of an acausal quantum mechanics"[36] suggests, contrary to Nietzsche's view, it *is* possible for the human mind to break through long-shared conventions of time and space, just as non-Euclidean geometry broke through the sacrosanct mathematics of millennia,[37] and quantum theory required a new, more complex and nonsuccessive definition of causality, one based on probability.[38] Relativity and quantum mechanics seemed, in Nietzsche's

36. Jungnickel and McCormmach, *Intellectual Mastery of Nature*, 2:246, 347, 328, 347. There is a vast body of literature on Einstein's theories of relativity. One thorough treatment of special relativity is by Arthur I. Miller, *Albert Einstein's Special Theory of Relativity: Emergence (1905) and Early Interpretation (1905-1911)* (Reading, Mass.: Addison-Wesley, 1981). Einstein's own semipopular version is *Relativity: The Special and the General Theory*, trans. Robert W. Lawson (New York: Bonanza, 1961).

37. For a discussion of the development of non-Euclidean geometry, see Douglas R. Hofstadter, *Gödel, Escher, Bach: An Eternal Golden Braid* (New York: Vintage, 1980); Jungnickel and McCormmach, *Intellectual Mastery of Nature*; and Morris Kline, *Mathematics: The Loss of Certainty* (Oxford: Oxford University Press, 1980).

38. Today, relativistic quantum mechanics combines the two revolutionary developments in modern physics—a combination that would have been resisted

metaphor, to wash away the support of the edifice of physical science and mathematics. Since the edifice in Nietzsche's view is founded on metaphor, he might respond that new metaphors have merely replaced the old, solidified ones. Yet some of the threatening questions raised by these revolutionary theories were anticipated in Nietzsche's own text. How, then, to interpret the crossover between Einstein and Nietzsche indicated by the quotation (above) from Einstein about a physical worldview moving *away* from anthropomorphism? The answer is that Nietzsche had already carried out the deconstruction in language that relativity and quantum mechanics were to do in physics, logic, and related epistemologies. They provided experimental evidence for his contention that the most basic human notions — space, time, logic, and causality — were mere habits.

Planck, with his discovery of quantum discontinuity, had been the "father" of the later development of quantum mechanics. He was also the first theoretical physicist to welcome Einstein's theory of relativity and was largely responsible for hastening its acceptance against heavy initial resistance among physicists. According to Planck, the relativity theory provided "the crown,"[39] and harmonious completion of the world-picture of classical physics because it provided a solution for unanswered questions and unresolved inconsistencies in previous theories. It was difficult to accept only because it required revisions of habitual, intuitive [*anschaulich*] notions. "The discovery was made by Albert Einstein, that our ideas of space and time, on which Newton and Kant had based their reasoning as the absolute, given forms of our intuition, in a certain sense have only a relative meaning because of the arbitrary nature of choice of reference systems and

---

by Einstein, who strongly opposed the epistemological and metaphysical implications of Heisenberg's and Bohr's "Copenhagen Interpretation of Quantum Theory" (see Heisenberg, *Physics and Philosophy*, 44–58). For a succinct presentation of their differences, see Niels Bohr, "Discussion with Einstein on Epistemological Problems in Atomic Physics," in *Albert Einstein: Philosopher-Scientist*, ed. Paul Arthur Schilpp (La Salle, Ill.: Open Court, 1949), 199–241.

39. "Physikalische Gesetzlichkeit," *Vorträge*, 199.

measuring procedures. This discovery attacks the roots of our physical thinking perhaps more deeply than anything else." For Planck, the common usage of "relativity" was a misunderstanding, for the "relative" — like all physical principles — required and depended upon the *absolute*, in this case the speed of light. His argument is apparent even in the title of a lecture presented in 1924 in Munich: "From the Relative to the Absolute." But in his conclusion to this lecture Planck adds that what we believe is absolute today may prove to be relative tomorrow and "give way to a higher absolute concept."[40] In this interplay we see the characteristic duality in Planck's thinking. We will find it in his views on quantum theory and its threat to causality, and his views on logic and on scientific laws. It is equivalent to the unresolved polarity in Nietzsche's text between metaphor (or the literariness of language) as the absolute, and the relative as the sciences with which he cannot help allying himself.

It had become clear to Planck some years after his own discovery that quantum theory, in contrast to relativity, brought a complete break with the foundations of classical physics. In his Nobel Prize acceptance speech of 1920, Planck explained what his "quantum of action" meant: ". . . something completely new, previously unheard of, which seemed destined to fundamentally reorder our physical thinking which, since the establishment of infinitesimal calculus by Leibniz and Newton, has rested on the presumption of the constancy of all causal connections."[41] Even more, it was "an exotic, threatening explosive device which has . . . torn a gaping fissure, from top to bottom, through the entire edifice [of classical physics]."[42] Planck's discussion of the changes in the

---

40. "Vom Relativen zum Absoluten," *Vorträge*, 181, 182.

41. "Die Entstehung und bisherige Entwicklung der Quantentheorie," *Vorträge*, 199. Translated versions available as "The Origin and Development of the Quantum Theory," trans. H. T. Clarke and L. Silberstein (Oxford: Clarendon, 1922); in Max Planck, *A Survey of Physical Theory*, trans. R. Jones and D. H. Williams (New York: Dover, 1960), 102–114; and in *The World of the Atom*, ed. Henry A. Boorse and Lloyd Motz (New York: Basic, 1966), 1:491–501.

42. "Physikalische Gesetzlichkeit," *Vorträge*, 199.

physical world-picture connects to Nietzsche's remarks through two central concepts above all: anthropomorphism and causality. Quantum theory meant a giant step away from anthropomorphism/*Anschaulichkeit*[43] — from connection to the world of the senses — and toward greater abstraction with mathematical formalism playing an increasingly important role. Paradoxically, according to Planck, the greater abstraction has meant approaching closer to the "real world." This seems to carry Nietzsche's ideas full circle — via mathematical abstraction, taking a detour around intuition, the "essence of things" is being approached as anthropomorphism is left behind. The dependence of quantum mechanics on probability calculations "appears to renounce the demand for strict causality in favor of a certain indeterminism."[44] Planck's conviction that science requires determinism, however, leads him to see a new kind of determinism (he has switched from the term "causality") in quantum mechanics.[45] It depends upon a modification of the concept of the predictability of one event from a previous event; the modification rests on an altered use of the term *event*, from an individual measurement to an imagined process.[46] The physicist's questions must be formulated differently, for the question of what happens *between* two quantum states is no longer

---

43. It is difficult to imagine, today, how large the question of "Anschaulichkeit" loomed and how its loss was dreaded. Jungnickel and McCormmach quote a poignant speech of last ditch resistance to the loss of "clear images" in physical theory, given by one of the leading theoretical physicists of the time, H. A. Lorentz, at the Fifth Solvay Congress in 1927 where the state of quantum mechanics was heatedly discussed (or its validity disputed) by all the leading actors, including Bohr, Heisenberg, and Einstein. (Jungnickel and McCormmach, *Intellectual Mastery of Nature*, 371.) For further discussion of the "Anschaulichkeit" controversy, see Paul Forman, "*Kausalität, Anschaulichkeit,* and *Individualität,*" and Arthur I. Miller, "Visualization Lost and Regained: The Genesis of the Quantum Theory in the Period 1913–27," in *On Aesthetics in Science*, ed. Judith Wechsler (Cambridge, Mass.: MIT Press, 1978), 73–101.
44. "Das Weltbild der neuen Physik," *Vorträge*, 210, 222.
45. Two seminal studies on the causality-determinism issue are Mario Bunge, *Causality and Modern Science*, 3d. rev. ed. (New York: Dover, 1979); and Ernst Cassirer, *Determinism and Indeterminism in Modern Physics*, trans. O. Theodor Benfey (London: Oxford University Press, 1956).
46. "Die Kausalität in der Natur," *Vorträge*, 255.

relevant. Because of the wave function there is no meaning in asking for the simultaneous position and velocity of a particle. Strict laws still govern the behavior of particles; however, those laws are calculated differently and expressed in different symbols. On these two central points—the move *away* from anthropomorphism/*Anschaulichkeit* and the retention of a new kind of nonsequential determinism—Planck again provides a "deconstructive" reading of Nietzsche on science. Like Einstein, Planck answers Nietzsche by recasting the questions. His interpretation of the new physics offers variations on anthropomorphism/*Anschaulichkeit* and determinism/causality that would need to enter Nietzsche's discussion.

Over the course of the twenty-plus years since Planck had given his Leiden lecture in 1908 there was a marked shift in his central concept, the physical world-picture. That famous lecture was called "The Unity of the Physical World-Picture" and referred to the fixed goal of science as a "constant, unified world-picture" that "contains certain features which can never be effaced by any revolution, either in Nature or in the human mind" (Toulmin, *Physical Reality*, 25). By contrast, his 1932 London lecture "Causality in Nature" contains descriptions of the physical world-picture in a Nietzschean tone: "the so-called physical world-picture which, to a certain extent, represents arbitrary thought constructions, an idealization as model, created for the purpose of escaping from the uncertainty attached to any individual measurement and making possible a precise determination of concepts"; it is "only a crutch," "a provisional and changeable creation of the human imagination." Science means continually striving, he concludes, "toward a goal that we are able to sense poetically, but are never able completely to grasp rationally."[47] It is justifiable to see in this development once again the intermingling of the scientific with the literary, of the Planckian with the Nietzschean.

---

47. "Die Kausalität in der Natur," *Vorträge*, 255, 256, 264, 269.

Let us return to Nietzsche's definition of a law of Nature. It began with a question:

> What is for us, in general, a law of Nature; it is in itself not known to us, rather only its effects, i.e., its relations to other laws of Nature which, again, are only known as relations. Thus all these relations again and again refer only to each other and are in their essence completely incomprehensible to us; only whatever we ourselves bring to them, such as time, space, sequence and number are really known to us. (885)

The laws of Nature are the focal point of Planck's thinking and writing. Over the course of many years he explores the idea of laws in his lectures. His starting point is always the "dualism" between reversible and irreversible processes, the former being a theoretical concept and the latter representing the processes of nature that show an increase of entropy, or the unidirectional flow in the direction of greater disorder described in the Second Law of Thermodynamics. In the course of his investigations Planck clarified and extended the Second Law to its modern version and discovered the quantum of energy. His work depended upon the adoption of statistical methods to measure the probability of any state occurring. The division of causality into deterministic or absolute causality (governing reversible processes) and statistical or probable causality (governing irreversible processes) posed epistemological problems to which Planck's thoughts always returned. Processes governed by statistical probability can only be known approximately, that is, by average values; the behavior of one individual molecule in a solution or an electron in a radiation field cannot be predicted. Statistical probability, therefore, represents a different kind of causality, one in which individual behavior is not predictable, but only the collective, or average behavior of a large number of entities. This dualism between "necessity and probability," Planck admits, is an "unsatisfying" element that has been introduced into the physical laws. But he goes on to explain that even probability calculations are exact in their formulation and strict in their proofs; "if the probability of a specific event following another specific event is 1/2," that means "in all cases when the first event occurs, exactly 50 percent will lead to the second event." The larger the number of cases observed, of course, the more exact the relationship will be. If it were possible to observe simultaneously *all* microscopic events in the world (as opposed to the macroscopic events of daily life), absolute determinism would be apparent. Physics, like any other science, cannot do without "the premise of absolute laws"[48] and Planck finds these in the laws of statistical probability as well. Planck's conviction is expressed differently in a later lecture that takes "the quantum hypothesis" fully into account. He asks the question Nietzsche had asked before: "What do we understand by physical laws?" His answer is that a physical law expresses a relation between "measurable physical units," "that permits one of these units to be calculated when the others are known by measurement." "Relation," of course, is also Nietzsche's answer. In the same lecture Planck continues:

First of all we may not at all regard it as a foregone conclusion that physical laws exist at all, or that even if they have existed up to now, they will always continue to exist in the same way in the future. It is completely conceivable, and we could not do the least thing to prevent it, that Nature one fine day could outwit us with the occurrence of a completely unexpected event . . .

Further:

. . . whatever we can test and measure in Nature can never be expressed by definite numbers, but always contains a certain indefiniteness caused by the unavoidable sources of errors in the measurements. We conclude that through measurements we will never succeed in deciding whether a law is absolutely valid in Nature or not. And we get no different result when we test this question from the standpoint of the general theory of knowledge. If we . . . are not even in a position to provide proof that

---

48. "Dynamische und statistische Gesetzmäßigkeit," *Vorträge* 90. Translated as "Dynamical Laws and Statistical Laws" in Max Planck, *A Survey of Physical Theory*, 56–68.

laws exist in Nature at all, we will succeed all the less in proving at the outset that such laws are absolute.

A working physicist, however, requires the presumption of "strictly causal laws" "in the interest of the healthy progress" of physics.[49] On this presumption he builds his "system of concepts and theorems, the so-called physical world-picture." "Thus the physicist must presume that the real world obeys certain laws incomprehensible to us, even when he has no prospect of completely grasping these laws or even at the outset of establishing their nature with complete confidence."[50] Planck in dialogue with his own text and with Nietzsche has led us to consideration of laws that exist but cannot be known, and laws that do not exist except as conventions based on habit. These considerations take us to the heart of Kafka's *The Trial* and provide further elaboration of its story of absent but all-powerful law.

J. Hillis Miller, in *The Ethics of Reading*, proposes "that there is a peculiar and unexpected relation between the affirmation of universal moral law and storytelling. . . . the moral law gives rise by an intrinsic necessity to storytelling, even if that storytelling in one way or another puts in question or subverts the moral law."[51] The idea of the law, an absent presence in Miller's and the other texts he examines, is represented in the Miller text by an epigraph from *The Trial*. The epigraph is from the section of *The Trial* that is "the exegesis of the legend"[52] "Before the Law," concluding with the impossibility of final interpretation. The Kafka text is a determining presence and point of reference throughout the Miller text, connecting its exploration of moral law and story telling to ours of the notion of law as realized in Nietzsche's essay

49. "Physikalische Gesetzlichkeit," *Vorträge*, 183–84, 184, 194, 195.

50. "Positivismus und reale Außenwelt," *Vorträge*, 235.

51. J. Hillis Miller, *The Ethics of Reading* (New York: Columbia University Press, 1987), 2.

52. Kafka's term, in *Tagebücher 1910–1923*, ed. Max Brod (Frankfurt am Main: S. Fischer, 1986) entry for 13 December 1914, 326.

and Planck's lectures. Miller's readings are "deconstructive," thereby necessarily focusing on language. And they begin with Kant, whose views determined the moral imperative as well as what was considered the law of nature in classical physics as inherited by Planck, and as inherited and disowned by Nietzsche. Our concern here is not Kant per se, but the inheritance of Kantian "law" as something that some contemporary developments in the sciences are leaving behind. Miller's reading leads him to find an unreliability in Kant's reading of his own texts that demonstrates the undecidability of the law. With Bloom's scheme of misreading as his point of departure, Miller finds the endpoint of his readings in the idea that the "reading is subject . . . to the law to which the text is subject. This law forces the reader to betray the text or deviate from it in the act of reading it, in the name of a higher demand that can yet be reached only by way of the text. This response creates yet another text which is a new act" (120). The procedure Miller describes is a recursive one—"a process that operates on the product of its own operation."[53] Inevitably, this must be our procedure as we read and reread the texts at hand, then take them, via their definitions of law, to yet another reading. We find, then, in the Miller text a bridge that spans our several texts and laws—from Kafka to science. He provides a "definition" of the law—"The law is the Absolute, empty air or an undifferentiated expanse of shining snow [an image from Henry James]" (121)—and a guide to reading Kant subversively that connect us, for example, to Prigogine and Stengers who argue for a new kind of science and against the "closed and limiting conception of science" (*Order Out of Chaos*, 86) that Kant's approach represented. The idea of law in science must be revised to take into account the rich and complex diversity of the natural world, for which *pattern*, *process*, and *system* are more applicable terms than *law*. The model of classical physics and other reductionist sciences

---

53. Humberto R. Maturana and Francisco J. Varela, *The Tree of Knowledge: The Biological Roots of Human Understanding*, trans. Robert Paolucci (Boston: New Science Library, 1988), 253.

is no longer sufficient and should be replaced by the systems perspective of biology. Referring to early developments in chaos theory, Gleick writes: "The tradition of looking at systems locally—isolating the mechanisms and then adding them together—was beginning to break down" (*Chaos*, 44). "[T]he complexity of the real phenomena studied in the life sciences outstripped anything to be found in the physicist's laboratory" (60). "These experimenters, the ones who pursued chaos most relentlessly, succeeded by refusing to accept any reality that could be frozen motionless" (196). The productivity that has been discovered to reside in nonlinearity, disorder, chaos, and noise points up the limits of restrictive definitions of Nature's laws.

Evelyn Fox Keller writes:

The very concept of "laws of nature" is, in contemporary usage, both a product and an expression of the absence of reflectivity. It introduces into the study of nature a metaphor indelibly marked by its political origins. The philosophical distinction between descriptive and prescriptive laws is invoked to underline the neutrality of scientific description. But nonetheless, laws of nature, like laws of the state, are historically imposed from above and obeyed from below. (*Reflections on Gender*, 131)

Imputing to the "laws of nature" metaphor and historical contingency in the service of a hierarchy of dominance takes us right past Planck's physics of practice (as opposed to "reality" or absolute laws that can never be known) back to the heart of Nietzsche's "On Truth and Lie"—to his description of the "great edifice of concepts that shows the rigid regularity of a Roman columbarium." The "concept" is "bony and 8-cornered like a die," though it is "only the residuum of a metaphor." "Within this dice game of concepts, 'truth' means to use every die as it is designated, to count its points exactly, form correct classifications, and never violate the order of castes and hierarchy of ranks. Just as the Romans and Etruscans cut up heaven for themselves with rigid mathematical lines and banned a god to such a limited space as if to a sanctuary . . . " (882). The story Nietzsche tells is of laws that "freeze," that disenchant the world, that rob people of the belief, once held by the ancient Greeks, in the enchantment of Nature by myth. According to Prigogine and Stengers, who credit Nietzsche with prescient insights into a science yet to come, "A disenchanted world is, at the same time, a world liable to control and manipulation. Any science that conceives of the world as being governed according to a universal theoretical plan that reduces its various riches to the drab applications of general laws thereby becomes an instrument of domination" (*Order Out of Chaos*, 32). No observer of the world today could deny that what is left of the natural world has been subject to a disenchantment by exploitation and abuse that has closer affinities to death than to life.

Prigogine and Stengers, as well as Keller, take on bringing together physics and biology in a redefinition of the sciences and their idea of "law." Keller adds the requirement of self-conscious language:

What is special about many, if not all, scientific communities is precisely the widely shared assumption that the universe they study is directly accessible, represented by concepts shaped not by language but only by the demands of logic and experiment. On this assumption, "laws of nature" are beyond the relativity of language—indeed, they are beyond language: encoded in logical structures that require only the discernment of reason and the confirmation of experiment. The corollary is that the descriptive language of science is transparent and neutral; it does not require examination. This may be convenient for the practical demands of scientific work, but . . . it is in fact an inseparable part of an objectivist ideology. (*Reflections on Gender*, 130–31)

Changing views of the meaning of *law*, an awareness of language as creator of its own unreliable realities, and the incorporation of a biological perspective are features of new views of science for which Nietzsche's "On Truth and Lie" is an ancestral text. They are also personified in the 1984 Nobel laureate in biology, Barbara McClintock, whose biography Keller wrote. For one thing, she has a passion for the individual, different, the exceptional in her research, avoiding the kind of compulsion for the general that Nietzsche saw in human conceptualizing that ignored the uniqueness of each leaf. McClintock's biology is the biology of the whole organism, a biology of difference, a biology dependent upon reading and understanding a language foreign to her molecular biologist colleagues. Her discovery of transposed genes in corn remained long inaccessible to her colleagues because they did not share her way of seeing and expressing the patterns she saw. We can regard her as a model reader because, like Nietzsche, she is aware of "the limits of verbally explicit reasoning," and of the limits of the kind of science that "can give us at most only nature-in-pieces; more often it gives us only pieces of nature." What we label scientific knowledge is lots of fun. You get lots of correlations, but you don't get the truth. . . . Things are much more marvelous than the scientific method allows us to conceive." Among the key words in McClintock's science are *transposition*, and *chiasmata* (points where chromosomes can be seen to cross).[54] We can see where Nietzsche shares with explorers in the late twentieth century some of the same matters his text explores by its subversive, self-undermining, and metaphorical path. We have seen a series of model readers: Max Planck, the epitome of the scientist committed to the worldview of his science, yet at the same time indicating other possibilities in his texts that carry his thinking beyond narrow limits; Nietzsche, who provides for the Planck we posed as reader a text that could guide Planck and us to a subversive reading of scientific texts; a series of contemporary scientist-readers, beginning with Niels Bohr; and J. Hillis Miller, whose strategy of reading "authors reading their own work" (10) leads us from consideration of the "law" (of a text or outside a text) to the "law" in Kafka's text that we shall explore, in the hope of being like the above readers, committed to the "trans-" and crossing points which in this case will be the crossing points where a literary and a technical text by Kafka "read" each other.

54. Evelyn Fox Keller, *A Feeling for the Organism: The Life and Work of Barbara McClintock* (New York: W. H. Freeman, 1983), xiv, 205, 203, 222.

CHAPTER 3

The Trial in the Stone Quarry

Perhaps it strikes you that I talk almost like a jurist . . . I profit
greatly from it, of course, but I'm losing a great deal of my vigor as an
artist.
— the painter Titorelli, speaking to Josef K., *The Trial*

In the history of culture the discovery of zero will always stand out as
one of the greatest single achievements of the human race.
— Tobias Dantzig, *Number: The Language of Science*

The quotations above are enlarged by their advertent or inadver-
tent irony. The loss of Titorelli's "vigor as an artist" is no real loss
since that "vigor" has produced merely clones of a single dour
landscape and judicial portraits that are iterative falsifications of
the rank and appearance of judges. Yet its apparent meaning raises
the problem of an incompatibility of discourses that plagued
Kafka, who by day wrote as a jurist and by night as an artist and
whose art suffered in consequence — at least according to the conventional wisdom and to Kafka's own testimony.

The second quotation seems to contain an ultimate paradox
that is not incompatible with Kafka's texts. Yet it also has a meaning grounded in the evidentiary history of mathematics. Modern
mathematics would not have been possible without the development of "place-value notation" that rests "on the invention of a
symbol for the absence of a digit, or a zero sign"[1] (as opposed, for
example, to the way Roman numerals function by the addition of

Epigraphs from Franz Kafka, *Der Prozeß*, ed. Max Brod (Frankfurt am Main:
S. Fischer, 1986), 130 (translations mine); and *Number: The Language of Science*, 4th
rev. ed. (Garden City, N.Y.: Doubleday, 1954), 36.

1. Karl Menninger, *Number Words and Number Symbols: A Cultural History of
Numbers*, trans. Paul Broneer from the rev. German ed., 1958 (Cambridge, Mass.:
MIT Press, 1969), 371.

units). But in addition to signifying nothing, the zero also increases by ten-fold a number that it stands to the right of. Thus "poets and philosophers have been fascinated by the zero, by its curious changes in numerical value and by the magic which it can create, although in itself it is nothing" (Menninger, *Number Words*, 403). In the European Middle Ages, zero was considered a work of the devil and met with long and stubborn resistance before Arabic numerals were finally accepted. Long considered an unsolvable mystery, zero retains its peculiar and special status today.[2]

The topics of these two epigraphs and their chiastic relationship — the apparent meaning of the first is truthful though founded on the shifting ground of irony, and the apparent meaning of the second is paradoxical though founded on a mathematical certitude — mark the connections our reading finds between two texts by Kafka: *The Trial* and an approximately twenty-two page (depending upon whether illustrations are counted) technical text included in the annual report for 1914 of Kafka's employer, the Workers Accident Insurance Institute for the Kingdom of Bohemia in Prague [*Arbeiter-Unfall-Versicherungs-Anstalt für das Königreich Böhmen in Prag*]. The report, "Accident Prevention in Stone Quarries," was written in early 1915, concurrently with parts of *The Trial*, and resemblances between them, such as the execution of Josef K. in a stone quarry, have been noted.[3]

The handwritten manuscript of *The Trial* was recently sold at auction for a record breaking $1.98 million.[4] Had Kafka's writings been limited to those he produced in the course of his work for the Workers Accident Insurance Company, they would not have broken auction records, nor been considered the repository of

---

2. See Graham Flegg, *Numbers: Their History and Meaning* (New York: Schocken, 1983), 267.

3. The most extensive collection of Kafka's technical writings and commentary on them is *Franz Kafka: Amtliche Schriften*, ed. Klaus Hermsdorf (Berlin: Akademie, 1984). Hermsdorf discusses resemblances between the stone quarry text and *The Trial* in his Introduction, 40. I refer to the pagination in the Hermsdorf volume; all translations are mine.

4. *New York Times*, November 18, 1988.

major currents of twentieth-century thought. Yet Kafka had been immersed in the discourse of his profession for years before he began his true vocation, and the writings of the bureaucrat and jurist are inseparable from the nighttime writings whose language and import they inform.

Without the estrangement of the days, no production of the nights. Without the restrictions of formulaic language, little freedom to create meaning beyond subject matter. Paradoxically, those discourses subject to the most stringent "laws" — formulaic discourses such as mathematics, logic, and the bureaucratic/legal/technical discourse used by Kafka — are those that can support the greatest freedom. The degree of freedom from context depends upon the degree of formal regulation.[5] The professional discourse that Kafka incorporated produced texts as a combination of the determinism and irreversibility of stories with the freedom and reversibility of its own logical system.

Kafka's texts, in particular *The Trial*, also have the paradoxical properties of the notion of zero. Sections of the text can be shown to arrive at zero, or nothingness, canceling themselves after following complex logical and defining procedures, thereby subverting the idea of knowledge. Yet, like zero, their procedures result in multiplication as well — the suggestion of another kind of knowledge.

In the dialogue between Kafka's technical and literary texts — and within each text — we find a further version of the scientific-literary dialogue that proposes a rereading by means of cross-disciplinary patterns and procedures, and that leads us yet further into a web of relations that defy disciplinary boundaries as they suggest a rewriting of what "literary" or "scientific" may mean.

Kafka's own sense of the importance of the stone quarry text is revealed in his having sent a copy of it to his betrothed, Felice

---

5. See Howard Margolis, *Patterns, Thinking, and Cognition: A Theory of Judgment* (Chicago: University of Chicago Press, 1987), especially 90.

Bauer, as a representative sample of his writing.[6] Such a text, however, was published without attribution to an individual author, and its form might depend upon the research of coworkers and, perhaps, even editorial changes. It necessarily adhered to stylistic and organizational requirements of the insurance industry, and included the perspectives and terminology of multiple disciplines.[7] Kafka's work in investigation, claims adjustment, and policy matters encompassed "organizational, scientific, technical and social-ethical duties" (Hermsdorf, *Amtliche Schriften*, 21). Among Kafka's responsibilities was, for example, writing an insurance policy for private automobile owners, making him the first specialist in Bohemia for automobile insurance. His writing depended heavily on statistics, on principles of mechanical engineering, and rudimentary physics. In view of the demands of his work, Kafka requested permission, in 1909, to attend daytime lectures at the Prague Technical University in order to acquire the necessary expertise.

All of Kafka's professional labors were by their nature dependent upon the interpretation of laws. The first technical text Kafka wrote in his job was on the subject of insurance in the construction industry. Hermsdorf finds in this early product evidence of motifs that appear in the later literary writings: "the contradictions, ambiguity, and inscrutability of the laws" (27). To us later readers, Kafka seems to be characterizing his own future literary texts when he writes the following in his critique of the new private automobile insurance law of 1908:

. . . this regulation . . . provided more room for free interpretation than was advantageous in a matter that is followed actively by so many interested parties. While at the same time, considering the too brief treatment of the complicated subject, it offers too few guidelines for proper exegesis.[8]

---

6. Letter of May 30, 1916, *Briefe an Felice*, ed. Erich Heller and Jürgen Born (Frankfurt am Main: S. Fischer, 1967), 660.

7. See Hermsdorf, *Amtliche Schriften*, 43–44.

8. "Einbeziehung der privaten Automobilbetriebe in die Versicherungspflicht."

The Trial offers interpreters the same challenge to pursue elusive meaning as that offered by the typical regulation in the civil laws of Bohemia.

Kafka's work required the transgression of disciplinary boundaries and the integration, in his texts, of the apparently incompatible discourses of precise technology and diffuse law. Perelman sees in these discourses two unalterably opposed models of reasoning. One representing the tradition of Plato and Descartes adheres to "the model of geometry and mathematical reasoning" in which there can be only one correct opinion when two are opposed on the same matter. The other, very different tradition "follows a juridical, rather than a mathematical, model. Thus in the tradition of the Talmud, for example, it is accepted that opposed positions can be equally reasonable; one of them does not have to be right."[9] One depends upon establishing the certainty of facts, the other upon the weighing and judging of arguments that have different degrees of truth or merit, and being obliged to reach a decision although neither the case nor the law itself may provide an answer. Each rests upon a different model of knowledge.

"The form is not separable from the content," writes Perelman, "language is not a veil which one need only discard or render transparent in order to perceive the real as such; it is inextricably bound up with a point of view, with the taking of a position" (45). On this basis, we must examine the relations of language in "Ac-

---

Übernahme bzw. Ablösung der Privat-Automobilversicherungsverträge nach Paragraph 61 U.V.G.," in Hermsdorf, *Amtliche Schriften*, 124–32.

9. Chaim Perelman, *The New Rhetoric and the Humanities* (Dordrecht: Reidel, 1979), 12. This is only one, called *ba'ya*, of the many different types of argument to be found in the Talmud. Rabbi Louis Jacobs explains the *ba'ya* as follows: "in this type of problem the two halves are so equally balanced that no reason exists for favouring one over the other. There are more than a thousand of these problems scattered through the Talmud. It is highly probable that such contrived problems were set consciously as an intellectual exercise, especial skill being required to see that the two halves were, in fact, equally balanced." (Louis Jacobs, *The Talmudic Argument: A Study in Talmudic Reasoning and Methodology* [Cambridge: Cambridge University Press, 1984], 17.)

cident Prevention in Stone Quarries," keeping in mind that there could be multiple ways of expressing the same statistics and conveying the same information, although any alternative language would impart different meaning, or tell a different "story."

Kafka introduces the topic by explaining the financial and legal limits on the power of the Institute to intervene to reduce hazards and improve occupational safety. Its efforts have, however, met with some success, specifically in improving the safety of agricultural machinery and planing machines in the wood processing industry. But because the Institute lacks independent powers to initiate and enforce action, its efforts depend upon the support of outside bodies, thus requiring lengthy start-up times and preparations before achieving any results. These limitations apply especially to its efforts to convert the stone quarries in its territory to more "rational" operations. A table shows insurance payments for accidents between 1890 and 1911 to be staggeringly high. Yet a large portion of these accidents, according to the author, could have been avoided by rational mining operations [*rationeller Abbau*] and minimal supervision. In some cases the simplest technology — protective goggles, for example — would prevent common injuries. Yet both employers and workers, for different reasons, resisted adopting even this simple measure.

Kafka's case relies for evidence upon numbers, statistics, and percentages, and his solution to the violations they reveal is thorough and repeated instruction. A situation in which common sense has not been applied ought to be amenable to correction by rational means. The term *rational* is used frequently.

The term *however* is also common because qualifications that indicate limitations on carrying out rational measures are a dominant feature of the text. For example, rational mining demands frequent audits, since safety installations must be adjusted to continually changing conditions (soil, water, rock formations, etc.). The official audit system, however, is not set up for frequent checks. Many of the quarries where conditions are worst are not even accessible to checks because they are categorized as "agricultural quarries" not subject to safety regulation. In addition, there are no authoritative principles that can be applied to the safety audit of quarries.

Several ordinances were passed, in 1905 and 1908, to alleviate this situation; however, in practice, they encountered the same obstacles to safety audits mentioned above.

Moreover, the shortcoming was apparent that is inherent in nearly all ordinances, namely that nothing was done to publicize them [*daß für die Verbreitung ihrer Kenntnis nicht gesorgt war*] and owners only found out about the regulations [*von den Bestimmungen der Verordnung erst Kenntnis erhielten*] when an accident had taken place that could easily have been avoided if safety regulations had been followed. (246)

In this excerpt we have a model for some of the central procedures of this text and of *The Trial*. The term *knowledge* [*Kenntnis*] is repeated twice. But this knowledge exists by presumption only; it has no locale and a zero degree of extension in space and time. It is a knowledge one speaks of as not being there and its not being there is the only reason for mentioning it. No one had taken care that it existed or that it was received until its reception no longer had meaning. The event in the conclusion happened first in time and its happening robbed knowledge of its meaning and purpose for existence. But, continuing backward to the beginning of the sentence, the final result is that the initial presumption that there is knowledge of ordinances that can be disseminated no longer has validity or support; it has been deconstructed. The deconstruction depends upon the use of the past perfect tense and the subjunctive mood in the last two clauses [*wenn sich ein Unfall ereignet hatte, der bei Befolgung der Schutzvorschriften leicht hätte vermieden werden können*]. In Kafka's texts when the notion of knowledge is introduced, it is eventually reduced by various devices of grammar and logic to a degree zero and verb tenses help effect that reduction. Frequently the most past (the first in time) event occurs as the latest or last in a sequence of which it appears to be the result. The past perfect tense gives away its true position. In Kafka's texts the subjunctive mood is the one that provides reliable information, and that information, since it is in the subjunctive, must necessarily be contrary to fact.

Remarkably, these textual procedures adhere to and are products of the formalistic textual models prescribed in the Bohemian insurance industry. They are also the means by which the futility of official attempts to prevent accidents in stone quarries is conveyed in language. This conjunction of meanings anticipates the conjunction of meanings in Kafka's literary texts. The grammar, the syntax, the verb tenses and mood, and the focus on a central but absent word or concept all convey a sense of the inevitable undermining of rational solutions, even the notion of reason itself.

The "Stone Quarries" text is marked by the conventions of its genre: frequent use of the passive voice and general avoidance of naming a subject, from which the necessity arises to personify the protagonist, i.e. the Institute. An ineffectual patriarch, the Bohemian Workers Accident Insurance Institute "believes," "casts its glance," "does not let [something] out of its sight," "associates itself," "is convinced," "decides," and produces statistics that "speak." The passive voice and personification of an institution mean that the assignment of responsibility is avoided. There are many other examples of this schematic language being personalized and requiring anthropomophisms. The language of science is also necessarily marked by the conventions of its genre, including strict formalisms. We find in Max Planck's papers on theoretical physics a similar preponderance of passive voice and the trope of personification of the central actors, which in his case are the physical features of thought experiments, i.e., quanta of energy, oscillators, heat and light, and many others. At least theoretically, responsibility plays no role in these procedures that purportedly follow impersonal "laws of nature." In the conventions of Kafka's "Stone Quarries" text, responsibility is not named, but that does not mean it does not exist; it is merely offstage somewhere, unacknowledged and unassigned. In a thought experiment in theoretical physics there is an unnamed responsibility of selection and choice by the manipulator whose manipulation is by necessity an imposition of force and thus a responsible determinant of results. In both kinds of text, responsibility is an absent and unnamed, but nevertheless relevant, category.

"Accident Prevention in Stone Quarries" and Planck's papers also share the frequent use of various terms for law or laws. In one single paragraph of Kafka's text there are eleven different nouns that refer to types of laws, regulations, or requirements, and many of these nouns are repeated.[10] In addition there are a variety of verbs with the same import. Laws are associated with rational planning and procedures. For example, the Institute joins with a government office to take a draft plan for safety regulations under advisement. They succeed in coming to an agreement that awaits approval from yet another government office. This draft plan is based upon statistics that were used to categorize conditions in quarries according to the degree of danger. The same classifications were used for the means by which these dangers might be counteracted. The draft plan carefully distinguishes between the essential and the nonessential, since the instructions must be brief and easily understood. To emphasize their importance, the regulations are accompanied by diagrams. The regulations, which depend upon principles of geology, engineering, the physics of explosives,[11] and other technical categories, consist of sixteen requirements or prohibitions for work in quarries expressed in nine different forms of imperative, several of them repeated more than once (256–57). We must conclude that knowledge, facts and certainty, reason, and guides to action—if they reside anywhere —reside in the laws.

However, the above-mentioned paragraph that contains

---

10. The nouns are: *Runderlaß, Vorschriften, Bestimmungen, Verordnung, Zulässigkeit, Genehmigungsbescheid, Bedingungen, Anforderungen, Vorschreibung, Detailvorschriften,* and *Anordnungen* (246–47).

11. This was a topic of great interest to Planck as well. In his textbook on heat radiation he discusses explosion as an example of the increase of entropy, i.e., the transformation of a system from a less to a more stable state. (Max Planck, *Vorlesungen über die Theorie der Wärmestrahlung,* 2d rev. ed. [Leipzig: Johann Ambrosius Barth, 1913], 48.)

eleven nouns of law and regulation is immediately preceded by the previously quoted sentence whose language erases the notion of knowledge. Thus there is an oscillation from knowledge-subject-to-erasure to knowledge-as-technical-certainty, as factuality, evidence, organization, and guidelines for action—in other words knowledge as a pragmatic category of communicable, learnable rationality in the context of laws.

Resonance is the energy transmitted between two oscillators of the same frequency. In the sentence that does away with knowledge there is oscillation in language between terms that refer to reason, and the deconstruction of such terms and concepts. In the paragraph with eleven nouns for requirements, regulations, and laws, there is a structural process that acts like an undertow to destabilize the imperatives of the law and the notion that knowledge means power to change. It begins with the statement that obstacles must be countered within the limits of what is attainable. A regulation passed from one imperial government office to another gives responsibility for executing its stipulations to this second office, and points out in particular that when applications for operation of a quarry are approved, that approval must contain conditions insuring operating procedures that are economically rational and in keeping with the welfare of the public. So far so good; so far so rational. However, the word *allerdings* introduces the next sentence and alerts us to the possibility that all that rationality may be retracted. *Allerdings* is one of Kafka's key connectors, both in this text and in *The Trial*. It is his great qualifier—most closely translatable as "however," "though," "of course," or something like "on the other hand"—and appears an extraordinary number of times (eighty-eight) in the relatively brief text of *The Trial*.[12] I would go so far as to maintain that the worldview Kafka's texts impart results from *allerdings* and related connectors that serve to qualify and undermine whatever assertions have preceded them.

---

12. Walter Speidel, *A Complete Contextual Concordance to Franz Kafka Der Prozess* (Leeds: W. S. Maney, 1978), 847.

"Of course [*Allerdings*] in this regulation—as is, in any case, necessary for the initial transitional years—it is emphasized no less clearly that the requirement of rational mining methods may not create any needless impediments to the operation of the business" (247). The detailed regulations must take into consideration the terrain, the qualities of the rock and its location, the manner in which the business is conducted, and "all other local conditions." "Finally," in the course of the discussion of the relevant paragraph "it was made clear" to the office in charge that "while the operation of the individual quarries and pits would have to be brought gradually into conformity with the specifications of the regulation [*nach und nach den Bestimmungen der Verordnung zwar angepaßt werden müsse*], it nevertheless would remain to be weighed most carefully whether considering the circumstances of the business, the directives are workable without jeopardizing its de facto and its economic potential" (247).

What we have before us is a progression typical of Kafka's texts: from a statement that seems to be a reasonable position, to its gradual demolition by means of one qualification after the other until finally the initial premise has been completely retracted. And all along the way each new qualification sounds reasonable. But by the time the conclusion has been reached, an initial apparent relationship between cause and effect is so diluted that an entirely different order of truth has evolved. Namely, in the case above, a contrary one:[13] there will be *no* effective safety regulation, since the deciding factor is profit and power lies with the owners. Of course this truth or grounding is never stated directly. It lies in the subtle irony of the successive terms *allerdings*, and *zwar* and the subjunctive *müsse*, as well as the superlative *most carefully*. The voice of reason is drowned out by its own words.

There is a sense in which Kafka's texts can be seen as self-

---

13. This procedure is equivalent to yet another type of Talmudic argument, as described by Jacobs: "The *on the contrary* argument seeks to demonstrate that, far from the premiss yielding the suggested conclusion, it yields the exactly opposite conclusion" (*Talmudic Argument*, 14).

consuming artifacts. Their language turns back on itself, undoes, and rewrites itself in a recursive process akin to the process of reading. Scientific papers also promote their theses by a series of "if . . . then" postulates, followed by further "ifs," each of which has the effect of further qualifying or rewriting what has preceded. In the case of Kafka, however, the procedure is spun out until it undermines standard logic and replaces accepted forms of knowledge.

The power of Kafka's texts lies in their capacity for resonance, that is, to produce the energy that results from the communicable oscillations between sections of text such as the two discussed above. Each such section of text is itself a system that follows a pattern of oscillation between apparently irreconcilable poles. That pattern may be linear, as in the second example, or nonlinear, as in the first example where the central term *knowledge* is extinguished from several directions. It is in the *relation* of the systems — their dialogue — that the full force of the text as a larger system emerges. And that relation is a chiastic one, as in the quotations at the beginning of this chapter. The chiasmus describes the inverse relationship between these two sections of text. The first follows a nonlinear pattern such as described by Perelman:

Nonformal argument consists, not of a chain of ideas of which some are derived from others according to accepted rules of inference, but rather of a web formed from all the arguments and all the reasons that combine to achieve the desired result. (*New Rhetoric*, 18)

The section of text that undermines knowledge is an example of this web that is characteristic of nonformal argument. Yet it is driven by formal linguistic and logical procedures. The second section of text follows the linearity characteristic of what Perelman calls "quasi-logical arguments" (19), yet it is driven by a political statement, considered outside the realm of logical operations.

The initial impression that a reader of "Accident Prevention in Stone Quarries" might have is of a pervasive and inescapable hierarchy on all levels, whether it be among institutions, units of government, and interest groups, or in terms of the fixed order of values, with unbiased expertise, evidence, proof, and praxis at the top and prejudice and disorganization at the bottom. A transgressive reading, however, may find the stability of hierarchy undermined by the subversive chiasmus inherent in relations of language and logic. The most decisive chiastic relationship is between figure and ground, as in the opening quotations. Kafka's textual procedures privilege neither the one nor the other. The chiasmus indicates a relationship that is not a parallel, nor an analogy, though it partakes of both and subverts both, nor is it repetitive, contradictory, or antithetical. Like the optic chiasm, efficacy and fulfillment (that is, sight) come only with the connection and reversal. As in Bohr's theory of complementarity, two mutually exclusive systems may be required for explanation. A single discourse or logical system is insufficient.

Let us see how author Kafka *interprets* the text discussed above. We resume with the paragraph that follows the words "without jeopardizing its de facto and its economic potential" (247):

As a transitional regulation this implementation order was very valuable. Since, however, it temporarily only included a further elaboration of the specifications of the regulation, but no plan of organization for its implementation, its practical value was limited to a certain dissemination of knowledge [*Kenntnis*] of the regulation and to a more stringent procedure for approving quarry operations. Beyond that it had no effect, even though the actual observation of the quarries was only supposed to occur when operations had begun, thus, after the approval.

For that reason the Institute had to see its task, in addition to the further dissemination of the safety rules, as organizing their implementation and extending this organization to agricultural quarries.

The details of the implementation of the audits could be temporarily reserved for a later time.

The next possibility that offered itself was disseminating the regulation in the form of posters. Since, however, similar attempts with regard to safety measures for agricultural machinery had not, up to now, proved successful, this method was disregarded. What mattered here was not so much to inform [*zur Kenntnis zu bringen*] owners and workers with a brief except in the form of a poster, but rather in the first place to compel observance of the safety rules. (247 and 250; intervening pages are illustrations)

We have here a sample of Kafka reading the law. He produces an interpretation that, like the several exegeses of "Before the Law" in chapter 9 of *The Trial*, is self-undermining. Each proposal that promises effective action is retracted—the first is legislation without execution, the second indefinite postponement, the third the failure of knowledge. Knowledge and the law are incompatible; they cancel one another. There is an implicit hierarchy of priorities with action, organization, and, finally, force ("to compel observance") at the top, information and knowledge at the bottom, and no mediation in between. Time here and elsewhere in "Accident Prevention in Stone Quarries" is indefinite ("temporarily"), open-ended, and subject to revision. There is a dialectic between options of order and responses of disorder. The text is constructed as a recursive process that originates with an assertion about "transitional regulation" and elaborates itself in a spiral of proposal and retraction, ending with compulsion. The process gets from origin to destination and tells its real story via connectors such as however [*aber*], but [*aber*], beyond that [*darüber hinaus*], even though [*trotzdem*], only [*erst*], thus [*also*], however [*jedoch*], up to now [*bisher*], not so much . . . but rather [*nicht so sehr . . . vielmehr*], in the first place [*überhaupt*]. Finally, there is an enormous disproportion between textual effort expended and end result (zero). In continuing, the text notes the problem of "indifference" toward safety rules that, the Institute does not doubt, could best be resolved in personal instruction by professionals. "Temporarily, however, it was still necessary to dispense with that" (250). The three qualifiers in this one brief sentence tell the entire story of attempts to improve safety in Bohemian stone quarries.

   The rest of the stone quarry text is characterized by a dialogue—better, an argument—between what might be called reason and unreason, faith and scepticism, or logic and antilogic—categories that could be subsumed into a great dispute between order and disorder. The reigning figure is paradox. For example, in one photograph described by the author, a quarry appears to be mined more correctly than others, although it is actually in greater breach of the regulations. Another photograph shows conditions under which correct mining methods are of no value; on the contrary, they increase the danger because they increase the workers' sense of security. Another example is a quarry that was so successful in deceiving the Institute that audits resulted in its continual reclassification to a lower risk (and lower premium) category while its safety record deteriorated and its accident rate climbed. In these cases, information or even photographic evidence was without effect, or the effect was the opposite of predictability, order, or reason.

While one side of a safety equation goes up, the other goes down. Paradox in the form of chiasmus dominates the discourse and the conditions it describes. "Yet [Allerdings] the Institute, for its part, after its experiences so far, still believes in the possibility of such an improvement" (263). In opposition to the antilogic of paradox stands faith that rests upon rational and scientific principles. These principles are cataloguing, evidence, instruction, and, above all, models. (Although at the same time the "organs of public safety will have to be involved to a greater extent" [263].) The author places his faith primarily in the principle of the demonstration model, supported by instructional lectures. He expresses faith in expertise, documentation, detail, evidentiary proof (in this case provided by photography), the reliability of cause-and-effect relations. Principles are demonstrated, models illustrate, and knowledge is enhanced in a process of reason that matches the laboratory or theoretical physics experiment. As in the above invocation of force ("organs of public safety"), however, contradictions appear in the model for rational control of human error and greed, and enlightened application of technology for the general welfare.

"Even though, for the time being, this [the improvements suggested above] cannot be carried out, the Institute can register not insignificant progress in this area" (266). An introduction to the final and summary page of the article, this sentence contains within itself the dispute that is never resolved. The text appears to follow a juridical as opposed to a mathematical model. Actually, it follows neither and undercuts both. For every proposed solution, there is a "however," "yet," or "although," for every failure of rationality there is a bolster of "in spite of." On the last page the target is "biases" that are to be replaced by "objective intervention" (266) of experts (even though "temporarily" no means are available to allow for them to visit sites).

The last word of the text, like the last word in one of Max Planck's essays, is *progress*.[14] May we not then argue backward, knowing that what appears last is emphasized most, and assert that the text arrives at, and thus affirms, its goal, which is the notion of progress? Indeed, the text has constituted a historical narrative, beginning with earlier and less successful attempts to improve conditions, and showing progress over the years with improved legislation, additional knowledge, and increased cooperation among interested parties. A story follows a deterministic course, or it would not be a story. But within that course are the whorls of a unique antilogical textual logic that subverts the apparent stability of the story.

It is generally believed that formal languages are context-free and, thus, neutral operators in contrast to natural language with its multiple meanings. In the case of Kafka's texts, critics have found an irreconcilability between the causal logic of grammatical norms and syntax, and the course of the narrative.[15] We find, by contrast, that not only can a formalized language be laden with

---

14. Typical concluding concepts (although word order in German may prevent them from being in exactly the last position) in Planck's essays are: progress (182), knowledge (136), forward (124), the light of truth (68), and unity (245). They are all to be found in *Vorträge und Erinnerungen* (Darmstadt: Wissenschaftliche Buchgesellschaft, 1965).

15. Theo Elm, "Der Prozeß," *Kafka-Handbuch*, ed. Hartmut Binder (Stuttgart: Kröner, 1979), 2:423.

meaning, but natural language can be manipulated in a manner as rigorous as formal logic, though perhaps following sequences that are not included in the Aristotelian or Euclidean versions. Natural language itself is an abstract system.

The obvious fact is simply that a speech does not mention every feature of stimulus. Since the ranges of stimulation and of predisposition are to all practical purposes continuous, and language can provide only a discrete set of forms, this *abstract* character of language is inevitable: not all the features of a situation appear in the report.[16]

Bloomfield also points out that logical systems, such as mathematics, remain dependent upon language: "our formal systems serve merely as written or mechanical mediations between utterances of language. . . . Even such a thing as a tabulation of numbers is linguistic; apart from the verbal character of the elements, the arrangement leads to a linguistic interpretation." Speaking of a formal system, such as symbolic logic, as a "language" obscures that fact that "interpretation, initial and final, of the procedure is made in terms of some natural language (such as English), and the system as a whole is meaningless to a reader to whom it has not been interpreted in these terms" (44–45).

Mathematics has been proved to breach its own logical consistency.[17] There is no quintessential *logic*; there are *logics*. For example, in chaos theory there is a logic of disorder — the pattern that ensues after time in a system that appears to have lost all order and system. Chaos is "orderly disorder created by simple processes."[18] It is driven by oscillations in a nonlinear process that eventually creates an unexpected pattern. With the study of chaos came the discovery of the universality of pattern formation, in nonlinear

---

16. Leonard Bloomfield, "Linguistic Aspects of Science," *International Encyclopedia of Unified Science* 1, no. 4 (Chicago: University of Chicago Press, 1939), 37.

17. For a historical overview, including well-known examples such as non-Euclidean geometry and Gödel's theorem, see Morris Kline, *Mathematics: The Loss of Certainty* (Oxford: Oxford University Press, 1980). Also see Douglas R. Hofstadter, *Gödel, Escher, Bach: An Eternal Golden Braid* (New York: Vintage, 1980).

18. James Gleick, *Chaos: Making a New Science* (New York: Viking, 1987), 266.

equations and in nature and biological systems, however disordered and unpredictable initial conditions appeared to be.

According to Margolis, "pattern-recognition is all there is to cognition" (*Patterns*, 3); it is not a mere initial, intuitive stage prior to the development of logical rigor. "Rule-following processes, including logic, must be reduced to pattern-recognition, not the reverse" (4); "logic . . . is a by-product of the capacity for informal reasoning (pattern-recognition applied to patterns of language)" (61). Resnik, among others, maintains that mathematical knowledge is dependent upon pattern recognition and cognition.[19]

Where, then, does knowledge reside in Kafka's texts — literary or technical — that seem to deny knowledge? A kind of knowledge must exist in his texts, since textuality, language use, and literacy itself are forms of knowledge. But knowledge is most certainly disassociated from the place where it is conventionally presumed to reside: in laws and guidelines, strictures and regulations. Knowledge appears as subversive patterns such as described by the terms *paradox, chiasmus, oscillation*, and *complementarity* that cannot be encompassed without disruption in hierarchy, mastery, and law. As in chaos theory, these patterns act as boundaries between systems: "The boundary between two or more attractors in a dynamical system served as a threshold of a kind that seems to govern so many ordinary processes, from the breaking of materials to the making of decisions. . . . This branch of dy-

19. Michael D. Resnik, "Mathematical Knowledge and Pattern Cognition," *Canadian Journal of Philosophy* 5, no. 1 (September 1975): 25–39; "Mathematics as a Science of Patterns: Ontology and Reference," *Noûs* 15, no. 4 (November 1981): 529–50; and "Mathematics as a Science of Patterns: Epistemology," *Noûs* 16, no. 1 (March 1982): 95–105. Whorf found every language to be a "vast pattern-system": "the forms of a person's thoughts are controlled by inexorable laws of pattern of which he is unconscious. These patterns are the unperceived intricate systematizations of his own language." *Language, Thought, and Reality: Selected Writings of Benjamin Lee Whorf*, ed. John B. Carroll (Cambridge, Mass.: MIT Press, 1956), 252. While Whorf's conclusions have been qualified in the half-century since he carried out his investigations, they remain stimulating theses about the relationship of language and pattern.

namics [the study of fractal basin boundaries] concerned itself not with describing the final, stable behavior of a system but with the way a system chooses between competing options" (Gleick, *Chaos*, 233). We read in this situation—as we did in Derrida's view of Kafka's text as being involved in "the paradoxical logic of boundaries" (see my chap. 1)—a story of productive transgressions between the borders of the scientific and the literary. "Life near or at a boundary, however, is considerably more complicated. The borders, much more than simple dividing lines, consist of elaborate swirls and whirlpools . . . ."[20] "Accident Prevention in Stone Quarries" straddles these boundaries as a logical-mathematical-literary system.

In mathematical terms, zero is a potential "attractor" in a "dynamical system"—a role it plays in Kafka's text as well. Like the vortex of a whirlpool, it can draw the elements of grammar into a pattern whose central conceptual consequence is zero. Zero has the peculiar property of signifying both nothing and a multiple increase. A very recent example of the paradoxical quality of the notion of zero is called *zero-knowledge proof*, a method for revealing that a theorem is provable, without actually revealing what the proof is.[21] It entails knowledge without knowledge, arrived at in the course of a dialogue between prover and verifier. In the dual role of zero we find a mathematical equivalent of the workings of a Kafka text such as "Accident Prevention in Stone Quarries," which consists in complex self-cancellations that direct boundary crossings between many oppositions including knowledge and absence of knowledge, order and disorder, and the literary and the scientific.

---

20. Ivars Peterson, *The Mathematical Tourist: Snapshots of Modern Mathematics* (New York: W. H. Freeman, 1988), 167.
21. See Peterson, *Mathematical Tourist*, 214. Also see "When Ignorance is Bliss," *The Economist*, June 20, 1987, 93–94; Oded Goldreich, Silvio Micali, and Avi Wigderson, "Proofs that Yield Nothing But their Validity and a Methodology of Cryptographic Protocol Design," *Proceedings of the 27th Annual Symposium on Foundations of Computer Science* (Washington, D.C.: IEEE Publications, 1986), 174–87; and Peter Wayner, "Zero-Knowledge Proofs," *Byte* 12, no. 11 (October 1987): 149–52.

II

> . . . since very small differences in initial conditions are magnified quickly, unless the initial conditions are known to *infinite precision*, all known knowledge is eroded rapidly to future ignorance.
> —Mitchell J. Feigenbaum on the subject of iteration in nonlinear systems

The Trial is anticipated in "Accident Prevention in Stone Quarries," but the relationship is a reciprocal one, the literary text displacing by parody the language of the technical text, and vice versa. The text of *The Trial* adds iteration and self-parody to the procedures for deconstructing definitions that might lead to knowledge. It also adds, when we read it as a "scientific" text, some fundamental concepts of mathematics and physics to its arsenal of interpretive proposals to the reader.

We can examine *The Trial* as we did "Accident Prevention in Stone Quarries," as a collection of alternative logics evolving from disorder and breakdowns in Logic. It travels farther than the technical text toward communion with Planck's scientific writings, is more rigorously structured and more drastic in its nonliterariness as a literary text. The matter of knowledge is directed, as in the technical text, by the zero attractor.

The formulaic-legalistic, labyrinthian, and self-canceling discourse of "Stone Quarries" also characterizes much of the text of *The Trial*, in particular those sections of text that have to do with the Court and its workings, such as the disquisition by the painter Titorelli on three mutually exclusive and mutually defeating types of "acquittal," and the lawyer Huld's ruminations on the inscrutable judicial hierarchy. Beginning with the last word of "Stone Quarries"—*progress*—*The Trial* can be read as engaged in a deconstructive dialogue with the technical text. The word *progress* (the German is in the plural) appears in *The Trial* for the first time in Josef K.'s review of the course of his meetings with Huld,

Epigraph from: "Universal Behavior in Nonlinear Systems," *Los Alamos Science* (Summer 1980): 21.

prior to his decision to dismiss the lawyer. The lawyer's speeches "were repeated at every visit. There was always progress [pl.], but the nature of this progress [pl.] could never be communicated" (*Der Prozeß*, 107). Josef K.'s meaning is, of course, ironic, and shows one consequence of the character's noting iteration in the text—to undermine the notion or events repeated. Progress is also a fruitless hope in the dialogue Josef K. has with the abject businessman, Block, who was able to see "no progress" in his own trial, to which K. replies: "But what kind of progress did you want to see?" "That is a very reasonable [rational] question" the businessman responds "only rarely can one see progress [pl.] in these proceedings. But at that time I did not know that. . . . I wanted to have tangible [graspable] progress [pl.], the whole thing was supposed to draw to a conclusion or at least make a real advance" (152). Among other things, this could be a description of the final stance of the author of "Stone Quarries."

Let us examine the evolution of *progress* in this brief dialogue: (*a*) there is no answer to the question about a "kind of progress"—indicating that such a thing cannot be verified or described; (*b*) progress is associated with the verb for domination and control: *grasp*; (*c*) it is associated with the negatives *no* and *rarely* (*seldom*); (*d*) the question about "kind of progress" is called a rational question but Block's smile when he says this indicates either that he believes the scepticism implied in the question is justified, and/or he considers the question foolish; (*e*) the second term of reason, *know*, is connected to a negative and refers to a state of delusion prior to knowing; and (*f*) finally, the last remark describes a scissors (or chiasmus) motion, whereby one line, translated literally, is "inclining to a conclusion" [*sich zum Ende neigen*] and the other is "taking the proper upward climb" [*den regelrechten Aufstieg nehmen*] — crossing inevitably like two changeable vectors in a graph, and, in this case, options that cross and cancel each other.

It does not take a close examination of the text to realize that the notion of progress is deconstructed in *The Trial*. Procedures similar to the deconstruction of progress are carried out on the term for *sense, meaning, purpose*, or *point* [*Sinn*] as it is passed in one section of dialogue through several grammatical forms, being drained of meaning along the way (16), and on the terms (also as proxies for the concepts and their realization in the narrative) *guilt, guilty, innocence, innocent, acquittal, acquit,* and *free* (128, 131, 136–37). What is enacted upon progress here, however, has an emblematic function: (1) It is characteristic of the exploration of individual terms, which amounts to their dissection without resulting in new or "graspable" knowledge; and (2) it subverts two concepts considered essential to science: (*a*) repeatability, which is the prerequisite for the verifiability and thus the legitimacy of any experiment, and (*b*) progress, which is the ideological foundation of all science. Thus it seems that the fundamental move in the text of *The Trial* is antiscientific.[22] It *seems* so. But I shall argue that upon further examination, *The Trial* can be read as engaged in a legitimizing dialogue with the scientific, the logical, and the mathematical. It is important to note that the conversation between Josef K. and Block takes place in the context of a profoundly dubious chapter in which all manner of sacred objects, such as religious worship, God, and biblical exegesis are, by implication, subjected to grotesque parody. It must be assumed, therefore, that there can be a reading that would propose the contingency of any segment of the chapter upon that radical dubiousness. All readings and all proposals will imitate trying to walk on quicksand—for all practical and impractical purposes there is no ground.

The first syntactic indication of the character of the Court appears in the attempt of Josef K.'s guards to persuade him to hand over his clothes to them:

---

22. The word *scientific* is used only once (*science* never), and that usage must be read as ironic since it appears in the speech of Huld who calls the peculiar beauty acquired by the faces of the accused "a strange, to a certain extent a scientific phenomenon" (158). As is always the case with Kafka, however, even this simple comment opens many interpretive options—from irony, with a character designating as "scientific" a perception whose source is superstition or mysticism—to a reading that presumes a biological phenomenon is involved.

"It is better if you give the things to us than handing them over to the depot," they said, "because there is often embezzlement in the depot and in addition after a certain time they sell everything without considering whether or not the respective proceedings have been concluded. And how long such trials last, especially recently! Of course [*allerdings*] in the end [*schließlich*] you would receive the proceeds from the depot, however these proceeds are, first of all, minimal [*erstens an sich schon gering*] because the sale is decided not by the amount of a bid, but by the amount of the bribe, and furthermore such proceeds, experience shows [*erfahrungsgemäß*], dwindle when they are passed year to year from hand to hand." (9)

Josef K. paid no attention to this talk. But if he had he would have noted the comedic suspension of authenticity introduced by "they said" — as if the two could make the speech in unison — that encourages us to read the text schematically — as a premise, followed by exceptions, followed by contradictions and retractions, until finally the initial premise diminishes toward nothing. This is accomplished, as it was in the "Stone Quarries" text, by means of connectors that serve as qualifiers, such as "in addition," "of course," "in the end," "however," "first of all," "already" [*schon*, not translatable in the text], "furthermore," and the subjunctive "would receive." In this segment of text can be found, *in nuce*, the story of *The Trial* insofar as it is linear and diminishing, dwindling as the proceeds do.

As we saw in "Stone Quarries," there can be a more complex and nonlinear, self-canceling textual logic. One example is located early in the story and also involves Josef K.'s relation to his guards, who are stand-ins for the Court:

It surprised K., at least from the train of thought of the guards it surprised him that they had driven him into the room and left him alone here where he had a ten-fold opportunity to kill himself. Although [*allerdings*] at the same time he asked himself, this time from his own train of thought, what kind of reason [*Grund*][23] he could have to do it. Perhaps because

---

23. The term *Grund* also means "foundation, basis, ground, land, or bottom." In *The Trial* it is used primarily in the negative with words such as *no* or *without*,

the two were sitting next door and had intercepted his breakfast? It would be so senseless [*sinnlos*] to kill himself that even if he had wanted to, he would not be capable of it because of its senselessness [*Sinnlosigkeit*]. If the limited intelligence [*geistige Beschränktheit*] of the guards had not been so obvious, one could have assumed that they too, because of the same conviction, had seen no danger in leaving him alone. (13)

This section's dense and convoluted weave of syntax and meaning, grammar and logic offers a model of counterlogical procedure that epitomizes the entire text of *The Trial* at the same time as it demonstrates an alternative to conventional logic and ways of knowing.

The text is divided into two parts by reference to two seemingly opposed "trains of thought." Yet the division is potentially annulled, in the end, by the most reliable mood in Kafka's verbal arsenal — the subjunctive — through its offering of the option that "one" (i.e., an individual of superior intelligence) might share "the same conviction" as the guards, were it not for the impression made upon the intelligent party that the opponent is unintelligent. That is, it is not a lack of intelligence that matters, but its "obviousness" to the narrator, in spite of which the narrator is able initially to identify with the thinking of the unintelligent party. Thus the opposition set up at the outset is seriously weakened, if not abrogated; K. has deconstructed his own premise, and the text seems to arrive at the opposite pole from where it began.

As a consequence of these annulments, we read the following as a progression of ideas in one mind or "train of thought": surprise at apparently being offered the opportunity to commit suicide, checking and being unable to find a reason for doing so, finding the whole matter absurd, deciding that it revolved around the term *sense* (or *meaning, purpose, point*) in its negative forms

---

adding to the notion that certainties are undermined. For a list of the contexts of *Grund*, see Speidel, *Concordance*, 350.

senseless and senselessness, which drive and determine the outcome of this life-threatening question. That is, at bottom, or in
the center, serving as an "attractor" geographically (near the middle of the section), rhetorically, and in terms of meaning is
senseless-senselessness. If we trace the central sentence back into
the indicative voice, we find it states that the speaker is not capable of an act, irrespective of his wishes in the matter, because that
act has no sense or meaning, point or purpose. Yet the entire
thought is expressed in the subjunctive, and, moreover, in the
past subjunctive ("would have been senseless," "had wanted to"),
indicating that the state of affairs could have changed in the later
time—past indicative—with which the text begins.

Indeed, as the subsequent narrative shows, that past indicative
signals the most dramatic oscillation in *The Trial*—to something
that looks like grounded certainty, that consequently suspends
again all deconstructive operations and strategies. Inexplicably
and under the most flimsy of circumstances, Josef K. has raised
the possibility of his suicide. The counterlogical operation of this
section of text directs us toward its beginning and thus reinforces
the absurd suggestion of a suicide. At this point the one thing
Josef K. is sure of and truly knows has been introduced—the certainty of his execution and the advisability of his suicide. This certainty, marked at four points, proposes determinism and irreversibility in contradiction to the freedom and reversibility of the
text's logical system. Our textual dialogue is taken up, reversed,
and transposed when Josef K. twice mentions "executioner(s)"
and ultimately delivers himself to his executioners, while maintaining his unwillingness to kill himself. First, in his rhetorically
crafted demagogic courtroom speech, K. lists what he sees as the
job titles of the Court's staff, "perhaps even executioners, I don't
shy from saying the word" (44). Venting his frustration in conversation with Titorelli, Josef K. asserts: "A single executioner
could replace the entire Court" (132). In both cases, no one else has
ever mentioned execution, just as suicide was not mentioned in
the early scene. These seemingly bizarre suggestions are the one
conviction of Josef K.'s about which he is not in error. The execu-

tion, finally, entails notions of shirking duty and responsibility, of refusal to do other's work, and of making a "last error" (194) by not committing suicide.

This iterative form is reinforcing, just as iteration in the sciences means reinforcement, and indeed, determines validity, that is, whether or not results are considered "science" at all. We have seen in Kafka's texts another type of iterative procedure that results in emptying words of their definitions and doing away with meaning. That type signals erosion of knowledge, as mentioned in the opening quotation. A third type signals erosion by parody. When Josef K. is overcome by faintness in the foul air of the court chancery, he is supported on each side by officials half carrying him toward the exit. The scene is reenacted at the end when the two grotesque figures resembling tacky vaudevillians[24] take him forcefully between them to half lead, half carry him to his place of execution, the stone quarry. When K. arrives at the Courtroom for the first time, unannounced, he is admitted (though he has neither identified himself nor even asked for the Courtroom) by the woman who says: "After you I have to close up, no one else is permitted to go in" (37). The equivalent statement is made by the doorkeeper of the Law when he announces to the dying man from the country that he has to close the door since no one else could gain admission; the entrance was meant only for the man from the country. These mutually parodying repetitions have the effect of redefining one another. A fourth iterative procedure has to do with time. The habitual recurrence of events is frequently indicated by such terms as *always, whenever,* or *usually,* and the past tense of verbs. The effect is threatening, as if there were no way out of a trap. By contrast, repetition or recurrence in science means reassurance that everything is in order. All together, iteration itself is made to seem dubious in Kafka's text. Its different forms cast doubt upon each other and upon the notion of iteration as a means for arriving at sure knowledge.

---

24. The models for such figures in Kafka's time would have been in the early silent movies he saw and in the Yiddish theatre.

We might be reminded by this result of Kafka's procedures that in the realm of the scientific as well, more intractable problems of knowledge, its reliability and ramifications are at stake than are generally recognized in the concentration upon proofs of validity in experiment.

On a smaller scale, transpositions present themselves as chiasmi that range from one that relies on classical logic to those that follow subversive procedures. The girl who helps Josef K. during his spell of weakness in the chancery of the Court phrases her solicitation in the form of a chiasmus that is also an Aristotelian syllogism:[25] "that is nothing out of the ordinary, almost everyone gets an attack like that when he comes here for the first time. You're here for the first time? Then it's as I said, nothing out of the ordinary" (61). Here our emblem of subversion is tamed within an affirmative logical order; the syllogism contains the potential of "four" inside the embrace of its "three," indicating, perhaps, a human inclination to prefer, in general, the tripartite over the quadripartite.[26] By contrast, a dialogue between Huld

---

25. A simple definition of syllogisms is "arguments purporting to be valid because of the relationship between three classes. These relationships are asserted in a total of three statements, two expressing premises and the third being the conclusion" (Peter A. Facione and Donald Scherer, *Logic and Logical Thinking: A Modular Approach* [Woodbridge, Conn.: Ox Bow, 1984], 170).

26. An interesting historical case is that of the Irish mathematician, Sir William Rowan Hamilton, who had been infatuated "with the idea of a triadic arrangement of elements or categories in mathematics and philosophy," and considered that a "triadic arrangement of metaphysical categories" might "organize and arrange all possible human knowledge," yet made his great contribution to algebra with the discovery of quaternions (Thomas L. Hankins, "Triplets and Traids: Sir William Rowan Hamilton on the Metaphysics of Mathematics," *ISIS* 68 [June 1977]: 175). Hankins also finds this phenomenon, which he calls "a prominent theme or principal idea that dominates and controls the direction of the individual's thought," elsewhere in the history of science. He concludes that "[o]ften the theme will have power in the mind of the scientist for a variety of reasons which are not purely scientific but are aesthetic and metaphysical as well. . . . Such themes are probably at work to a greater or lesser degree in all conceptualization" (175). In a variation on Conan Doyle's title, Umberto Eco and Thomas A. Sebeok edited a volume with the title *The Sign of Three: Dupin, Holmes, Peirce* (Bloomington: Indiana University Press, 1983).

and Block that takes the form of a chiasmus undermines itself and represents in its brief space the entire self-defeating story of Josef K.: "[Huld] you've come at the wrong time." "[Block] Wasn't I called?" . . . "[Huld] You were called" . . . "[Huld] Nevertheless you've still come at the wrong time" (163). From this predicament, as for the man from the country before the law, there is no way out. Both rhetorical patterns show the recursion inherent in the *abba* pattern. That is, *ba* are already contained in *ab* and derived from them by various grammatical operations upon the original, such as turning a statement into a question, or a question into a statement, or connecting it adverbially with a *then*, or a *nevertheless*.

When we impart to the chiasmi the authority of being miniaturized versions of "Before the Law" or of *The Trial* itself, we are operating in the manner of the mathematical principle of fractals, the geometry of complex forms that are scale dependent.[27] The possibility that Kafka's texts—*The Trial* and "Stone Quarries"—can be read analogously to new principles in mathematics supports, again, the notion of their "nonliterary" rigor and language that engages in a dialogue of equals between the literary and the mathematical-logical-scientific. Recursive symmetry of scale is part of chaos theory. Feigenbaum came upon the universal mathematical function of how chaos evolves by means of iteration (no matter what the medium—from heartbeats, to turbulence in liquids, to clouds) and revealed "a universality in how large-scale features related to small details. The shift in focus is from the particularities of a given function to the relation between different recursive levels in the iterative process."[28]

---

27. Benoit B. Mandelbrot, the discoverer of fractals, explains them in an unusual mathematical "essay" that has characteristics of a self-conscious literary work: *The Fractal Geometry of Nature*, rev. ed. (San Francisco: W. H. Freeman, 1983).

28. N. Katherine Hayles, "Chaos as Orderly Disorder: Shifting Ground in Contemporary Literature and Science," *New Literary History* 20, no. 2 (Winter 1989): 308. Unfortunately, Hayles's new book, *Chaos Bound: Entropy, Information, and Complexity in Contemporary Literature and Science* (Ithaca, N.Y.: Cornell University Press) was not yet available at the time of this writing.

Hayles sees a connection between these developments in mathematics and contemporary literary theory: "The movement from scale-invariant models to scale-dependent paradigms has an obvious correspondence to the movement in critical theory away from totalizing theories." She cautions, however, to remember that the "new scientific paradigms"

. . . have not renounced globalization. Chaos theory, for example, simply achieves totalization in a different way, by focusing on recursive symmetries between levels rather than by following the motions of individual molecules. . . . what makes [chaos theory] noteworthy is the discovery that *despite* this disorder, universal structures can still be discerned. The thrust toward globalization is apparent in the name Feigenbaum chose for his discovery that chaotic systems can be described through universal constants: he calls it "Universality Theory." (310–11)

These ideas bring us to our own readings that operate on the notion of symmetries of scale and examine the practice and consequences of iteration. They inevitably, at the same time, tend toward "globalization" by pointing to an overall process of dialogic interchange that can follow certain patterns, some of which are mutually reinforcing, such as chiasmus and oscillation, and others that appear to stand in opposition, such as hierarchy and its manifestation as law.

"In the place of hierarchies of truth . . . [*The Trial*] . . . offer[s] dialogically agitated fields of knowledge,"[29] that are worked out in oscillations that also explore the idea of knowledge. For example, the woman who resides at and serves the

29. Robert Markley, "From Kant to Chaos: Physics, Metaphysics, and the Institutionalization of Knowledge," presented at the seventh annual GRIP conference, Minneapolis, April 1989. I took the liberty of inserting "*The Trial*" in the original text that reads as follows: "To differentiate postdisciplinarity as political action from postmodernism as a theoretical analytic, we might group the new conceptual models drawn from physics and information theory under the rubric of 'interphysics' to emphasize their resistance to being co-opted into the traditional dialectic of physics and metaphysics. In the place of hierarchies of truth they offer dialogically agitated fields of knowledge."

Court asks Josef K. whether he believes that his efforts will improve the Court (chap. 3). Josef K. responds that "actually" [or "strictly speaking"—*eigentlich*] he has not been hired to improve the court; "in fact" [*tatsächlich*] he never would have become involved of his own free will. "But because I was supposedly arrested—I have namely been arrested—I have been forced to intervene here, and specifically [*zwar*] for my own sake. If, however, I can at the same time somehow be of use to you, I will naturally do so very gladly. Certainly not only [*nicht etwa nur*] out of charity, but in addition [*sondern außerdem*] because you can also help me" (47).

The oscillations are between "actually," correcting a misimpression, and "in fact," the true situation; between "supposedly" and its correction by the factuality of "namely." But the "namely" is an aside, set off and separated by punctuation. The "supposedly" connects with force and thus carries the thrust of the sentence, skipping over the "namely" of the actual situation. Would the intervention have been forced if it were not for the supposed arrest? The actual arrest seems to be a secondary matter. According to this syntax, "supposedly" dominates "namely"; that is, one may avoid the facts, or knowledge, but one has less power over the "supposedly" that connects to force. The oppositions are suspended in the unresolved "not only . . . but in addition." And the entire syntactical disputation was preceded (on the previous page) by Josef K.'s ironic comment that it is apparently intrinsic to this type of Court "that one is condemned not only in innocence, but also in ignorance" (46). His statement about ignorance is spun out in the succeeding dialogue among syntax, semantics, and punctuation.

As in the "Stone Quarries" text, oscillations in language are also oscillations between options that are never resolved. They are signaled by the many equivalents of "on the one hand . . . on the other hand," the most complete one being the self-canceling "even if perhaps not . . . nevertheless however probably" [*wenn auch vielleicht nicht . . . so doch wahrscheinlich*] (56). Kafka's text offers interpretive options to the reader. For example: "In embarrassment or impatience the examining magistrate shifted back and forth on his chair" (42–43). A completely different story of the Court's power is told according to which option—embarrassment or impatience—a reader (including the reader, K.) chooses. In the same scene, two different stances are proposed toward an action of the examining magistrate: "It could only be a sign of deep humiliation or at least it had to be interpreted as such" (40). That is we, as readers in the same boat as Josef K., may read with the expectations of realism and take signs as indubitably referential, or we can read self-reflexively, as meta-readers who know that there is an interpretive distance between ourselves and the text. The quintessential dilemma of choice can be found in the interpretations of "Before the Law" that constitute a parody of Talmudic exegesis.[30] The model Kafka's exegesis follows is of refutation proceeding recursively out of the preceding interpretation, with frequent references to the opinions and conclusions of authorities. Following the Talmudic manner, it allows for the coexistence of opposed opinions, but to the opposite purpose, namely to explain failure to reach an inaccessible Law, whereas actual Talmudic exegesis intends to invoke and clarify the omnipresent Law. To his end, Josef K., the interpreter, never finally resolves opposing choices to arrive at a confident reading of the Court and his trial. We note below in chapter 5 that Planck also describes interpretive options in his canonical text on heat radiation. As in the case of Kafka, the choices may be directly stated or inherent in textual operations.

---

30. In addition to the *ba'ya* mentioned above in "Stone Quarries" (n.9), Rabbi Louis Jacobs (*Talmudic Argument*) reviews some of the many other styles of argument to be found in the Talmud, a number of which can be seen in Kafka's parody. Jacob's list includes the "argument from authority" (13), the "argument by comparison," the "argument by differentiation," the "either/or argument," the "contrary argument," the "acceptance of an argument in part," the "argument based on an opponent's position," the "argument exposing the flaws in an opponent's argument," the "argument based on historical or geographical conditions, in which an attempt is made to demonstrate that these conditions affect the law and limit its application," the "argument against a statement of the obvious," and the "argument to resolve a contradiction between sources," (13–14) as well as others.

The words of Josef K., reflecting the operations of the whole text, can give the impression of a visitor from another planet, a stranger in whose eyes everything is new and for whom the language does not easily provide names. This condition is particularly striking in the opening scene, but also the scene in the cathedral (chap. 9) when Josef K. is attempting, despite inadequate light, to examine a large painting. The examination is notable for a number of reasons. First of all, because it is a piece-by-piece, detail-by-detail uncovering of an icon in the investigative manner of an art historian, with the significant difference that no collective names are used. We would expect the helpful, even necessary guidance contained in the art historical terminology familiar to any educated European and certainly to Josef K., who is an expert in this field. Yet, as is typical for the text of *The Trial*, and in agreement with Nietzsche's views about the distortion inherent in the metaphoricity of naming, collective terms are avoided. Instead, evidence is studiously collected and described as it might have been by Adam on the first day of creation. Science could not operate without collective concepts, as Josef K. does in this scene. A knowledge that is based neither on naming nor iteration is arrived at in language.

His investigation of the picture leads Josef K. to find inherent action. He observes of the figure of the knight in armor: "He was resting on his sword that he had thrust into the bare ground in front of him. . . . He appeared to be observing attentively an event that was taking place in front of him. It was surprising that he stood still and did not draw nearer" (175). He extrapolates from a static depiction that action has occurred and may occur again at any time. The comparable scientific principle is that of the congruence of matter with energy: matter is potential energy as expressed in Einstein's formula $E = mc^2$ that tells of the immense energy (c is the speed of light) contained in matter that ultimately was released in the explosion of nuclear fission. Josef K. finds potential energy in other pictures as well: a judge in one of Titorelli's portraits "seems to want to leap up in the next instant"

(94); the figures in a smutty drawing "project bodily" (48) out of the picture.

Josef K. can barely see the picture before him in the church and, indeed, only a small part of it at one time because of the poor lighting. It is pitch-dark inside the church and neither candles, nor the "eternal light," nor technology in the form of a flashlight provide sufficient light to see clearly. The light of an enormous candle only has the effect of "increasing the darkness" (175). This paradox of light failing to alleviate the darkness is a favorite device of Kafka's in *The Trial*. He uses it in the first scene in his lawyer's room (chap. 6, 91), in a scene with Leni in the lawyer's kitchen (chap. 8, 145), and in the scene where K. tells the lawyer of his intention to dismiss him (chap. 8, 159). In that scene, K. dims the candle with his hand, in order to have a better view of the lawyer. The inversion of the expected relationship of light to darkness has implications with respect to knowledge and science. We could infer, for example, that it indicates that our enlightenment and rationality serve to obsure understanding—a tale told frequently in the course of *The Trial*. On the other hand, we could also maintain that we are dealing with optical realities, or with an analogue of responses of radiation in a black-body as it is heated to the different frequencies of the light spectrum. In a paradox equivalent to Kafka's, "the formula Planck sought described the worst possible source of illumination, and so could serve as a zero-point standard for rating new electric lamps."[31] That is, technological advantage (and profit) connected in the case of Planck's black-body research to the least illumination as expressed in the notion of zero as a base level standard for evaluation of light.

It could be possible to interpret Kafka's light-darkness paradox as a legitimate physical statement, for the physical relations of light are not those we easily perceive with the naked eye. When

---

31. J. L. Heilbron, *The Dilemmas of an Upright Man: Max Planck as Spokesman for German Science* (Berkeley: University of California Press, 1986), 6–7.

the man from the country is dying in front of the entrance to the law "he doesn't know whether it is really getting darker around him or whether his eyes are deceiving him." But he is sure of recognizing "in the darkness a radiance" (183) from the door of the law. That radiance depends upon the darkness.[32] Were the surroundings themselves bright in the eyes of the man from the country, the radiance would be weak or imperceptible. In chapter 5 I examine relations of light in Max Planck's standard textbook on heat radiation. We find that, in his Foreword, Planck prefers the literary and conventional metaphor — "a thoroughly dark, inaccessible region into which only the introduction of the elementary quantum of action promises to cast some light"[33] — which also reflects a rhetorical stance that informs his scientific writings. Planck's text examines, with mathematical precision, the physics of light rays, but it is also implicated in the inherited literary rhetoric of light. In Kafka's text, the human eye is unable accurately to assess relations of light. Light is a consistently ambivalent phenomenon, just as it was proved to be by Einstein's application of quantum theory to the photoelectric effect, showing light to behave both as wave and particle.

In *The Trial*, concepts and definitions are suspect, light is suspect, pictorial evidence is suspect (just as in "Stone Quarries" where pictorial evidence dissolves in paradox). Numbers, too, are suspect, their relevance canceled. Chapter 2 is marked by games with twos, fives, and tens. In the courtroom are two windows, two men block K.'s path between the two opposing parties, and a messenger tries twice to convey his message — all on the same

---

32. Clayton Koelb, in the context of a different kind of argument, expresses a similar view of the relation of light and darkness in "Before the Law": "One can only point in the direction of truth or perhaps merely surround the place where truth might be with a darkness so that the true radiance might be glimpsed, if only by contrast and at a distance. . . . One might therefore reveal the truth, though indirectly and by accident, simply by wrapping up something unknown in a dense enough darkness." (*Kafka's Rhetoric: The Passion of Reading* [Ithaca, N.Y.: Cornell University Press, 1989], 179.)

33. *Vorlesungen Über die Theorie der Wärmestrahlung*, 2d rev. ed. (Leipzig: Johann Ambrosius Barth, 1913), ix.

page (37). On the fifth floor K. discovered the courtroom where the first thing he saw upon entering was a clock that showed ten o'clock (36). But it all seems to depend, in K.'s opinion, upon coincidence, since he had been told that the Court is attracted by guilt, and thus, he reasons, whatever floor he chooses by chance must be where the Court is located. For the building itself he had no number, yet he found the correct one on a street of identical buildings. Businessman Block, whose case is five years old, has secretly hired five additional lawyers to assist in his case. Yet, he asserts that he can entrust it less to the five than if he had only one (151). Multiple petitions in his case turned out to be useless. Numbers and their multiples, which seem to be hard evidence and in which we place our faith, are irrelevant or useless and might as well be replaced by chance.[34] By implication we could also argue that with his treatment of numbers, Kafka casts off the limits of ordinary arithmetic in favor of a commitment to the play of chance and necessity.[35]

The Trial also permits the reader the option of a switch from reading for the play of "postmodern" scientific textual models to a contrary strategy, namely reading positivistically for scientific or technological references and parallels. There are, for example, references reminiscent of Darwinian biology and the concept of psychosomatic illness. Leni displays her webbed fingers, which K. calls a "game of nature" (96). K. intends that his superior, the deputy director of the bank, must be reminded as often as possible that K. was alive and "like all living beings [he] could one day surprise with new capacities, however innocuous he might seem today" (212, uncompleted chapter). After his unpredictable reaction to the physical ordeal of the stale air in the offices of the court, K. wonders (in a thought full of ironic meaning) whether "[h]is

34. For a history of the failure of mathematics to achieve infallible reasoning methods and a uniformly agreed upon foundation in logic—though not in Kafka's sense—see Morris Kline, *Mathematics*.

35. See, for example, molecular biologist Jacques Monod, *Chance and Necessity*, trans. A. Wainhouse (New York: Vintage, 1972) for the role of this pair in relatively recent scientific developments.

body wanted to revolt and subject him to a new trial, now that he had so easily handled the old one" (66). Biological notions are present in the text, as are the latest achievements of early twentieth-century technology—the telephone, automobile, and "copy machine." These, in turn, mark the contrast between modernity and the musty, Dickensian[36] mode of the Court.

In conversation with Titorelli, Josef K. makes demands like a scientist. He requires of the painter's testimony probability, reliability as evidence, and freedom from contradiction. He would like to subject it to truth-testing and refutation. In the face of the unreliability of theory, history, and literature to predict acquittal (the painter warns against "generalizing," testifies to the undependability of accounts of the past, and of "legends" [132–33]), K. depends upon a scientific method with the same standards as Max Planck. (Like literature, according to some views, the "legends" in the painter's tale are "not provable," "contain a certain amount of truth," and are "very beautiful" (133). Titorelli himself does not read [has never read the Law] and prefers *not* knowing what the supreme court is like, yet he seems to "know" a lot more than Josef K.)

Moreover, Josef K. acts like an author of a scientific paper. He plans at one point to produce a written defense that includes an autobiographical statement:

In it he wanted to present a brief description of his life and in the case of every in any way important event explain for what reasons he acted the way he did, whether this way of behaving according to his present judgment should be rejected or approved, and what reasons he could state for either one or the other.

[Er wollte darin eine kurze Lebensbeschreibung vorlegen und bei jedem irgendwie wichtigeren Ereignis erklären, aus welchen Gründen er so gehandelt hatte, ob diese Handlungsweise nach seinem gegenwärtigen Ur-

---

36. It is obvious that *The Trial* has a great deal in common with Dickens's *Bleak House*. Sometimes one can have the feeling that Kafka's texts are like an amalgam of the lushness of Dickens and the spareness of Beckett.

teil zu verwerfen oder zu billigen war und welche Gründe er für dieses oder jenes anführen konnte.] (98)

As in a scientific paper, we find a brief introductory statement of intention, we find "reasons," explanation, evaluation, and the goal of completeness. Josef K. is following one of Max Planck's favorite lines of reasoning, that is to propose a category, then to define it by way of a bifurcating pattern — a larger concept is divided into two subcategories, and each of those into further subcategories. *The Trial* also shares some semantic (and metaphysical?) distinctions with Planck's texts, for example opposition between "theoretical questions" and "reality," which Planck may refer to as "abstract ideas" versus "nature." Both deal freely with notions of "apparent" versus "real," and apply the term *infinite* to relations of size or quantity, sometimes paradoxically, such as Kafka's "it made infinitely little impression on him" (209, uncompleted chapters).

On the matter of time, however, as realized in the notion of *future*, Kafka and Planck part company again. The future can properly be called the foundational metaphor of physics. Prediction is its raison d'être and ideological imperative. "[A]s far as a physicist is concerned, the important quality of a theory is the predictions it makes."[37] "Physics is the drive to predict the behavior of the world stripped of most of its complications" (Gregory, *Inventing Reality*, 197). Kafka, by contrast, manages to bracket entirely the notion of *future* from his texts, both in its metaphysical and its rhetorical-syntactical manifestation. His antilogic cancels linear evolution, and his complex manipulations of tenses and syntax have the effect of repealing chronology and the idea of space and time as separate categories. By virtue of the possibilities of German syntax, the usual sequences are suspended and the future is annulled. An example of these procedures (whose translation, unfortunately, requires contortions of the English language) follows:

37. Bruce Gregory, *Inventing Reality: Physics as Language* (New York: Wiley, 1988), 47.

Somewhat soothed by this thought, K. gave orders to the attendant, who had been holding open [simple past tense in German] the corridor door for him for a long time, to notify the manager when he [the attendant] has a chance, that he [K.] was [present subjunctive] on a business errand, and then, almost happy at the thought of being able to devote himself entirely to his case for a while, he left the bank.

[Durch diesen Gedanken ein wenig beruhigt, gab K. dem Diener, der schon lange die Tür zum Korridor für ihn offenhielt, den Auftrag, dem Direktor gelegentlich die Meldung zu machen, daß er sich auf einem Geschäftsgang befinde, und verließ, fast glücklich darüber, sich eine Zeitlang vollständig seiner Sache widmen zu können, die Bank.] (121)

Contrary to their placement and tenses, the events take place in the following sequence: (1) the door has been held open for an extended period of time with an indefinite beginning and end, (2) K. feels soothed, (3) K. gives the order, (4) he departs from the bank happy, (5) he can devote himself to his case, (6) he is on a "business errand", and (7) the director receives notification. Furthermore, the business errand, a fiction expressed in the subjunctive of reported speech, is only actualized when the director receives notification, and thus could also be seen as simultaneous with that event. At first glance, the sentence appears, while complex, perfectly reasonable. A process-oriented reading, however, discovers that time and space are jumbled in defiance of chronology and the convention that movements in time coincide with movements in space. In such arrangements there is no room for a future that, as soon as it might suggest itself, is neutralized or rescinded.

Like "Stone Quarries," the text of *The Trial* is marked by the play of the language of reason with its opposites. Words such as *reason*, *judgment*, *understanding*, and their verbal forms, for example, seem to dominate K.'s discussion with his landlady of the early-morning arrest. In his attempt to rationalize, K. refers to office telephones and other appurtenances of the young, upwardly mobile urban professional. Yet the entire segment of text, as we saw above in chapter 1, is driven by a discourse of irrationality as shown by its avoidance of naming the central topic—the arrest. In the course of a longer—page and a half—segment of text, Kafka plays first with multiple verb forms in the realm of knowing and understanding [*wissen*, to know; *kennen*, to know, be acquainted with; *auffassen*, to comprehend, grasp; *bedenken*, to consider], then suspends their cumulative effect with the phrase "for which the intellect is no longer sufficient" [*für die der Verstand nicht mehr ausreicht*] (149), which introduces a page full of nouns from the opposite realm: "superstition, opinion, sign, belief, error," and even "superstitious opinions" (150). By their historical antiquity (referred to in the context), by their position (at the end of the discussion of the topic), by their iteration and the greater space they occupy, it seems the "superstitious opinions" and their ilk carry the day.

We must recognize, however, that there is also playfulness in these linguistic disputations. Not only Kafka's, but Planck's texts can, by the operations of their language, be playful. Linguistic playfulness implies an unnamed but present and richly productive disorder, pointing beyond each reading to untapped dimensions of interpretive possibilities. Playfulness resides also in the very oscillation between alternatives. For example, naming, while undermined elsewhere, is supported in a sequence that opens the sixth chapter where K. reviews, in his imagination, his uncle's appearance, manner, and likely behavior, eventually blending indistinguishably the imagined uncle and the one who actually appears in K.'s office at the bank. This obviously accurate review in the mind's eye closes with K.'s correct naming of his uncle in a way that self-descriptively asserts the preeminence of the imagined uncle over the real one: "It was his [Josef K.'s] habit to call [literally, to name] him 'the phantom from the country' " (80).

A brief speech by Josef K. revolves around the verb *to know* [*wissen*] in the sense of knowing facts or information, and its conjunction with naming. In conversation with Miss Bürstner he maintains: "What I know [*weiß*] I already told you. Even more than I know, because it wasn't an investigating commission at all, I'm calling [*nenne*] it that because I don't know any other name for it" (28). Knowing means naming, or having the ability to name. Josef K.'s speech starts out with knowing, then rescinds that knowing because, it turns out, it is a case of *not* knowing, that is, of having no name. The order of the operation is significant, because it opens with the proposition that there is knowing, deconstructs that proposition, yet despite that deconstruction, must continue anyway without the name on which knowing depends. Naming means controlling. Josef K. is unable to name, and therefore is not in a position to control.

Block says of the legal hierarchy: "everyone can call ("name") himself 'great' if he so chooses" (152). That arbitrary naming has no significance for a lawyer's real status. In fact, *un*naming may be more reliable than naming. Josef K. himself, we learn, is a text subject to refutation. His uncle Karl, who appears very knowledgeable about the Court, warns K. about his seemingly cavalier attitude toward the trial: " 'Do you want to lose the case ["the trial"]? Do you know what that means? That means that you are simply expunged' " [*einfach gestrichen*] (84–85). The past participle, *gestrichen*, applies primarily to written language and includes the meanings "deleted, crossed out, canceled," and "taken off the list."

In an earlier chapter the text explores K.'s identity in a logical-grammatical process that cancels the existence of that self. It is nighttime and K. is reenacting for Miss Bürstner the scene of his arrest that morning:

I am the Supervisor, two guards are sitting over there on the trunk, three young people are standing near the photographs. A white blouse, that I mention only in passing, is hanging on the window latch.

Thus the text begins with the erasure of K., who has assumed the identity of the Supervisor.

And now it begins. Oh, I'm forgetting me. The most important person, well then I, am standing here in front of the little table. The Supervisor is sitting in a very comfortable position, legs crossed, his arm hanging here over the back of the chair, a really crude type.

Here the subject is forgetting itself; we cannot know whether that subject is the original K. or his new identity as the Supervisor. The *I* in the nominative case has transposed itself into the accusative or object case. With the reminder that that *I* is the center, it returns in the nominative case, but not quite as the subject. The little comma in the text after *I* (strange as it looks in English) serves to associate the now restored nominative *I* with its appositive, "the most important person," and at the same time separate it from the subject standing at the table. In this brief space of text an identity has gone through five transformations.

And now finally it's really beginning. The Supervisor is calling as if he had to wake me up, in fact he's shouting; unfortunately, if I want to make it comprehensible to you, I have to shout too, by the way it's only my name he's shouting that way.

K., "immersed in the role," ends the demonstration by slowly and loudly calling his own name, "Josef K.!" (28–29). The third revision of the beginning of the scene brings an identity split between something like an ego and a superego, or victim and persecutor, with the final total identification of the object with the subject, so that even the object's name is denigrated. It is "only" whose name? The name has become worthless as its original owner, subsumed in a new identity, calls upon himself as an outsider. K. acts like an erasable text. Inside and outside are collapsed in this linguistic dismantling of the notion of identity.

In another place the text comments on its own procedure, exploring in it a nonlinear logical-grammatical sequence.

[h]e had only come . . . out of the desire to ascertain that the interior [*das Innere*] of this Court system was as repulsive as its exterior [*sein Äusseres*]. And it appeared, indeed, that he had been right in that assumption, he did not want to intrude further [*nicht weiter eindringen*], he was op-

pressed [cramped, confined—*beengt*] enough by what he had already seen. . . . (60)

The sequence follows from the noun of interiority that is equated with the noun of exteriority—canceling their difference—to the verb for forcible entry into the interior, which is negated, although the subject is characterized by a predicate adjective that implies narrow, confining interiors. As the text moves through the sequence of nouns, verb, and adjective it loses the consistency of logical development, concluding with an adjective that cancels the negative of the more powerful preceding verbal form, and also cancels the noun for "exterior," since that final adjective tells exclusively a story of interiority that is apparently what the whole thing is about—*not* about inside versus outside, as it initially seemed.

The Court, like K. himself, behaves like language with its gesture that invites at the same time it excludes.[38] Language is by its nature exclusionary: it sets up tribes and nations, disciplines and fortunes, or simply excludes the "other"—the uninformed, the innocent, the speaker of a different tongue. To use language, as Kafka and Nietzsche knew, is to lie. "Lying is made the order of the world" says Josef K. (188). The reader is informed by a desire for inclusion—to decipher, to decode, to break through the exclusionary barrier. In an ironic inversion that contradicts conventional views, Planck's texts, driven as they are by tropes and rhetorical strategies, appeals to the reader, and a personal narrator, are weighted toward inclusion in contrast to Kafka's texts with their peculiar logical patterning that seems to prefer the gesture of exclusion. Planck means for his "laws" to be accessible, whereas Kafka's "law" is absent and inaccessible, merely a reference point. "Before the Law" tells the story of failure to break the barrier of exclusion, failure to enter the text and share its discourse.

---

38. Leonard Bloomfield writes: "The dichotomy of including and excluding statements inheres in the nature of language." Bloomfield is analyzing the operations of calculation or "a scientific dialect" in terms of the operations of ordinary language ("Linguistic Aspects," 50).

All other characters in *The Trial* seem to understand and accept the Court system without question—all except Josef K., whose growing inability to comprehend, even to hear, signals his demise. K.'s relationship to the Court is like Kafka's to language—that of someone for whom what is familiar to everyone else is strange, foreign, and new, like a visitor from another planet who lacks ready names, generalizing concepts, and thus easy control, yet who seeks proper designation with a rigor bordering on absolute. The trial and thus the Court's existence, however, are dependent upon that uncomprehending observer. K. maintains (in his courtroom speech) that "it is only a trial [*ein Verfahren*] if I recognize it as such" (39). That remark, which can perhaps be seen as merely a feature of persuasive rhetoric, is reinforced much later in the text (chap. 7) by K.'s reflecting: "The contempt he had earlier felt for the trial no longer obtained. If he had been alone in the world, he could have easily disregarded the trial, though [*allerdings*] it was also certain that in that event the trial would never have arisen at all" (108). Here we have conceptualizing in common with the Copenhagen interpretation of quantum mechanics (see chap. 2) that, at a certain level, phenomena cannot be considered to have existence independent of observation. Here, as elsewhere in *The Trial*, a distinct boundary between literary and scientific conceptualizing cannot be drawn. In the Court system not only is everything related to everything else, as in field theory, but conservation of energy obtains. As explained to K. by Titorelli, the Court never forgets and "no file is ever lost" (136).

"The trial must continuously be turned in the little circle to which it has artificially been confined" (138), according to K.'s informant Titorelli. The notion could be a metaphor for the thought experiment of a theoretical physicist that takes the measurements of a continuously operating system artificially confined to a small radiation cavity. It also suggests Bloomfield's explication of the "miniature linguistic systems" of logic and mathematics. What is defined as acceptable is "true" only within the agreed upon limits of the system.

Such a discourse produces a calculation, made for its own interest, or as a model, or with a view to eventual use; about the outside world it tells nothing. We may be sure of its correctness because it moves only within the verbal agreements upon which it is based. (Bloomfield, "Linguistic Aspects," 46)

In accord with the avoidance of ready naming in *The Trial*, Bloomfield asserts:

So far as concerns anything accessible to science, the only infinite classes are classes of speech-forms; such situations as are referred to by terms like *limit*, *dense*, and *continuous* arise only from our agreements as to the use of speech-forms and will be sought in vain in that outer world which is studied by science. (Bloomfield, "Linguistic Aspects," 53)

The language system of *The Trial*, like that of science according to Bloomfield, is self-enclosed and internally consistent. The consistency, however, is one of language patterning, not a consistency that panders to the inclination of readers to seek determinism in the narrative.

Kafka's texts locate knowledge in the play of linearity with nonlinear disruption. In demonstrating the value of disruption they offer a redefinition of "rigor" at the same time as they violate their own references to law. According to Whorf, "[t]here are here no laws of thought. Yet the structural regularities of our sentences enable us to sense that laws are *somewhere* in the background."[39] In the "Stone Quarries" text, for example, many types of hierarchy are subverted by language, which is itself a hierarchical system in its grammar and syntax and recursive patterns. Language, itself laws, can only subvert laws by means of its own antilogical logical processes. Subversion of hierarchy is usually associated with anarchical tendencies. In the case of Kafka, however, law is subverted not with disorder, but with order and precision that are generated, however, from outside the law.

---

39. Benjamin Lee Whorf, *Language, Thought, and Reality*, ed. John B. Carroll (Cambridge, Mass.: MIT Press, 1956), 238.

As a consequence of the dialogue, the give and take, the oscillation process knowledge is not resident and fixed, but shifting and in motion. Its very flux and play make it infinitely productive. Kafka's are texts in praise of flux over the innate desire for permanence and fixed analytical schemes, thus their dynamic patterns connect to some of the latest developments in scientific thought more than half a century after Kafka's death. Oscillation is as essential to physical as to chemical and biological systems. It is the orderly process that can evolve into a chaotic system, and it is the order to which that system ultimately returns. "Dissipative dynamical systems" evolve irreversibly in "a far more complicated evolutionary regime than simple decay."[40] Their opposites are "conservative," or reversible systems. In Kafka's texts we have seen the dynamic interplay of reversible logical systems with irreversible, dissipative stories. These are also extrapolations from the central theoretical concerns of Max Planck.

Kafka's textual procedures validate only themselves and the problematizing of language. Accordingly, a reader must attend critically to language, to its peculiarities as an agent of other than ostensible meanings, and by that means, as Kafka did, touch on the possibilities of kinds of knowing other than that which resides in everyday instructions, rules, strictures, and ordinances. Since other kinds of knowing potentially threaten hierarchies, convention, exclusive dialects, privilege, and presumptions of mastery, Kafka's language-centered, language-obsessed texts can provide us only with a less than respectable, irreverant, and even slightly disreputable, underground access to discourses of science.

---

40. Pierre Berge, Yves Pomeau, and Christian Vidal, *Order within Chaos: Towards a Deterministic Approach to Turbulence*, trans. Laurette Tuckerman (New York: Wiley, 1984), 22.

CHAPTER 4

Planck and His Readers —
Kafkaesque?

. . . the corpus of scientific writing is one of the more remarkable of
human literary accomplishments.
— Charles Bazerman, *Shaping Written Knowledge:*
The Genre and Activity of the Experimental Article in Science

We cut nature up, organize it into concepts, and ascribe significances as
we do, largely because we are parties to an agreement to organize it in
this way — an agreement that holds throughout our speech community
and is codified in the patterns of our language. . . . This fact is very
significant for modern science, for it means that no individual is free to
describe nature with absolute impartiality but is constrained to certain
modes of interpretation even while he thinks himself most free.
— Benjamin Lee Whorf, "Science and Linguistics"

These quotations direct our attention to two premises in our
reading of Planck's scientific articles that are not found in the canonical readings by historians and philosophers of science: the
literariness of scientific texts and the dependence of scientific
description and interpretation upon the patterns and peculiarities
of a natural language. These assertions are neither new nor startling. They are in accord with the greater attendance to language
as a shaping force that Whorf predicted in his writings half a century ago. Philosopher of science Mary Hesse, for example, has
explored both rhetorical structures in scientific texts and the dependence of scientific classifications and interpretations upon
syntax.[1]

Epigraphs from *Shaping Written Knowledge: The Genre and Activity of the Ex-*
perimental Article in Science (Madison: University of Wisconsin Press, 1988), 13; and
Language, Thought, and Reality: Selected Writings of Benjamin Lee Whorf, ed. John B.
Carroll (Cambridge, Mass.: MIT Press, 1956), 213–14.
   1. See the introduction to her *Revolutions and Reconstructions in the Philosophy of*

The obvious objection is that modern scientific communication is conducted primarily in mathematics, and thus can be seen
as largely independent of natural language. This objection can be
countered by arguments such as Richard Rorty's (chap. 1) that
science only defines itself as science once it has been accepted and
transmitted in language. Whorf calls upon Bloomfield as a wit-
ness to this circumstance:

> As Leonard Bloomfield has shown, scientific research begins with a
> set of sentences which point the way to certain observations and experi-
> ments, the results of which do not become fully scientific until they have
> been turned back into language, yielding again a set of sentences which
> then become the basis of further exploration into the unknown.[2]

The privileging of mathematics as the "language" of science is
historically and ideologically contingent. Elkana, for example,
points out that the notion of a privileged language of nature
evolved from Luther's emphasis on interpreting the language of
the Bible, or deciphering God's word. Later, and up to the present
time, the "guiding metaphor"[3] for physical scientists has been
Galileo's famous remark: "The Universe, which stands continually open to our gaze, cannot be understood unless one first
learns to comprehend the language and read the letters in which
it is composed. It is written in the language of mathematics. . . . "[4] What Elkana calls "the language of science fallacy"
evolved in the nineteenth century "with the professionalization of
science" and reinterpretations of science in terms of Victorian
ethics. With these developments "came the conflation of the

Science (Bloomington, Ind.: Indiana University Press, 1980) where she discusses
the "theory-ladenness" of data that necessarily obtains since "every set of predi-
cates in a natural or any other descriptive language implies a *classification* of the
contents of the world" (viii).

2. "Linguistics as an Exact Science," *Language, Thought, and Reality*, 221.

3. Bruce Gregory, *Inventing Reality: Physics as Language* (New York: Wiley,
1988), 17.

4. From "The Assayer," in *Discoveries and Opinions of Galileo*, trans. Stillman
Drake (New York: Doubleday, 1957), 237–38. As quoted in Gregory, *Inventing
Reality*, 17.

method of science and the language of Nature into the 'language of science.' There was only one method of discovery; and if you learned it well, you were on the sure path to the making of discoveries."[5] The power of a privileged language of Nature readable only by the mathematically versed scientist can be seen in the frequent rephrasing by modern physicists of Galileo's notion, a recent example being Nobel laureate Richard Feynman as quoted above (chap. 2, n. 11). In agreement with Elkana, Rorty, Arbib and Hesse, and many other scholars, this study rejects the notion of a privileged, "objective" language, whether it be mathematics or any other that is meant to give access to "raw data" or "bare facts." Although mathematics is often called a "language," it lacks the shifting and multiple, indeterminate and context-dependent meanings of a true language. Mathematics can more properly be called a kind of rhetoric in its relations to the language text in scientific articles.[6]

Historically, changes in science are accompanied by, fostered by, and only recognized by changes in language. Wilda Anderson has examined this process in the work of Lavoisier, Maurice Finocchiaro in the work of Galileo.[7] We have seen an exploration of the relation between language and quantum theory in the writ-

5. Y. Elkana, "The Historical Roots of Modern Physics," *Proceedings of the International School of Physics "Enrico Fermi": History of Twentieth Century Physics*, ed. C. Weiner (New York and London: Academic Press, 1977), 255.

6. A recent change in views is indicated by the fact that some professors of mathematics are finding that language precedes mathematical conceptualizing. In order to foster understanding, they are requiring students to verbalize and write about math, rather than the traditional memorization of equations and development of quantitative skills. See "Math Professors Turn to Writing to Help Students Master Concepts of Calculus and Combinatorics," *The Chronicle of Higher Education* 35, no. 23, (February 15, 1989): A14.

7. Wilda C. Anderson, *Between the Library and the Laboratory: The Language of Chemistry in Eighteenth-Century France* (Baltimore: Johns Hopkins University Press, 1984); Maurice A. Finocchiaro, *Galileo and the Art of Reasoning: Rhetorical Foundations of Logic and Scientific Method* (Dordrecht: D. Reidel, 1980). There are many other studies, including a noteworthy early one by Ernst Cassirer, "The Influence of Language upon the Development of Scientific Thought," *The Journal of Philosophy* 39 (January–December 1942): 309–27.

ings of Bohr and Heisenberg (chap. 2). Elkana reminds us of the historicity of the language-science relationship by pointing out that in the seventeenth century Boyle and Wilkins, among others, determined the nature of the scientific report by establishing certain rules for inclusion and exclusion in the write-ups of experimental results:

> A rule was established that all factors possibly relevant to an experiment should be carefully noted down. But it was also established that the lengthy speculations and personal stories that had led an enquirer to a given experiment should not be included as part of the scientific report—which meant, incidentally, that the theory or metaphysical view according to which it was decided what factors were relevant to an experiment was suppressed. This also created an impression of the existence of "raw facts." (Elkana, "Historical Roots," 254–55)[8]

Many philosophers of science would agree with Elkana's statement that "any scientific theory has a hard-core metaphysics—that is, a view of the world that in its very formation is not testable—and if we remember that concepts have a meaning only within the framework of a given theory, then there are no theoretical results which are independent of the theory's metaphysics: Newton's laws do not have the same meaning in two cultures if 'time,' 'space,' and 'force' have different meanings" ("Historical Roots," 254).

The cultural relativism indicated in Elkana's remarks is reminiscent of the findings of Whorf and others on the cultural variations of conceptions of time, space, and so on, based on differences in language. Other cultural and sociopolitical factors, including, according to Elkana, "the social image of knowledge," (254) determine the choice of problems to investigate. Interpretations of results are also a function of the cultural nexus. Science in its multiple context-dependencies is also examined in the writings of Ludwik Fleck, Paul Forman, Thomas Kuhn, and Stephen

---

8. See also the discussion by Robert Markley in "Objectivity as Ideology: Boyle, Newton, and the Languages of Science," *Genre* 16 (Winter 1983): 355–72.

Toulmin.[9] These assessments of the relationship between science and language, and the context-dependency of the enterprise of science are the necessary premises of our association of texts by Kafka and Planck and our investigation of these texts for possible alternate sites and kinds of knowledge.

The views just expressed are assumed in the following readings of several of Planck's papers on theoretical physics. Beginning with one of the papers that introduced the quantum in 1900, they have been selected because of their importance and because they represent stages in Planck's thinking on the quantum and other topics. The last paper examined is Planck's report to the first Solvay Conference in 1911. This conference marked the beginning of widespread international acceptance by physicists of quantum theory, and thus is an appropriate cutoff point before we subject the 1913 edition of Planck's standard textbook on heat radiation to a language-based reading in chapter 5. The heat radiation textbook is treated separately from the journal articles (many of which had originated as lectures) because they are two distinctly different types of scientific writing. The journal article "is tentative; it is personally formulated as knowledge which has yet to be confirmed by the collective." The textbook, or handbook, however, "formulates the genuine core of the system of opinions of a discipline. It is impersonal, presents itself as secure and substantiated knowledge, which is to be taken as the basis for all further work of the thought-collective. . . . All journal science strives

9. Toulmin's suggestion of multiple explanations for the sciences is equally applicable to literature, thus underscoring the deepest level of communality and implying that rigid, inviolable boundaries are historical constructs that do not engage the deep connections: "In some respects, the natural sciences may be as they are, because human beings have the kinds of nervous systems they do; in others, because they have developed the kinds of cultures and institutions they have; in others again, because of the kinds of languages or channels of communication they possess." ("Ludwik Fleck and the Historical Interpretation of Science," *Cognition and Fact: Materials on Ludwik Fleck*, ed. Robert S. Cohen and Thomas Schnelle [Dordrecht: D. Reidel, 1986], 268–69.) See also Bazerman, *Shaping Written Knowledge*, on the cultural context of science.

towards the handbook. It wants to be accepted in the collective and to be counted in the basic corpus of its discipline."[10] Thus we would expect that Planck's journal articles would have more in common with the fragmentary nature of Kafka's texts.

The dialogue between Kafka's and Planck's texts as read from Planck's scientific texts is particularly intricate and provocative insofar as it provokes conventional notions about the nature of scientific texts. I take as a starting point the canonical readings of Planck's texts that do not recognize the literariness of the texts, but which do offer different interpretations of their meaning, thus proferring multiplicity, as is the case with interpretations of Kafka's texts. In the interpreters' disagreements we read a story of inevitable uncertainty, and of a Planck displaced in his historical role and in the sites where his texts' version of scientific knowledge are thought to be or have been located in a posited continuum of physical theory.

One of Planck's most reliable and respected interpreters is Martin J. Klein, who wrote between 1960 and 1966 three seminal articles on Planck and the discovery of the quantum. An excerpt from one of Klein's papers illustrates where his interpretation (representing the majority view) of Planck's discovery differs from the revisionist interpretation by Thomas S. Kuhn in his 1978 study of the history and meaning of Planck's discovery.[11] While there is no doubt today that "the concept of energy quanta that Planck introduced to the world in 1900 has taken the central role in the physical science of the twentieth century,"[12] we must remember that that judgment is from hindsight, in view of de-

---

10. Robert S. Cohen and Thomas Schnelle, "Introduction," *Cognition and Fact*, xxix. The editors are reviewing Fleck's findings and using his terminology, e.g. "thought-collective."

11. *Black-Body Theory and the Quantum Discontinuity, 1894–1912*, 1978, rpt. with new afterword (Chicago: University of Chicago Press, 1987).

12. Martin J. Klein, "Planck, Entropy, and Quanta, 1901–1906," *The Natural Philosopher* (New York: Blaisdell, 1963), 1:104–5. The other papers I have referred to are: "Thermodynamics and Quanta in Planck's Work," *Physics Today* 19, no. 11 (November 1966): 23–32; and "Max Planck and the Beginnings of the Quantum Theory," *Archive for History of the Exact Sciences* 1, no. 1 (September 1960): 459–79.

velopments that occurred after Planck's discovery. We must be-
ware, as Kuhn warns, of presuming that understanding dependent
upon later developments was part of the repertoire of the historical
actors. There are two major points of difference between Klein and
Kuhn. One has to do with Planck's understanding, in 1900, of the
revolutionary nature of what he had done. The second has to do
with how long it took for that revolution to be accepted by Planck
and incorporated into his concept of physics. On the first point
Klein detects the revolution in Planck's thought beginning in 1900;
on the second point, Klein gives us a date of 1906:[13]

> Planck's introduction of quanta constituted, then, only half of the
> revolutionary change in his thinking that began in 1900; the other half
> was his acceptance of the statistical interpretation of entropy. Naturally
> enough, it took time for the implications of both changes to be fully ab-
> sorbed into his physical outlook. This absorption occurred during the
> years between 1900 and 1906, from the time Planck first constructed his
> successful theory of the radiation spectrum,. . . . (Klein, "Planck," 84)

Kuhn moves the revolution from 1900 to 1906, finding it not
in the work of Planck, but in Einstein's interpretation and application of Planck's discovery. In a close analysis of Planck's papers
of 1900, Kuhn finds they lack "even the appearance of discontinuity" (*Black-Body Theory*, 357), and that Planck's first known state-

---

13. In agreement with Klein's chronology is yet a third version by atomic physicist and Nobel laureate Max Born who was a longtime friend, colleague, and ad-
mirer of Planck's: "Planck was perfectly clear about the importance of his discovery. We have not only the testimony of his wife but also an account of his son
Erwin, given to and reported by Professor Bavink. It was in 1900 when his father,
on a walk in the Grunewald, near Berlin, said to him: 'Today I have made a discovery as important as that of Newton.' Planck has, of course, never said anything
like that in public. His modest and reluctant way of speaking about his work has
caused the impression that he did himself not quite believe in his result. Therefore,
the opinion spread, especially outside Germany, that Planck 'did not seem to
know what he had done when he did it,' that he did not realize the range of his
discovery." Max Born, "Max Karl Ernst Ludwig Planck. Obituary Notices of Fellows of the Royal Society," 6 (1948): 161–80, reprinted in Henry A. Boorse and
Lloyd Motz, eds., *The World of the Atom* (New York: Basic Books, 1966), 1:473.

142 / Transgressive Readings

ment, and thus the first evidence of his understanding of "the discreteness of the energy spectrum and the need for discontinuity" (356) appears in a letter he wrote in 1908. Kuhn marshals evidence for this iconoclastic view. In particular, he notes that in the first edition of Planck's *Lectures on the Theory of Thermal Radiation* (1906) "neither restrictions on classically permissible energy nor discontinuities in the processes of emission or absorption were to be found in Planck's work. Those are, however, the central conceptual novelties we have come to associate with the quantum, and they have invariably been attributed to Planck and located in his work at the end of 1900."[14] Kuhn makes the point that Planck's "publication pattern" was such that the "conceptual novelties" would have shown up in the 1906 text: "Typically, he published reports on research programs in progress. Then, when he thought the program finished, he would sometimes present a systematic summary of the whole in an article or in a book. Between 1901 and 1906, however, he published nothing at all on black-body theory" (355).

Kuhn also cites as evidence for his case two changes in Planck's key terms—he switched from *energy element* to *energy quantum* and from *resonator* to *oscillator*. Using evidence from Planck's letters and his publications, Kuhn argues that the latter terms were prevalent in Planck's discourse only as of 1908–09, thus marking Planck's late acknowledgement of discontinuity.[15] Of Kuhn's main arguments, the third rests on the nature of his own "narrative": "Told in this way, the story makes better historical sense than the long-standard version." Kuhn finds that "the new narrative is more nearly continuous than its predecessor," and that his

---

14. Kuhn, *Black-Body Theory*, viii. Kuhn is using his correct translation of Planck's title *Vorlesungen über die Theorie der Wärmestrahlung*. I have referred to the collection as Planck's "heat radiation textbook," for two reasons: (1) indeed, the lectures were intended as, regarded as, and used as a standard text in physics; and (2) the authorized English translation by Morton Masius of the 1913 second edition has the title *The Theory of Heat Radiation* (New York: Dover, 1959, rpt. of 1914 pub. by P. Blakiston).

15. See Kuhn, *Black-Body Theory*, 200–201, 305, and 356.

"reinterpretation eliminates a number of the apparent textual anomalies and inconsistencies . . ." (354). Thus Kuhn's own agenda is one that accords well with classical physics—the criteria for validity in experiments and results include consistency and continuity, and elimination of anomalies and inconsistencies. It is the agenda with which he associates Planck up to a later date than that accepted by other historians. Implicit in Kuhn's historical narrative is a denial of the possibility of history as a discontinuous and disorderly, even chaotic, narrative.

There are several internal inconsistencies in Kuhn's system of dating the various moves Planck made toward or away from quanta. For example, Kuhn quotes from a letter Planck wrote in 1910 to his colleague, the prominent German physical chemist Walther Nernst: "I can say without exaggeration that for ten years, without interruption, nothing in physics has so stimulated, agitated, and excited me as these quanta of action" (134). In his footnote Kuhn comments: "I am indebted to Martin Klein for insisting that I face the problems this statement might present to my reconstruction" (289). It seems to a reader, however, that the problems indeed presented by this undermining of his chronology are not faced in Kuhn's text. In his advocacy of Einstein, Kuhn asserts of a passage in Einstein's 1906 paper "On the Theory of the Emission and Absorption of Light": "That passage is the first public statement that Planck's derivation demands a restriction on the classical continuum of resonator states. In a sense, it announces the birth of the quantum theory" (170). The natal metaphor is rich with (surely unintended) implications. It implies, for example, the question of whether birth (Einstein) or conception (Planck) are to be taken as the onset of life. With speculative hindsight (and what might be called the irrelevant conditional) Kuhn describes Einstein's research program as "a program so nearly independent of Planck's that it would almost certainly have led to the black-body law even if Planck had never lived" (171). At these and other points in his text, Kuhn's rhetoric contradicts his "historiographic-philosophical" convictions. One larger unposed question is Kuhn's reliance on the *absence* of certain evidence in earlier letters and documents, though Planck's entire library, including letters and diaries, was destroyed in a 1944 bombing raid on Berlin. My purpose is to show that Kuhn is also implicated in a story of misreading, just as he maintains of his predecessors.

It has been claimed by historians of science that Planck himself misread a paper by Lord Rayleigh that was of crucial importance to Planck's work in 1900, the reason being "that everything in Planck's background argues against his having been ready to receive Rayleigh's ideas."[16] That Planck's articles of 1900 were not generally understood by physicists for ten or so years after their publication can be attributed to a lack of clarity in Planck's formulations (Kuhn), but also, as Klein maintains, to the fact that at the time the attention of physicists was not directed toward the theory of radiation, but toward other, more exciting contemporary events — the discoveries of radioactivity, of the electron, and of radium, among others. In addition, Klein points out that scientific thought was powerfully influenced by antiatomists Ostwald and Mach who attacked Boltzmann's work, on which Planck's depended. That is, all kinds of political, social, and linguistic factors can determine misreadings. When Kuhn presented his revisionist views on Planck at a centennial symposium in honor of Einstein, they evoked an emotional, rather than a reasoned, response in defense of Planck by members of an audience of physicists and historians of science.[17] In an afterword to his book, Kuhn quotes a published report of the meeting that again misreads the Planck story. We are all practitioners of more or less creative misreading, and the story of Planck interpretations indicates that scientific development can also be narrated as a story of misreading.

Thus we can be considered to be part of a historical continuum of inevitable misreadings even as we venture beyond the confines of

---

16. Klein, "Beginnings of Quantum Theory," 467.

17. In Harry Woolf, ed., *Some Strangeness in the Proportion: A Centennial Symposium to Celebrate the Achievements of Albert Einstein* (Reading, Mass.: Addison-Wesley, 1980), 194–95.

the disciplines that have legitimized the readings of Planck's texts. My readings of Planck's papers are in chronological order, selecting from each those features which, together, suggest peculiar connections to Kafka's texts and an alternate version of the language of science.

From Planck's two "epoch-making papers of 1900 on quantum theory"[18] (even this standard summary remark represents an interpretation, as we have seen above), I have chosen to examine the longer and later paper — "On the Theory of the Energy Distribution Law of the Normal Spectrum" — which he presented as a lecture on December 14.[19] Characteristic features appear in this and in subsequent papers. First, the conclusion does not bring closure but points to future developments, showing the inevitably fragmentary nature of the scientific article: "To test it by more direct methods should be both an important and necessary task for further research" (45). Second, the introductory paragraphs are structured with rhetorical persuasiveness to convince the audience of the importance of the discovery, its firm grounding in the context of accepted physical problems and previous results, and of the necessarily limited nature of the task Planck has set himself within the bounds of the paper. This last point concludes as follows:

You will find many points in the treatment to be presented arbitrary and complicated, but as I said a moment ago I do not want to pay attention to a proof of the necessity and the possibility to perform it easily and practically, but to the clarity and uniqueness [*Eindeutigkeit*, which is more

---

18. Allen L. King, "Foreword," *Planck's Original Papers in Quantum Physics*, trans. D. ter Haar and Stephen G. Brush, ed. Hans Kangro (London: Taylor and Francis, 1972), v.

19. "Zur Theorie des Gesetzes der Energieverteilung im Normalspektrum," originally published in *Verhandlungen der Deutschen Physikalischen Gesellschaft* 2 (1900): 237–45. Both the original German version and an English translation are printed in *Planck's Original Papers in Quantum Physics*. I use the ter Haar–Brush translation, and pagination refers to that edition. The article also appears in Max Planck, *Physikalische Abhandlungen und Vorträge* (which I abbreviate *PAV*) (Braunschweig: Vieweg, 1958), 1:698–706. All other translations are mine.

accurately translated as "unambiguousness"] of the given prescriptions for the solution of the problem. (*Planck's Original Papers*, 39)

We find here a reversal of the expected figure-ground relationship—Planck is foregrounding style—"clarity and unambiguousness"—instead of the features we would think de rigeur in a scientific article—proof, necessity, performance, and practical envisioning of physical conditions. He is choosing to read his own conclusions in the manner we have chosen to read his text and Kafka's texts, that is by foregrounding the "way" they are written. Let us, in addition, take Planck's sentence as descriptive of "Accident Prevention in Stone Quarries" and *The Trial*. It works well as a self-description of the stone quarry text. By contrast, we would have difficulty finding "prescriptions for the solution of the problem" in *The Trial*. Our view of *The Trial* would be expressed, however, were Planck's sentence taken together with the findings of his readers who failed to recognize the "clarity and unambiguousness" Planck intended, that is, the text that purports to be revealed was actually shrouded, remaining unclear and ambiguous to interpreters. In the discrepancy between Planck's purported intention and its reception lies the ironic disjunction that is also embedded in the discrepancy between Kafka's language of clarity and its shrouded meanings. Third, the introductory paragraphs present the problematic dialogue between order and disorder that is a hallmark of Planck's concerns. That is, he is striving to calculate entropy, a measure of disorder, which requires him to apply probability calculations in order to arrive at orderly measurements of energy distribution, or certainty by means of measured averages from an otherwise incalculable mass of occurrences. The aid of two natural constants is required in order to arrive at the measurement of disorder. Fourth, as readers of theoretical physics, we must be willing to enter and accept a closed system or fantasy world with a certain magical appeal.[20] Planck transports us as follows:

---

20. In an 1889 lecture, Heinrich Hertz said of a fundamental electrodynamic

Let us consider a large number of linear, monochromatically vibrating resonators . . . which are properly separated and are conclosed in a diathermic medium with light velocity c and bounded by reflecting walls. Let the system contain a certain amount of energy, the total energy . . . which is present partly in the medium as traveling radiation and partly in the resonators as vibrational energy. The question is how in a stationary state this energy is distributed over the vibrations of the resonators and over the various colours of the radiation present in the medium, and what will be the temperature of the total system. (*Planck's Original Papers*, 39–40)

This imagined space is as fictional as the imagined space of any work of fiction, and is comparable, in particular, to the imagined space of *The Trial* that we must enter and accept in order to follow the distribution of energy over the system, and how the entropy of that system shows up in the increasing disorganization and dissipation of Josef K.'s energy. In Planck's later papers, the space has become a tropological feature of the text that he introduces with the phrase "in the accustomed manner" that alerts the reader to the fixed associations, or metaphor of the black, radiation-filled container. "The question" governing Planck's imagined system is quite plain, however, although difficult to answer. It is not clear there is a "question" governing Kafka's text, and if so, what that question might be, unless we return to Planck and ask what are "the given prescriptions for the solution of the problem?" Initially, then, the question would have to be "what is the problem?" But surely Planck's "problem" is equally elusive, for we would have to ask who invented that "problem" with black-body radiation, for whom is it a "problem" at all? We (with the exception

law: "Whatever one may think about the correctness of this [law], the totality of efforts of this kind constitutes a closed system full of scientific appeal; once you had wandered into its magic circle you remained imprisoned in it." ("Über die Beziehungen zwischen Licht und Elektricität," address at the 1889 meeting of the German Association, reprinted in Hertz, *Gesammelte Werke* 1:342. Quoted in Christa Jungnickel and Russell McCormmach, *Intellectual Mastery of Nature: Theoretical Physics from Ohm to Einstein* [Chicago: University of Chicago Press, 1986], 2:90, n. 81.)

of a few theoretical physicists of Planck's time) are likely to have equal difficulty recognizing the "problem" in Planck's text as in Kafka's.

Fifth, let us look closely at Planck's textual connectors:

> To answer this question we envisage first of all only the vibrations of the resonators, and assign to them on a trial basis certain arbitrary energies, namely to the N resonators. . . . [my translation]

> [Zur Beantwortung dieser Frage fassen wir zuerst nur die Schwingungen der Resonatoren ins Auge, und erteilen ihnen versuchsweise bestimmte willkürliche Energien, nämlich den N Resonatoren. . . .] (8)

As we did in the case of Kafka's texts, we note within a brief space of text an influential series of qualifiers—"first of all" [*zuerst*], "only" [*nur*], "on a trial basis" [*versuchsweise*], "certain" [*bestimmte*], "arbitrary" [*willkürliche*], "namely" [*nämlich*]. The statement is dominated by the trope of "grasping (or seizing) into the eye"—a favorite metaphor of Planck's and particularly ironic in this context since none of these occurences are observable. On the basis of this highly qualified beginning a series of theoretical calculations are carried out that lead to the equation for the entropy of the system. The mathematics are precise, but the operation (of calculating probability) and its results are underdetermined by language. (It is necessary, though, to also note the peculiar use of "arbitrary" in this and other scientific papers, for it means the opposite of everyday usage. When elements are "arbitrary" it means an operation is most convincing because it works under a large or infinite number of conditions.)

Sixth, the mathematical equations appear to be the switch-points to a reliable, commonsense realm: workable equations provide proof, determine what will be considered true. They seem outside the speculative fantasies and the qualified language, and can be compared to those passages in *The Trial* that describe elements of a commonsense world in between the slippages into the fantastic or the indecipherable. Yet equations also play the role of rhetorical tropes in their relationship to the language text, and thus are infected by the ambiguity of rhetoric. If one examines Planck's papers for each language statement that introduces an equation, a pattern of tropological relations of equations to text becomes apparent—realized as metonomy, synecdoche, metaphor, or analogy.

Seventh, finally and inevitably, Planck's metaphysics—the metaphysics of theoretical physics—distances his text from Kafka's. As in his essays, Planck injects the notion of *truth*. He writes about the possibility of using a (mathematically) simple case "to test the degree of approximation to the truth"—an unspecified, apparently transcendental concept (10).

These are some examples of crossings and partings between Planck's and Kafka's texts. Strategies to get at the textual relationships include finding that Planck's papers can be read as telling a story of Kafka's text—not, as one might expect, of Kafka's technical but of his literary text, *The Trial*.

Planck's 1908 paper, "On the Dynamics of Moving Systems," predicts the possibility of utilization of "atomic energy."[21] In this paper Planck concludes "that every body contains a colossal quantity of internally stored energy—Planck called it 'latent' energy—which ordinary physical and chemical processes hardly affect."[22] One American physicist called Planck's result "the 'first valid and authentic derivation' of the relationship between mass and energy."[23]

Rhetorical gestures of inclusion—"we imagine" [*wir denken uns*], "our next task" [*unsere nächste Aufgabe*], "we can" [*wir kön-*

21. Born in Boorse and Motz, *World of the Atom*, 477. Planck's paper is "Zur Dynamik bewegter Systeme," *PAV* 2:176–209; first published in *Annalen der Physik* 26, no.4 (1908): 1–34.

22. Summary by Stanley Goldberg, who reviews this paper in his article "Max Planck's Philosophy of Nature and His Elaboration of the Special Theory of Relativity," *Historical Studies in the Physical Sciences*, ed. Russell McCormmach (Princeton: Princeton University Press, 1976), 7:140.

23. H. E. Ives as quoted in Goldberg, "Planck's Philosophy," 140.

nen], "we want to" [*wir wollen*], and others—effectively insure reader involvement in the stages of the investigation. The effort is made out to be a cooperative one between two equal investigators—author and reader. Either in the form of the first person singular or plural, a personal narrator is consistently present in Planck's texts.

"We imagine" or "let us imagine" are common introductory prescriptions that remind the literary-minded reader again and again of the "willing suspension of disbelief" (Coleridge) required of the theoretical physicist. Even the very heart of the paper, section 18, which introduces the notion of atomic energy, requires of the reader a great leap of the imagination, in particular because of the hyperbolic "colossal" that would seem out of place in sober science:

> According to the theory developed here, one must imagine in the interior of every body a supply of energy whose amount is so colossal that the warming and cooling processes we normally observe, even quite profound chemical transformations that are associated with considerable amounts of heat, change that energy by only an imperceptible fraction.

> [Nach der hier entwickelten Theorie hat man sich also im Innern eines jeden Körpers einen Energievorrat vorzustellen, dessen Betrag so kolossal ist, daß die von uns für gewöhnlich beobachteten Erwärmungs- und Abkühlungsvorgänge, ja sogar ziemlich tief eingreifende, mit beträchtlichen Wärmetönungen verbundene chemische Umwandlungen, ihn nur um einen unmerklichen Bruchteil verändern.] ("Zur Dynamik bewegter Systeme," 205)

The first step toward atomic power has to be a great leap of faith—a willingness, as in Coleridge's thesis—to accept in the imagination conditions that do not accord with observable reality, to accept on faith, in this case, a quantity so staggering as to be describable only in terms of that which cannot affect it. Planck requires of his readers no less a suspension of disbelief than Kafka requires of his readers. In the "colossal" that everyday, known processes can affect only imperceptibly, we also have a description of the Court in *The Trial.*

Planck's paper, which can be considered a quintessential scientific paper, is replete with the uncertainties, contradictions, rhetorical tropes, logical contradictions, and mystery considered quintessentially literary. When a very important implication of the paper is mentioned, it is followed by the statement: "But this is not the place to consider more closely this and related questions" (198). Of a change in mass by means of a change in temperature, Planck asserts that it is "so minimal that it will probably forever elude direct measurement" (204). Another quantity (decrease in mass of a single atom of radium) is so small that "for the time being it lies outside the realm of possible experience" (207). Data remain tantalizingly elusive; crucial implications are not pursued—a device Kafka uses at the very end of *The Trial* when the questions (in the mind of Josef K.) whose answer would provide solutions to the mysteries of the text are raised but go unanswered.

Designation or naming, whether by words or symbols, is often a matter of choice introduced with a phrase such as: "we want to designate it here as the 'latent energy' of the body" (205). That is, within the bounds of certain conventions, there can be an arbitrariness to naming that brings us into the vicinity of Kafka's textual avoidance of naming, his sense of its arbitrariness. Even definitions are not always fixed in Planck's papers. For example, at the end of the paragraph that reviews the different criteria by which changes in mass might be evaluated, he concludes: "What one calls these different expressions [of mass] is naturally a matter of definition" [*Wie man diese verschiedenen Ausdrücke benennt, ist natürlich Definitionssache*] (202).

Contradictions appear that, as the narrator explains, result from the fact that a particular symbol has different meanings in other contexts. Actual but unacknowledged contradictions appear within the conventional scientific language, for example: "relatively completely insignificant" [*verhältnismäßig ganz unwesentliche*] (205). Planck uses such combinations without comment, which means they are part of the stock of conventional terms of the field, meaning that contradictions are accepted and built into the scientific language itself. A logical flaw appears in Planck's method of drawing conclusions. In this and other papers he likes to note the common features of two phenomena and conclude that, therefore, the two phenomena must have a common origin. While the physics that rests on such a method is not necessarily flawed, it does indicate that, generally speaking, the scientific paper should not be one of the first places we look for logical rigor.[24]

Planck can write with rhythms, hesitations, qualifications, and deep recursive boxes very similar in tone and effect to Kafka's texts. In "On the Dynamics of Moving Systems," Planck produced a sentence whose operations conjure up *The Trial* as well as the stone quarry text (although this coincidence is difficult to convey in translation). An English version could read as follows:

Because nothing hinders presuming, and it would even be, especially viewed from the standpoint of electrodynamics, very understandable that inside the chemical atoms certain stationary movements take place, in the nature of fixed oscillations which are not connected to any, or only to imperceptible radiation.

[Denn es hindert nichts, anzunehmen, und wäre sogar, namentlich vom elektrodynamischen Standpunkt aus betrachtet, sehr wohl verständlich,

---

24. The evidence from Planck's papers is supported by Leslie H. Kern, Herbert L. Mirels, and Virgil G. Hinshaw, "Scientists' Understanding of Propositional Logic: An Experimental Investigation," *Social Studies of Science* 13 (1983): 131–46. In their study "seventy-two scientists (psychologists, biologists, and physicists) from a large US midwestern state university completed a questionnaire designed to assess understanding of the principles of formal logic believed by philosophers of science to be essential to theory and hypothesis testing. . . . Across academic disciplines the participants' performance reflected substantial deficits in the appreciation of straightforward logical propositions. For example, nearly half of the scientists failed to recognize the logical validity of *modus tollens*, an inferential rule of propositional logic which, from a strictly normative standpoint, has been depicted as the only form of valid conclusive inference in theory and hypothesis testing" (131).

daß innerhalb der chemischen Atome gewisse stationäre Bewegungs-
vorgänge von der Art stehender Schwingungen stattfinden, die mit
keiner oder nur mit unmerklicher Ausstrahlung verbunden sind.]
(205–6)

For nearly every step forward there is also a step backward. The
initial grammatical subject is "nothing," which is followed by a
subjunctive that intensifies the idea from "nothing hinders" to
"would be understandable." The conclusion is a qualified negation that ties end to beginning by their mutual negativity. The
first half concerns human mental activities: presuming, viewing,
understanding; the second half concerns activities of the objects
of investigation: motion, radiation, connection. The first half is
static, contemplative (including "standpoint"); the second half is
active. They are tied finally by the human act of (non-)perception
—a syntactical undermining of the entire operation. The focal
point and geographic interior of the sentence is the word *inside*. All
together it is a complex masterpiece of recursive organization,
qualifiers, and hesitations equal to Kafka's sentences.

Rhetorically, Planck again parts company from Kafka's texts.
A characteristic trope—personification—is realized in a characteristic setting in the sentence "*the future must teach* whether such
an influence will ever be directly provable" (207). The notion of
future is a defining force in Planck's metaphysics and in his scientific papers. It is axiomatic for him and all physicists, for whom
theory means the capacity to predict. According to Bruce
Gregory: "When physicists say they understand a phenomenon,
they usually mean that they can write an expression describing
how the phenomenon unfolds in time."[25] For that reason Planck
would not notice the contradiction in the idea of the future as
pedagogue—once the future has pupils it has become the present
or the past. Kafka's texts seemed geared toward rescinding "future." We have seen that his textual logic can divert and absorb

---

25. *Inventing Reality*, 57. Bruce Gregory is Associate Director of the Harvard-
Smithsonian Center for Astrophysics.

the notion of *future* in maneuvers that create a field of space-time in which chronology is irrelevant.

Because for Planck the future is always extending into the present as a goal toward which the entire corpus of his work is directed, it is unusual to find definitive closure as we do in this paper. It concludes with the words: "in complete agreement with (51)" (209), the number *(51)* referring to a previously mentioned equation. That is, this paper is a completed whole that refers back to itself and brooks no interjection or continuation. Ironically, it may also represent Planck's most future-directed and (at the time of its composition) his least provable work.

Planck's 1910 paper "On the Theory of Thermal Radiation,"[26] was selected by Kuhn as an example of a key move by Planck toward accepting discontinuity: "By the beginning of 1910 Planck was at last firmly and publicly committed to the entry of discontinuity and the abandonment of some part of classical theory."[27] In the dramatic narrative of Planck's relationship since 1900 to the principle of discontinuity, this paper stands out as an example of the rhetorical possibilities of science as a political agenda. In that sense — the manner in which it pleads modesty, diminishes opponents, asks rhetorical questions, appeals for reader support, and locates itself in self-defense as moderate, or middle-of-the-road among competing agendas — it is comparable to Josef K.'s performance as political demagogue before the Court during his first hearing (with the difference that Josef K.'s speech turns out to have been directed only to himself, as his audience was immune to argument). John L. Heilbron writes of Planck's "Theory of Thermal Radiation": "In 1910 he expressed himself in the manner of a protector of a menaced and even losing cause."[28]

Planck begins by situating the paper as a response, on his part, to the "other side." One opposing standpoint (that of British

---

26. *PAV* 2, 237–47; first published in *Annalen der Physik* 31, no.4 (1910): 758–68.

27. Kuhn, *Black-Body Theory*, 200.

28. *The Dilemmas of an Upright Man: Max Planck as Spokesman for German Science* (Berkeley: University of California Press, 1986), 21.

physicist James Jeans) is called "extreme," "absolutely conserva-tive" (237). Yet, if one accepts its premise, Planck asserts, it is completely convincing and, among radiation theories up to now, "the most unified" and "most satisfactory." That is, it fulfills two of the major criteria in physics for a convincing theory. Now that praise has created a worthy target, the rhetorical attack follows: the theory, however, "contradicts experience" (238) and with that, it is finished, since "experience" is the most powerful determinant of validity in the hierarchy of values in physics and takes prece-dence over the values of unity and satisfaction. By contrast, in *The Trial* and Kafka's other texts, "experience" is one of the values most deeply compromised.

Now Planck is able to move ahead on the assurance of support by the majority, for the issue is "beyond question for me and for most physicists" (238). Not only does Planck marshal forces on behalf of the necessity for change, but also on behalf of the *kind* of change he supports: "all physicists" are unanimous in believing "that such change must be carried out as cautiously as possible, so that along with those parts of the theory that can be improved, [we do not] at the same time unnecessarily throw out valuable parts, indispensible for the future, which then later would have to be reclaimed with redoubled effort" (238).

Planck has positioned himself rhetorically as a political moder-ate, believing in change in small increments, fearing radical moves that might lead to throwing out the baby with the bathwater. In a strictly scientific text we find a quintessential political argu-ment, one we could easily associate with Planck's stand in support of Wilhelminian policies and German nationalism. Heilbron writes of Planck's values:

Planck identified his own development so fully with Germany's that the preservation of its cultural capital was inseparable from the preservation of his personal values and professional life. Over all these values stood the ideal of unity, which in the political sphere inspired belief in the inter-connectedness of all respectable branches of learning. Planck's pride in imperial Germany and his commitment to the academic ideal of the unity of knowledge were the pillars on which he raised his science policy. (*Dilemmas*, 4)

An overriding, unquestioned value for Planck is "the future," to whose interests others are to be subordinated. The penalty for not doing so is "doubling" your efforts. That is, a projection, a metaphor, or a metaphysical construct must determine present strategy in theoretical physics. The codeterminers are, by contrast, the traditional virtues in a well-run German household of discarding as little as possible and avoiding duplication of work (since there was already so much to do in the course of organizing and maintaining cleanliness and frugality).

The radiation formula arrived at "via experience" "points a finger" in the correct direction for reform of the theory [In welcher Richtung diese Reform der Theorie sich zu bewegen hat, dafür enthält die durch die Erfahrung gelieferte Strahlungsformel schon einen deutlichen Fingerzeig] (238). Thus, the characteristics of Planck's rhetoric can be found in this paper in abundance: the personal narrator, the rhetoric of persuasion, personification (a formula that has at least one "finger"), the appeal to unquestioned authorities ("the future," earlier physical theories), and above all, an appeal to anthropomorphic standards of judgment: unity, satisfaction, and experience. These standards contradict the demands of good science and good physics that Planck makes in his essays: they must strive to be as removed as possible from the anthropomorphic, from human-based standards. It is as if in his scientific papers—by virtue of the historically accumulated conventions of the genre and his own deepest political convictions—Planck cannot help realizing Nietzsche's portrait of science, thus highlighting the widely separated arms of their chiastic connection.

When Planck turns to the theories on the nature of light developed by Einstein and others (which propose that light, too, is not continuous but divided into discrete quanta), he applies the epithet "most radical" to them. They are apparently on the opposite side of the political spectrum from the Jeans theory called "absolutely conservative" and, by providing another parameter, permit a further distinction that leaves only the desirable middle location for Planck. One can interpret this paper as primarily a situating of Planck's political position in the history of that idea called the quantum that has gathered accretions along the way, coming to represent conflicting standpoints in the community of physicists, and eventually (in the late 1920s) becoming a full-blown philosophical position.

The attack on Einstein's theory reaches a crescendo with rhetorical questions: "How should one imagine, for example, an electrostatic field?" "Is a finite, specifically directed field force even at all definable?" (243). Accepting this theory, Planck maintains, would mean abandoning the most important recent successes of physics and turning back the clock by centuries. He paints a dramatic portrait of the battle, centuries ago, by Christian Huygens to achieve victory over Newton's theory of light. "And all of these achievements, that are among the proudest successes of physics, in fact of all of scientific research, should be sacrificed for the sake of some very contestable observations? That would require after all much heavier artillery in order to shake the by now very well-founded edifice of the electromagnetic theory of light" (243). Planck at his ironic, polemical best has launched from high ground an aggressive, military defense of his citadel, firing favorite metaphors at the opposing theory, making Einstein's "observations" seem to be a heretical attack on the temple of science itself. A hierarchy is apparent here which is not questioned in Planck's writings: the institution of science itself is at the pinnacle, supported by revered authorities, while the base consists of proven theories that are strong enough to resist "radical" renewal (compare with Nietzsche's description of the edifice of science in my chap. 2).

Planck turns then from heated polemic to a conciliatory tone, underscoring the moderation of his solution between the extremes: "It seems to me a more rewarding task to spare no effort to discover a modification of the theory which will do justice to the new facts, without sacrificing their most valuable components. And there the radiation theory developed by me still offers, in my opinion, the most favorable prospect for a fruitful further development" (243).

After discussing the main point of difficulty in his theory, pointing out that he does, in some respects, come close to the theories of Einstein and others (except that Planck maintains his commitment to the Maxwell-Hertz differential equations), Planck concludes by listing the six main points of the thesis developed in his paper. The engaged reader will by now be breathing easier, having been guided by Planck's peaceful conclusion to recovery from the rhetorical roller coaster of alternating polemical attack and conciliation. "On the Theory of Thermal Radiation" is undoubtedly driven by a kind of political rhetoric and purpose. Heilbron writes of Planck in 1910: "By then conservatism, always congenial, had become a duty for Planck under a general rule of his own devising. As scientists age and gain authority, he said, they must display 'an increased caution and reticence in entering into new paths' " (21). Heilbron is quoting from Planck's eulogy in 1906 for physicist Paul Drude. Only Planck did not assert, there, that scientists "must" display increased caution, etc., but rather that "with added years the consciousness of growing authority and increased responsibility *usually goes hand-in-hand with* continually increased caution and reticence in entering new paths" (*PAV* 3:314; italics added). That difference in translation alters the thrust of Planck's statement, showing a nondogmatic Planck and helping legitimize my readings of Planck's texts for breaches in the conservative language agenda and noncontainable countertexts.

On October 29, 1911, the first international conference on theoretical physics opened in Brussels. It was sponsored by Belgian industrialist Ernest Solvay at the urging of Walther Nernst. Nernst, who had spoken of "Planck's introduction of the hypothesis of energy quanta as an innovation in the same class as those due to

Newton and to Dalton,"[29] had called for the conference in order
to "discuss the needed reformulation of physics" (Kuhn, *Black-
Body Theory*, 231), in particular how to handle the quantum discontinuity. The first Solvay Congress "marked the coming of age
for the problems associated with the concept of quanta" (Klein,
"Beginnings of Quantum Theory," 37), and their evolution from
a strictly German to an international research subject. According
to Kuhn, the Congress and the developments it stimulated in the
years prior to the first World War meant that "the first stage of
the conceptual transformation leading from classical to modern
physics was complete" (*Black-Body Theory*, 232). That is to say an
event that is generally dated 1900 was actually a process that lasted
over fourteen years, coming to fruition before the war began and
in the year when Kafka began to write *The Trial*.

Naturally, Planck, as the originator of the quantum hypothesis, was one of those invited to participate both as an organizer
and a presenter.[30] His paper, "The Laws of Thermal Radiation and
the Hypothesis of the Elementary Quantum of Action," represented a further elaboration of Planck's "second theory" that proposed the quantum discontinuity only during the *emission* of radiation from oscillators, not during absorption, which proceeded
continuously according to classical laws. In a letter to his Dutch
colleague H. A. Lorentz, one of the most highly regarded physicists of the time, Planck explains this step in terms that reveal that
so-called subjective judgments, i.e., language that indicates an

29. Quoted in Martin J. Klein, "Beginnings of Quantum Theory," 37. The 1911
Solvay Congress is discussed in detail in Jungnickel and McCormmach, *Intellectual
Mastery of Nature*, 2:318–21.

30. Presenters included Einstein and other leading researchers in the field. The
proceedings of the congress were first published in French in 1912. (Reviewed
with great enthusiasm by Max Born in *Physikalische Zeitschrift* 15 [1914]: 166–67.)
The German translation appeared in 1914, and included an overview of developments in quantum physics from 1911 to 1913: *Verhandlungen des Conseil Solvay 1911:
Die Theorie der Strahlung und der Quanten*, ed. A. Eucken, *Abhandlungen der Deutschen
Bunsen-Gesellschaft für angewandte physikalische Chemie* no. 7 (Halle: Wilhelm Knapp,
1914). Planck's paper, "Die Gesetze der Wärmestrahlung und die Hypothese der
elementaren Wirkungsquanten," 77–94, can also be found in *PAV* 2: 269–86.

extrascientific agenda, are as integral to the enterprise of science as they are to any cultural or intellectual project:

> The discontinuity must enter somehow; otherwise one is irretrievably bound to the Hamiltonian equations and the Jeans theory. Therefore, I have located the discontinuity at the place where it can do the least harm, at the excitation of the oscillator; its decay can then occur continuously with constant damping.[31]

While this version of the quantum hypothesis proved short-lived, it did have a powerful influence, most notably upon Bohr's development of the Correspondence Principle. Kuhn explains the appeal of Planck's second theory by the fact that "it reduced the magnitude of the break with classical theory" (*Black-Body Theory*, 244). During the five years after the second theory appeared, "several long-lasting contributions to quantum theory were based upon it" (244). "The aspect of Planck's second theory that attracted the most and the longest lasting attention" (246) was its suggestion of a "zero-point energy." "Zero-point" as the most productive part of a theory connects to the operations of the notion of zero in Kafka's texts. Heilbron explains that the formula Planck sought for cavity radiation "described the worst possible source of illumination, and so could serve as a zero-point standard for rating new electric lamps" (*Dilemmas*, 6–7). As a result, even the imperial bureau of standards took an interest in Planck's calculations. The notion of the "zero-point" thus brings together histories of science, technology, and mathematics in a pattern of interlocking and overlapping effects that implicates the culture of Kafka's textual logics as well. Aspects of Planck's second theory remained influential and it continued to be described in physics textbooks until approximately 1920 (Kuhn, *Black-Body Theory*, 252). The role of the second theory, according to Kuhn, is that it:

---

31. Planck to Lorentz, 7 January 1910; as quoted and translated in Kuhn, *Black-Body Theory*, 236.

accounted for one or more esoteric aspect of nature with a simplicity and precision that gave its author and some of his contemporaries the confidence required to attempt its further development. Though these attempts, in each case, soon resulted in fundamental modification of the theory that had permitted their design, they had meanwhile assisted in the identification of additional quantum phenomena and in a deeper understanding of the nature of a still emerging new physics. (254)

We note that explanation, influence, evolution, and thus historical change in science is presented as a partly rational, partly aesthetic, partly ego-dependent process that fosters and depends upon such notions as "accounting for nature, simplicity, precision, confidence, design, identification," and "deeper understanding." This description of science overlaps with its own self-representation. To read another story we must turn to the inevitably subversive operations of language, irrespective of discourse.

Planck's Solvay paper can be read as a rhetorical masterpiece—a drama of fall and partial redemption in which a heroic struggle takes place between a protagonist (the second quantum hypothesis) and contending forces that are conquered one by one. Let us look at the introductory scene:

The principles of classical mechanics, made fertile and enlarged through the expansion of electrodynamics, especially the theory of electrons, have proved themselves in such a satisfying manner in all areas of physics that have to do with ordered (i.e., controllable in all details) processes, that the unremitting striving toward uniformity of the physical world picture had to suggest the hope that the same principles would, without significant modification and with equal success, be applicable to those fine physical phenomena whose laws can only be understood indirectly by means of the statistical method. Indeed, the development of the kinetic gas theory, which through the introduction of simple, bold ideas shifted the standard of visualization [*Anschauung*] and calculation to the scale of atoms and electrons, seemed for a time, on the basis of numerous results in various areas—all confirmed by experience—to justify brilliantly the expectations attached to it. Individual difficulties of a principle nature that surfaced here and there appeared—in view of the great abundance of hypotheses still available within the framework of classical dynamics—ultimately not insuperable.

Today we must say that hope has proved deceptive, and the framework of classical dynamics . . . seems too narrow to also encompass all the physical processes that are not directly accessible to our crude senses. The initial proof of this assertion, which can hardly be disputed any longer, is provided by the glaring contradiction between classical theory and observation which has revealed itself in the universal laws of the thermal radiation of black bodies.

The contradiction goes so far that. . . .

[Die Prinzipien der klassischen Mechanik, befruchtet und erweitert durch den Ausbau der Elektrodynamik, speziell der Elektronentheorie, haben sich auf allen Gebieten der Physik, wo es sich um geordnete, d.h. in allen Einzelheiten kontrollierbare Vorgänge handelt, in so befriedigender Weise bewährt, daß das unablässige Streben nach Vereinheitlichung des physikalischen Weltbildes die Hoffnung nahelegen mußte, die nämlichen Prinzipien würden sich ohne wesentliche Modifikation mit gleichem Erfolge auch auf diejenigen feinen physikalischen Erscheinungen anwenden lassen, deren Gesetze nur indirekt mittels der statistischen Betrachtungsweise dem Verständnis zu erschließen sind. Und in der Tat schien die Entwicklung der kinetischen Gastheorie, die durch Einführung einfacher, kühner Vorstellungen den Maßstab der Anschauung und Rechnung in die Größenordnung der Atome und Elektronen verlegte, durch ihre zahlreichen, auf verschiedenen Gebieten durch die Erfahrung bestätigten Resultate die an sie geknüpften Erwartungen eine Zeitlang glänzend zu rechtfertigen. Einzelne hier und dort auftauchende Schwierigkeiten prinzipieller Natur mochten bei der großen Fülle der innerhalb des Rahmens der klassischen Dynamik noch zu Gebote stehenden Hypothesen schließlich nicht unüberwindlich erscheinen.

Heute müssen wir sagen, daß jene Hoffnung sich als trügerisch erwiesen hat, und daß der Rahmen der klassischen Dynamik . . . zu eng erscheint, um auch die unseren groben Sinnen nicht direkt zugänglichen physikalischen Vorgänge alle zu umspannen. Den ersten, wohl kaum mehr anfechtbaren Beweis für diese Behauptung liefert der eklante Widerspruch, welcher sich in den universalen Gesetzen der Wärmestrah-

lung schwarzer Körper zwischen der klassischen Theorie und der Beobachtung gezeigt hat.
Der Widerspruch geht so weit, daß. . . .] (77)

In the case of a narrative as rhetorically intricate as Planck's, one can only begin to do it justice by suggesting multiple readings. In the first sentence we read an idyllic family story: the principles of maternal classical mechanics, made fertile by paternal electrodynamics, have expanded and thus provided satisfactory performance, albeit in a limited realm. Meanwhile, the prevailing cultural context provides an ideological basis in the drive to achieve and faith in a single deity ("uniformity") that offers hope that the product of the union will—without corrective surgery—succeed even where access depends upon averages rather than the knowledge of every detail.

There are subtle hints, however, that despite the support of a close relative—kinetic gas theory—all is not well with this ideal family: "seemed," "for a time," "difficulties of a principle nature that surfaced here and there," and the qualified "appeared . . . ultimately not insuperable."

These warnings are followed in the next paragraph by the knockout punch: "we" (the reader is enlisted for the first time to assure his or her cooperation in the exposure of promised hope as illusory) have no choice but to admit that the idyll is false, that the offspring of the traditional family unit has not proved capable of its duty of avoiding contradiction. Beyond just ordinary contradiction, the result is "glaring" contradiction that intensifies yet further—contradiction between theory and observation (or "experience") being the greatest sin of physical theory. Moreover, this contradiction is revealed in "universal laws," the ultimate authority over the social, as well as the physical, order.

After reviewing some details of the contradiction, Planck begins the next paragraph with the question he means his paper to address: "The question now arises of how the theory can reconcile itself with the facts, and the following report is to be dedicated primarily to that question. In the course of it I will try to discuss all the different attempts that have been directed toward this goal . . . " (78).[32] Initially, James Jeans's conclusions are dismissed, as are the other leading approaches, in the course of building a case for the need for a hypothesis that modifies classical theory. Gradually, one "model" after the other (including Einstein's) is examined for its contradictions and dismissed until, four pages before the end, Planck introduces his own "second theory" as a solution. Along the way, the argument becomes politicized with some of the same rhetorical devices we noted above in Planck's paper of 1910. For example, the argument against Einstein's "light quanta hypothesis" includes the metaphor of "shaking the foundations" of Maxwell's theory—a notion reprehensible to Planck that he expands by adding that Einstein's theory should be disregarded because it is still at a "primitive stage" (83). At another point, Planck refers to the "simplistic assumptions" (92) on which a formula of Einstein's is based. Despite Planck's early patronage of Einstein, his good working relationship with Einstein, and his role as the first theoretical physicist to appreciate and support relativity theory, there is clearly an unacknowledged, intense rivalry on Planck's part, reflecting, perhaps, their political differences.[33] Finally, in a conciliatory closing, Planck determines that no explanation has been entirely "satisfactory," that the solution to the problem will only be possible via a completely new hypothesis that contradicts current assumptions, and that there is

---

32. Planck's distinction depends upon facts being separate from theory. My point of view, by contrast, presumes the theory-ladenness of facts: the only facts that will be found and labeled as such are those that a particular theoretical net catches, just as we are only able to see what we have focused on and comprehend what we are prepared to comprehend. (See, for example, Harold I. Brown, *Perception, Theory and Commitment*.) Finally, factuality is determined by the acceptance of scientific texts. For texts to be accepted means they become "science," sources of established facts, potential makers of Nobel laureates, and sources of further legitimizing activities as they are cited by subsequent investigators. (See Bruno Latour, *Science in Action* [Cambridge, Mass.: Harvard University Press, 1987].) This does not mean that facts do not exist. It means their definition changes over time.

33. See Heilbron, *Dilemmas*, 31–32, for the early years.

"no doubt" that continuing efforts will lead ultimately to a hypothesis that is "free of internal contradictions" (94).

We have read "social" implications in the opening paragraphs with its extrascientific language tainted with multiple implications. The paper as a whole might suggest the archetypal pattern of a fairy tale or Western: Little Red Riding Hood or a small mining town, after a series of clues that something is amiss, faces siege by the wolf or gunslinger of contradiction. Finally, though, opponents are overcome and the sheriff or huntsman (Max Planck) arrives to do his best to free little radiation theory from contradiction. Planck has structured the article like a mystery narrative.[34] He holds off until near the end with a solution to the dilemma he has created, but maintains suspense by tantalizing the reader at key intervals with the solution to come. For example: "as already emphasized at the beginning of this report, a special physical hypothesis will have to be introduced that in some characteristic point stands in direct contradiction to the common — whether expressed or tacit — assumptions of classical dynamics" (90). There is reference to equations whose combination will produce "the law of the black equation" (88) — a nice, evocative title for the mystery theatre presented here.

The style of the opening paragraph is elaborate and formal, the

---

34. My description is reminiscent of the description in Bruno Latour's *Science in Action*: "The more we get into the niceties of the scientific literature, the more extraordinary it becomes. It is now a real opera. Crowds of people are mobilised by the references; from offstage hundreds of accessories are brought in. Imaginary readers are conjured up which are not asked only to believe the author but to spell out what sort of tortures, ordeals and trials the heroes should undergo before being recognised as such. Then the text unfolds the dramatic story of these trials. Indeed, the heroes triumph over all the powers of darkness, like the Prince in *The Magic Flute*. The author adds more and more impossible trials just, it seems, for the pleasure of watching the hero overcome them. The authors challenge the audience and their heroes sending a new bad guy, a storm, a devil, a curse, a dragon, and the heroes fight them. At the end, the readers, ashamed of their former doubts, have to accept the author's claim" (53–54). While I am in accord with Latour's above description of the workings of an individual scientific text, I disagree with the distinction he makes between a "regular text in prose and a technical document [as] the stratification of the latter" (48).

textual logic is linear. Positive-value terms such as *made fertile, ordered, controllable, satisfying, proved themselves, striving,* and *uniformity* culminate in *hope,* which points to the second paragraph where it is repeated in the first sentence but with the purpose of deconstructing the hopeful narrative of the first paragraph. Thus the key weak link in the apparently exclusively positive first sentence is, paradoxically, the word *hope.* The second sentence undermines its opening phrase, *in der Tat* ["indeed, in fact," or "really"] and its valorized qualities of "simple, bold, experience, confirmed," and "justify" by those warnings or expressions of doubt, such as "seemed" "for a time," "difficulties of a principle nature that surfaced here and there," and "appeared . . . not insuperable." From the next paragraph on, the undermining becomes overt and direct, rather than implied in textual contradictions. The narrator, whose purpose is to defeat contradiction, ambiguity, and nonevidentiary meanings, and construct an impregnable edifice of universal meaning, is himself by his language inextricably implicated in contradiction, multiplicity, and indeterminacy of meaning.

"Meaning"—perennially sought by interpreters of literature—is also one of Planck's overt concerns. He writes of a possible "deeper meaning" [*tieferer Sinn*] to the quantum hypothesis that depends upon the "fundamental meaning" [*fundamentale Bedeutung*] (93) of the constant, h. To arrive at meaning is the goal that inspires his argument. For example, he sets up for his disapproval the standpoint of other physicists—he calls it a "more phenomenlogical standpoint" (82)—who have given up the search for meaning:

One can be content with establishing the fact that the elementary domain of probability h has a finite, specifiable value, and dismiss all further questions about the physical meaning of this strange quantity. . . . I believe, however, that one may not stop at this opinion, since it is not conducive to further development of the theory, and it seems more than ever of the highest importance to look for connections between the elementary quantum h and other physical constants, and thereby to fortify and expand its meaning.

[Man kann sich nun mit der Konstatierung der Tatsachen, daß das Elementargebiet der Wahrscheinlichkeit *h* einen endlichen angebbaren Wert hat, begnügen und alle weiteren Fragen nach der physikalischen Bedeutung dieser merkwürdigen Größe ablehnen. . . . Aber ich glaube doch, daß man bei dieser Auffassung nicht stehen bleiben darf; denn sie ist einer Weiterentwicklung der Theorie nicht günstig, und es scheint gerade von höchster Wichtigkeit zu sein, nach Beziehungen des Elementarquantums *h* zu anderen physikalischen Konstanten zu suchen und dadurch seine Bedeutung zu befestigen und zu erweitern.] (82)

The philosophy or the metaphysics that drives Planck's (all physicists?) science is expressed in the terms *further questions, may not stop, further development,* and *to fortify and to expand.* We need not know about laboratory results or the so-called behavior of Nature in order to detect this metaphysical impetus, for it infects and shapes his language as well as the scheme and overall strategy of his scientific papers.

Finally, we turn to yet another reading strategy: reading Planck's text for the story of *The Trial.* There are three places in Planck's paper where the story of *The Trial* crops up. The first is a continuation of the quest for the meaning of *h.* Planck offers two options, of which he writes: "Depending upon the answer to this prequestion, the further development of the theory will be directed in completely different paths" (83). Alternative narratives, alternative outcomes are possible according to which answer to a "prequestion" is selected. That is, one must return to the status quo ante, to whatever was accessible to judgment even prior to the raising of a question. That is the locus and origin of all that is to come; a wrong answer means the future is wrongly determined. Josef K. is obsessed with this very notion—that his asking the correct questions and providing the correct answers at the very earliest stages would have determined and will determine the direction and outcome of his case. Throughout *The Trial,* the reader is made to have that discomforting and urgent desire that Josef K. ask the right questions and provide the right answers, or else all will be lost. Josef K.'s story begins before the beginning:

the prequestions are implied in the opening statement — "someone must have slandered Josef K., for without having done anything bad, one morning he was arrested." — and the narrative options from then on seem to turn on knowing how to respond to those implied questions: Did someone slander Josef K.? If so, who? Did he do something bad? If he did not, why was he arrested? What might the alternative narrative of Josef K. have been, had he, or anyone, correctly answered the prequestions? What, for that matter, might have been the alternative course of the narrative if we knew the correct order of the chapters? Planck's suggestion of alternative narratives is a rhetorical device, part of his persuasion of the reader that Planck's, rather than Einstein's, hypothesis is correct. It has the effect of lulling the reader into being convinced of the open-minded and objective stance of the narrator, and accepting Planck's construction of a rhetorically airtight case by the end of the paper.

The last sentences in *The Trial* include the statement "the logic, it is true, is unshakable" [*die Logik ist zwar unerschütterlich*] (*Der Prozeß*, 194), which is comparable to Planck's conclusion that there is "no doubt" that a hypothesis will be arrived at that is "free of internal contradictions." But the text of *The Trial* continues by adding further prequestions that remain unanswered: "Were there objections that one had forgotten?" "Where was the judge whom he had never seen?" "Where was the high Court that he had never reached?" (194). There are crossings and partings in both texts between notions of logical closure and open, alternate narratives, between determinism and indeterminacy. Ultimately the texts come together again by means of a key passage in Planck's text — a passage that, it can be argued, contains a story of Max Planck's physics, *The Trial*, and the beginning of the twentieth century:

But in spite of these evident successes the theory of the thermal radiation of black bodies which has been expounded up to now cannot by any means be viewed as satisfactory, and specifically at the outset for the reason that the assumptions from which, on the one hand equation (13), on the other hand equation (15), are derived contradict each other fundamentally. Because when deriving the first equation the energy of a single oscillator is assumed to be whole multiples of hv, when deriving the second equation, however, it [the energy] is assumed to be continuously variable, and it is not possible to decide on one of these two alternatives without, at least initially, making the deduction that is based on the opposing alternative illusory.

All models devised up to now suffer from this contradiction. . . .

[Aber trotz dieser augenscheinlichen Erfolge kann die bis jetzt vorgetragenen Theorie der Wärmestrahlung schwarzer Körper noch keineswegs als befriedigend angesehen werden, und zwar schon deshalb, weil die Voraussetzungen, aus welchen einerseits die Gleichung (13), andererseits die Gleichung (15) abgeleitet ist, sich im Grunde widersprechen. Denn bei der Ableitung der ersteren Gleichung wird die Energie eines einzelnen Oszillators als ganzes Vielfaches von hv vorausgesetzt, bei der zweiten Gleichung dagegen wird sie als stetig veränderlich vorausgesetzt, und es ist nicht möglich, sich für eine dieser beiden Alternativen zu entscheiden, ohne, wenigstens zunächst, die auf der entgegengesetzten Alternative fußende Deduktion illusorisch zu machen.

An diesem Widerspruch kranken auch alle Modelle, welche man bisher ersonnen hat,. . . .] (89)

Consider Josef K.'s predicament, his apparent choices, combined with the feeling of finality about choices made or not made, the seeming unavoidability of error, alternating with the impression of no choice at all, the reminders in the narrative that the existence of Josef K.'s trial—while inescapable— depends upon his acknowledging it, and thus the inevitability of making a "deduction that is based on the opposing alternative illusory." That quotation from Planck is the language of Josef K.'s condition: the language of *The Trial* (also of "Accident Prevention in Stone Quarries") insists that an interpretive act or "deduction"— inevitably based on an opposing alternative—be illusory. Consider also the nature of light that is both wave and particle, and how this relates to the necessity, in the subsequent Copenhagen interpretation of quantum mechanics, of choosing an alternative to measure—either position or velocity—the choice of which

170 / Transgressive Readings

makes the alternative not chosen "illusory" (see chap. 2). Some of the great philosophical issues restated by the implications of theoretical physics in this century—determinism versus indeterminism, continuity versus discontinuity, the status, reliability, and position of the subject and the object, and the limits to knowledge and interpretation—remain accessible to speculation, but not to final answers. "All models devised . . . suffer from . . . contradiction" is the only and central consequence of the interpretive model "Before the Law" in *The Trial*. Such contradiction is inescapable, for it inheres in language itself and, thus, in any possible description. All texts—as Derrida maintains of Kafka's—including the texts of theoretical physics, are necessarily both readable and unreadable.

CHAPTER 5

A Canonical Text and Its Subversion: Planck and Kafka in Concert

As we have seen, reference is the lesser part of meaning, patternment
the greater.
—Benjamin Lee Whorf, "Language, Mind, and Reality"

Tracing the evolution of Planck's second radiation theory, Kuhn
refers to its "canonical" formulation in the second edition of the
Lectures on the Theory of Heat Radiation that was completed late in
1912.[1] Scientific articles or papers, as timely presentations of work
in progress, are by their nature incomplete; a book, by contrast,
is meant as a summing up and fixing of the state of a field, and
thus can be termed *canonical*. The translator of the second edition
of Planck's lectures wrote in his Preface (1914) of its importance:
"Probably no single book since the appearance of Clerk Maxwell's *Electricity and Magnetism* has had a deeper influence on the
development of physical theories" (v). It is not exaggerated to

Epigraph from *Language, Thought, and Reality: Selected Writings of Benjamin Lee
Whorf*, ed. John B. Carroll (Cambridge, Mass.: MIT Press, 1956), 261.
    1. Thomas S. Kuhn, *Black-Body Theory and the Quantum Discontinuity 1894–1912*
(Chicago: University of Chicago Press, 1978), 236. Kuhn's discussion of the *Lectures* consists primarily of a comparison between the first edition, published in
1906, and the second, published in 1913, for the purpose of supporting his argument about the lateness of Planck's conversion to discontinuity (240–44). Kuhn
shows that the second edition is more cogent than the first, but also that "it is focused upon the quantum in a way that the first edition was not" (244). I have chosen to read the second edition for these reasons and because of its historical influence beyond its modest claim to be an introductory text. Planck's text is
Vorlesungen über die Theorie der Wärmestrahlung, 2d rev. ed. (Leipzig: Johann Ambrosius Barth, 1913). An authorized translation by Morton Masius, first published
by Blakiston in 1914, is titled *The Theory of Heat Radiation* (reprinted in 1959 by
Dover).

claim for the *Lectures* the status of an exemplary scientific text for its time. Kuhn writes of the *Lectures*:

> However other physicists may have felt about Planck's second theory, the second edition of the *Lectures* and the papers that followed it were widely and closely read. In the event, they provided important clues for the growing group that, since 1911, had been seeking a coherent formulation of quantum laws, one that would cover Planck oscillators, rotators, three-dimensional vibrators, sometimes the photoeffect, and from 1913, the Bohr atom. (*Black-Body Theory*, 251)

Kuhn reminds us, with his reference to "clues," that we have been reading for the structure of the mystery or detective story in scientific accounts; his reference to coherence associates the necessary prerequisite of the successful mystery story with the scientist's test for validity that selects for the historically prevailing definition of "coherence" and excludes or does not perceive the rest.

In earlier chapters my readings of Planck's essays and his scientific papers have been an attempt to "tease out" (Barbara Johnson, *The Critical Difference*) the dissonances between the types of text and within each text that indicate discourses other than those of scientific convention. These dissonances engage the conventions of science in a dialogue of mutual interrogation that produces a textual complex of dimensions that exceed the boundaries of a scientific text. Planck's prescriptions for the nature of science and the self-descriptions in his texts are always and again undermined by the operations of his language, *despite* his adherence to the strictest scientific conventions of his time. Science implies mastery, implies hierarchies of authority claims, laws, and values. Contradiction, paradox, and subversion are meant to be excluded from its presentation.[2] Yet, by the very use of language they can-

---

2. Whether the behavior of subatomic particles according to quantum mechanics can be interpreted as a paradox is another matter, as are paradoxes in mathematical logic. All physical theories, nevertheless, strive for internal consistency.

not be avoided, and in concert with their opposites, they tell a different story about Max Planck and theoretical physics. I would argue that the self-undermining is the meaning imparted by Planck's text to the scientific, just as the self-undermining operations in Kafka's texts impart meaning to the literary. If we can find evidence for multiple discourses in the epitome of a stable and established scientific text, then we have found the strongest argument on behalf of a Kafka-Planck dialogue. If I, like Planck, were attempting to approach as close as possible to "truth," I would maintain that it is the dialogue of mutual interrogation that comes closest. Perhaps, like Kuhn, I am suggesting a revisionist reading of Planck, but with the difference that I do not offer a revision of his place in the history of theoretical physics, but a revision of readings of Planck and by implication of readings of scientific texts in general.

The *Lectures* are divided into five sections (each of which contains from two to five chapters): "Fundamental Facts and Definitions," "Deductions from Electrodynamics and Thermodynamics," "Entropy and Probability," "A System of Oscillators in a Stationary Field of Radiation," and "Irreversible Radiation Processes."[3] In the Foreword to the first edition, Planck explains his intention to provide an introductory text, organized for didactic reasons to proceed from simple, well-known theorems to the more complex and problematic. The Foreword to the second edition elaborates considerably upon the first, emphasizing the "quantum hypothesis," and situating the author, in the familiar manner, midway between those physicists who reject his views on the quantum for "conservative reasons," and those who believe they must add "yet more radical assumptions." The cautious "standpoint" that the revised edition represents is anchored to classical authority, with the proviso that transgression, if absolutely necessary, is an option:

---

3. I am using the Masius translation here. Otherwise I use my own translations, drawing upon Masius for assistance with several technical terms.

Since nothing is more disadvantageous to the successful development of a new hypothesis than exceeding its boundaries, I have always advocated making as close a connection as possible between the quantum hypothesis and classical dynamics, and only violating the limits of the latter when the facts of experience leave no other way out. (viii)

Planck's critique of his first edition includes the speculation that it must have left the reader feeling dissatisfied, a situation he has tried to avoid by insuring complete internal consistency of the theory presented in the second edition, though he certainly does not want to claim that it does not need further improvement. We see here several of Planck's typical devices: the reference to his reader, and the expressed confidence in his own theories combined with a modesty disclaimer. They are followed again, in Planck's typical rhetorical mode, by an offensive strategy. We must look closely at the offensive paragraph to see an example of Planck's rhetorical and logical procedures and to find an unacknowledged contradiction between conformity and subversion that denies Planck's claim to the middle, and shows him instead to be engaged in a pattern of oscillation — not situated at a midpoint, but containing within his language unresolved dichotomies of the twentieth century itself.

Before presenting the paragraph in question let me point out that it has six main segments, arranged like the skins of an onion — the outermost "skins" (at the opening and conclusion of the paragraph) serve to connect to the preceding and subsequent paragraphs and are the most pronouncedly rhetorical or narrative. The four interior "skins" form a chiasmus — a tropological scheme to be found here and there throughout the *Lectures*. The core of the quantum-theoretical "onion" is a statement about laws and models that reverses Planck's political self-positioning in this book and the previous papers we have examined. In addition to being a contradiction, it is also a riddle and a paradox that denies the representational nature of scientific language and reaches out (if contradiction, riddles, and paradoxes had hands) to Kafka's texts as brothers under the skin.

Thus, while the new edition of this book may not claim to bring the theory of heat radiation to a conclusion that is satisfactory in all respects [or: satisfactory to everybody], this deficiency will not be of decisive importance in judging the theory. For anyone who wanted to make his attitude concerning the quantum hypothesis depend, for example, upon whether the meaning of the quantum of action for elementary physical processes is made clear in every respect or can be visualized through a simple dynamic model, misjudges, I believe, the character and the meaning of the quantum hypothesis. *A really new principle does not allow itself to be expressed via a model that functions according to old laws.* And with regard to the ultimate formulation of the hypothesis, one should not forget that even from the classical point of view the physics of the atom has always remained in reality a thoroughly dark, inaccessible region into which the only introduction of the elementary quantum of action promises to cast some light. (italics added)

[Wenn somit auch die neue Auflage dieses Buches nicht den Anspruch erheben darf, die Theorie der Wärmestrahlung zu einem allseitig befriedigenden Abschluß zu bringen, so wird dieser Mangel bei ihrer Beurteilung doch nicht als entscheidend ins Gewicht fallen. Denn wer seine Stellungnahme zur Quantenhypothese etwa davon abhängig machen wollte, ob die Bedeutung des Wirkungsquantums für die elementaren physikalischen Vorgänge nach allen Richtungen klargestellt ist, oder gar an einem einfachen dynamischen Modell versinnlicht werden kann, der verkennt, wie ich meine, den Charakter und die Bedeutung der Quantenhypothese. *Ein wirklich neues Prinzip läßt sich eben nicht durch ein nach alten Gesetzen funktionierendes Modell wiedergeben.* Und was die endgültige Formulierung der Hypothese betrifft, so darf man nicht vergessen, daß auch für die klassische Auffassung die Physik der Atome in Wirklichkeit stets ein überaus dunkles unzugängliches Gebiet geblieben ist, in welches erst die Einführung des elementaren Wirkungsquantums einiges Licht zu bringen verspricht.] (ix, italics added)

An intrepid explorer with flashlight (the quantum casts *and* explains light, although it remains partially in darkness itself) dares to enter uncharted territory despite the objections of the faint at heart and petty in spirit who will not be satisfied until they see a precise map of the route. This is hardly the self-portrait of a conservative, as Planck is consistently referred to in the literature. For this endeavor, a kind of faith is required—faith in "character" and "meaning." That character and meaning is contained in the core sentence of the paragraph: *not* a dichotomy between new principle and old laws, but—separated from that direct confrontation by three layers of interference—the rejection of *representation* [or "expression"—from the verb *wiedergeben*] that depends upon a model that functions according to old laws. Representation, functioning, and modeling come between new principle and old laws, and thereby indicate how far distant "laws" can be from interrogation, challenge, and change. The distance is so great that the laws appear immutable ("old," i.e., permanent). The distance appears so great that stages of knowing—representation, functioning, modeling—do not work to overcome it. What does work we are not told, only what does not work. How, or whether, a really new principle is to be represented (if not by a functioning model, if not by a model functioning according to old laws) is not indicated.

The conundrum of the laws is embedded in that subersive trope the chiasmus: the benighted make their judgment dependent upon (*a*) meaning that is clear in every respect; (*b*) a model. The response follows that (*b*) the kind of model they want cannot be expected to do the job; (*a*) clarity of meaning in the form of a final formulation is not available in territory that is generally acknowledged to be shrouded in mystery.

What could be more Kafkaesque?—self-contradiction, the denial of direct representation, the inaccessibility and apparent immutability of the old laws, their distance from new thought, the impossibility of clear meaning and final formulations, a protagonist with benighted opponents, dark, trackless territory. What could be more Kafkaesque than the subversive chiasmus?

What could be *less* Kafkaesque than the promise of casting "some light"? Let us remember that the application of light in *The Trial* further enhances the darkness and ignorance. Light, for Planck, is an object of study and a principle metaphor, as well as a metaphysics (enlightenment) folded in on itself as a source of enlightenment. What could be less Kafkaesque than Planck's prediction:

> Thus it follows from the nature of the case that it will require pains-taking experimental and theoretical work for many years and decades to gradually move forward in the new terrain. Whoever currently devotes his strength to the quantum hypothesis must, for the time being, be content with the consciousness that complete success of the labor spent will probably only benefit a future generation. (x)

For Planck, while the present may be inadequate, the future will inevitably be better. In Kafka's texts there is no future prospect—not even where it seems to appear (yet is also deconstructed) in the "Stone Quarries" text—nor is there terrain in which progress can be made, where effort will bring benefits, where hard work is its own reward, yet where it will also be crowned with "complete success." Kafka never tells such a story.

Nor does Planck always follow the subversive convolutions of the chiasmus. The *Lectures* often progress by means of more conventional patterns—linear arguments that begin with a general assertion, then bifurcate into smaller subunits as the assertion is broken into its individual parts for proof; passages that accumulate assertions to arrive at a definition; or frequent back-references to supporting material in previous sections and anticipatory references to the arguments yet to come. The first two of these strategies can also be found in *The Trial*.

Planck's arguments for theoretical moves always depend upon a whole series of limiting conditions, some very speculative. If any one of them turned out to be incorrect, the carefully constructed mathematical-physical case for the second quantum theory would collapse. Favorite phrases are "let us assume," "we may assume," and "on the assumption that." In Kafka's texts, by contrast, there is no relationship between the power of an argument and the validity of its assumptions—such a connection is simply not a relevant category. *The Trial* does not offer testable premises to its protagonist or its reader. Who can say, however, that the intricate but fragile structure of Planck's assumptions is more "scientific"? The extreme restrictions on conditions that are necessary to build a theoretical structure are as reductive and artificial (or fictional) as the statements of standard logic (predicate, propositional, syllogistic) that may, by necessity, operate with only the most simple language relationships.

The rhetorical structure of the *Lectures* is that of a mystery (what is the "meaning" of *h*?) whose solution is gradually unfolded under the pretense of having to be worked out by solving one "question" after the other. The imperative of certain questions and problems is presumed and they direct the inquiry. The narrator, however, also offers a choice of narratives, or, in his aggressive metaphor, strategies for "attack." We may focus upon events in a particular space during a specified time, or alternatively upon the "history" or "story" of one ray from cradle to grave:

. . . we can attack the problem from two different sides: we can either focus on a specific location in space and inquire about the different rays which cross through this location in the course of time, or we can focus on a specific ray and inquire into its history, that is, its genesis, propagation, and destruction.

[. . . [wir] können . . . das Problem von zwei verschiedenen Seiten angreifen: wir können nämlich entweder eine bestimmte Stelle im Raume ins Auge fassen und nach den verschiedenen Strahlen fragen, welche im Laufe der Zeit diese Stelle durchkreuzen, oder wir können einen bestimmten Strahl ins Auge fassen und nach seiner Geschichte fragen, d.h. nach seiner Entstehung, seiner Fortpflanzung und seiner Vernichtung.] (4)

The latter option is chosen for the sake of greater "convenience." It also offers greater rhetorical power—via the trope of personification in the biography of a ray. Access to either narrative is by means of the eye—"grasping into the eye" [*ins Auge fassen*], which I translate as "focus on"—a favorite metaphor of Planck's that is also used by Kafka in his personification of the Insurance Institute in "Stone Quarries." The metaphor is ironic, for neither can the

Institute see, nor can the rays be seen; the metaphor of sight makes claims far exceeding the scope of possible knowledge.[4] Theory itself is personified in the *Lectures*: theory has a "task" that it will have fully "accomplished" only when it "gives account" (180) of an additional process. A pencil [*Bündel*] of rays has an "origin," "paths," and a "future fate" (40). Like a postmodern writer, Planck also offers more than one narrative perspective. He offers the mutually exclusive standpoints of an imaginary "electrodynamic observer" and a "thermodynamic observer" whose interpretations will be completely different since they attribute different meanings to the same terms. The "dilemma" of the incompatability of probability calculations with electrodynamic theory is explained by this relativity of definitions: "For on closer inspection it turns out that what is understood in electrodynamics by 'initial and boundary' conditions, as well as by the 'course over time' of a process, is completely different from what is denoted by the same words in thermodynamics" (110–11).

One thinks of definitions as the most solid part of science. Naming, however, is arbitrary: "let us call it," and "let this stand for" (in the case of a mathematical symbol) are the means of setting up categories and types upon which to erect definitions and theorems. We have seen that the text of *The Trial* reflects upon its own arbitrariness of naming. On the subject of naming in mathematics and physics, Gregory points out that "ontology recapitulates taxonomy — the way we divide the world in language tells us how we think the world is 'really' put together" (*Inventing Reality*, 174). In Planck's dialogue with certainty, the side where definitions are unequivocal, where "the absolute" (44) exists, "all . . . questions are answered" (19), conclusions and con-

---

4. Bruce Gregory writes of the metaphor's use in physics: "The 'all-seeing eye' is a metaphor, so much so that it never appears to us to be an assumption, but seems simply to be 'the way things are.' It is this metaphor, acting as an undisclosed assumption that allows us to talk about how our theories reflect the way the world really is" (*Inventing Reality: Physics as Language* [New York: Wiley, 1988], 190).

firmations "follow with necessity" (58), there is "complete agreement," and "all details are known" (161) alternates with the same language of qualifiers that we find in Kafka's texts[5] and with admission that what the narrator has described "will only approximate the actual conditions" (14), or that the central definition — the definition of a black-body — defines something that does not exist (45).

From the beginning, the *Lectures* proceed by setting up stipulative definitions, meant to be prescriptive, followed by operations of the text on those words. For example:

> By the "state" of a physical system at a certain time we understand the embodiment of all those mutually independent quantities through which the course over time of processes taking place in the system under given boundary conditions is clearly determined; thus a knowledge of the state is precisely equivalent to a knowledge of the "initial conditions."

> [Unter dem "Zustand" eines physikalischen Systems zu einer bestimmten Zeit verstehen wir den Inbegriff aller derjenigen voneinander unabhänigen Größen, durch welche der zeitliche Verlauf der in dem System stattfindenden Vorgänge, bei gegebenen Grenzbedingungen, eindeutig bestimmt wird; die Kenntnis des Zustandes ist also genau äquivalent der Kenntnis der "Anfangsbedingungen."] (119)

The language is the language of certainty; knowledge itself is defined self-reflexively by its "precise equivalence" to knowledge. This time the language is undermined by the concepts. In this section, Planck is treating the notions of entropy and probability that measure irreversible processes. As Prigogine and Stengers explain, the notion of irreversibility means that "initial conditions arise from previous evolution and are transformed into states of the same class through subsequent evolution."[6] That

---

5. Such as *allerdings, einerseits . . . andererseits, indessen, nämlich, zwar,* and others. Cf. chap. 3.

6. Ilya Prigogine and Isabelle Stengers, *Order out of Chaos: Man's New Dialogue with Nature* (New York: Bantam, 1984), 310.

is, in the recursive process there are never "initial conditions" that hold still long enough for us to have "knowledge" of them; they are in a state of continual transformation and as soon as we designate them as "initial conditions," they no longer fit that name (see Coda, below). Secondly, Planck's definition of "states" leads next to two subcategories: the microscopic and the macroscopic. The latter is the one that interests Planck because measuring it requires consideration of entropy and the calculation of probability: "The macroscopic processes take place unambiguously, in the sense of the second principle [of thermodynamics], when and only when the hypothesis of elementary disorder[7] is satisfied." ["Die makroskopischen Vorgänge verlaufen nur dann eindeutig, im Sinne des zweiten Hauptsatzes, wenn die Hypothese der elementaren Unordnung erfüllt ist, sonst nicht"] (119). The definition of the subcategory of macroscopic states arrives at its central thesis and conclusion in "disorder." In other words, there is in this passage a dialogue between discourse attempting to impose order and concepts resisting that imposition of order.

Kafka seemed, according to his *Diaries*, to be engaged in a constant struggle to quell disorder by means of language. He wrote: "The stability that even the slightest writing causes for me, however, is beyond doubt and wonderful." ["Die Festigkeit aber, die das geringste Schreiben mir verursacht, ist zweifellos und wunderbar."][8] Like a scientist, he tested language for the "false" and the "unprovable" (*Tagebücher*, 248–49). Obsessed with words, he was not content with language as he found it, but had to reshape it toward the greatest possible precision of definition, which, however, he deconstructed in the process. Many passages in the *Diaries* that are organized around a central term with grammatical variations, seem — by means of a private antilogic — to test and explore that term in search of a definition. At the end of the pas-

---

7. Translated by Kuhn as "primitive disorder" (*Black-Body Theory*, 242) and by Masius as "elemental chaos" (*Theory of Heat Radiation*, 121).

8. Franz Kafka, *Tagebücher 1910–1923*, ed. Max Brod (Frankfurt am Main: S. Fischer, 1986), 245, Entry for 27 November 1913.

sages, no conventional definition has been reached after extensive grammatical and syntactical exploration reminiscent of materials testing under various conditions. One such passage explores "nothing" and "nothingness" (also "insignificance," "nullity," and "invalidity"):

Dying would mean *nothing* [pronoun, nom. case] other than surrendering a *nothing* [noun, accus. case] to a *nothing* [noun, dat. case], but that would be impossible to feel, for how could one even only as a *nothing* [noun, nom. case] consciously surrender oneself to *nothing* [noun, dat. case] and not just to an empty *nothing* [noun, dat. case], but to a roaring [foaming] *nothing* [noun, dat. case] whose *nothingness* [noun, nom. case] consists only of its inconceivability [incomprehensibility]. (italics added)

[Sterben hieße nichts anderes, als ein Nichts dem Nichts hinzugeben, aber das wäre dem Gefühl unmöglich, denn wie könnte man sich auch nur als Nichts mit Bewußtsein dem Nichts hingeben und nicht nur einem leeren Nichts, sondern einem brausenden Nichts, dessen Nichtigkeit nur in seiner Unfaßbarkeit besteht.] (246)

There is a profound order in the defining language and a profound disorder in the concepts the language explores. "Nothing" seems to be a kind of waterfall characterized by incomprehensibility without which it would be something. Here, where definition is a form of play, we see also the deep connection with Nietzsche. Kafka's play with "nothing" is no less serious, no less confident or truthful than Planck's play with the definition of a "black body" that does not exist, or with precision and knowledge in a field of elemental disorder.

Kafka sets out in a similar way to define "peace," "silence," "quiet" [*Ruhe*] and finds nothing but the self-referentiality of a word that, nevertheless, and at the same time, incomprehensibly, is equivalent to mercy (or grace):

When I imagined today that during the lecture I would be absolutely still [*ruhig*, adj., silent, peaceful], I asked myself what kind of stillness [*Ruhe*, noun, nom., silence, peace] it will be, on what [where] will it be based [founded, justified], and I could only say that it will only be a stillness [*Ruhe*, noun, nom., silence, peace] for its own sake, an incomprehensible mercy [grace], nothing else.

[Als ich mir heute vorstellte, daß ich während des Vortrags unbedingt ruhig sein werde, fragte ich mich, was das für eine Ruhe sein wird, wo sie begründet wird, und ich konnte nur sagen, daß es bloß eine Ruhe um ihrer selbst willen sein wird, eine unverständliche Gnade, sonst nichts.] (249)

Three "definitions" are provided for the word *Ruhe*: one is *Ruhe* pointing at itself, the second is *Ruhe* pointing at an analog, the third draws boundaries around the first two, beyond which *Ruhe* does not exist. Knowledge, according to convention, and certainly in science, resides first of all in definitions. The initial steps toward definition—dividing and naming—are taken in this passage. Then, however, the only definition comparable to a scientific, or dictionary definition, that is, one that provides an analogous term, offers incomprehensibility. Self-reflection, a metaphysics of incomprehensibility, and nothing seem as distant as possible from Planck's kind of defining. Yet we have found countertexts within and in addition to Planck's ostensible text, whose language and representations engage just those extrascientific options.

A dialogue between the literary and the scientific can be read as a series of mutual representations, analogues, or isomorphic narratives. The counterlogic we have seen as process in Kafka's texts can be read in Planck's physics and in his rhetoric. He provides instructions on how to read the story of rays; it requires, paradoxically, ascertaining the future in order to determine the past:

In order to learn more details about the origin and the paths of the individual rays of which the radiations . . . consist, it is most practical to follow the opposite course and inquire into the future fate of that pencil [a bundle of rays] which is aimed in exactly the opposite direction to pencil *I*, and coming, thus, from the first medium . . . encounters the surface element . . . of the second medium inside the cone. . . . . For since every optical path may also be traversed in the opposite direction, one obtains by this observation all paths along which rays can pass into pencil *I*, however complicated they may otherwise be.

[Um nun näheres über die Herkunft und die Bahnen der einzelnen Strahlen zu erfahren, aus denen sich die Strahlungen . . . zusammensetzen, ist es am zweckmäßigsten, den umgekehrten Weg zu gehen und nach dem künftigen Schicksal desjenigen Strahlenbündels zu fragen, welches dem Bündel *I* gerade entgegengesetzt gerichtet ist, also vom ersten Medium kommend innerhalb des Kegels . . . auf das Oberflächenelement . . . des zweiten Mediums trifft. Denn da jeder optische Weg auch in umgekehrter Richtung gangbar ist, so erhält man durch diese Betrachtungn sämtliche Bahnen, auf denen Strahlen in das Bündel *I* hineingelangen können, so kompliziert sie auch im übrigen sein mögen.]
(40–41)

The meetings and partings, the comings and goings in opposite directions of the rays of radiation produce a pattern like that produced by the grammar, syntax, and counterlogic of the passage in Kafka's "Stone Quarries" text that deconstructs the notion of knowledge (chap. 3).

In Planck's discussion of "electrodynamic processes in a stationary field of radiation" he presents arguments for the common description of black radiation as consisting of regular periodic oscillations. He explains why this description is "completely justified" and lends itself to forming convenient and clear observations. Then he proceeds by degree to tear down the arguments he just advanced, concluding that: "One could, on the contrary, be equally justified in maintaining that in all of nature there is no more irregular process than the oscillations of black radiation" (107).

While Planck undermines his opening proposal by concluding with an opposite proposal, it is clear that there is a great difference, despite a similarity of pattern, between this type of undermining and the type we find in Kafka's texts. This is transparently a rhetorical strategy for convincing the reader, in the Socratic manner, by opening with a premise that is generally accepted, the refutation of which is thereby made all the more powerful. Planck's argument is dipolar, and amounts, in the end, to supporting all interpretations, rather than none. By contrast, such a pattern in Kafka's texts — a paradigmatic example being the previously mentioned "Stone Quarries" passage — has the effect of negating all interpretations. It collapses in on itself, imploding on its own central term.

The passage in which Planck traces the history of radiation rays is isomorphic with equivalent segments of Kafka's texts not only by means of a shared overall pattern, but also because language is organized in such a way that it traces the process it wants to describe. Planck describes, self-reflexively, such congruence:

This complicated method of consideration lies wholly in the nature of the case and corresponds to the complexity of the physical processes in a medium irradiated in such a manner.

[Diese Kompliziertheit der Betrachtungsweise liegt aber ganz in der Natur der Sache, und entspricht der Kompliziertheit der physikalischen Vorgänge in einem solcherweise durchstrahlten Medium.] (96)

This comment bespeaks confidence in the representational nature of language. Might it also be a description of Kafka's writing? Let us take faith in representation one step further and find, in a passage of the *Lectures*, a text that tells at least three stories beyond the story of the behavior of radiation — a story of reading, a story of interpretation, and a story of Josef K.:

At the boundary surface . . . the rays of pencil J are partly reflected and partly transmitted regularly or diffusely, and thereafter, in both media, are partly absorbed, partly scattered, partly again reflected or transmitted to different media, etc., according to the configuration of the system. Finally, however, after having branched into many individual rays the entire pencil J will be completely absorbed in the n media.

[Die Strahlen des Bündels *J* werden an der Grenzfläche . . . teils reflektiert, teils durchgelassen, regulär oder diffus, hieraufin beiden Medien teils absorbiert, teils zerstreut, teils wiederum reflektiert oder in andere Medien durchgelassen usw., je nach der Konfiguration des Systems. Schließlich aber wird das ganze Bündel *J*, nachdem es sich in viele einzelne Strahlen verzweigt hat, in den *n* Medien vollständig absorbiert werden.] (41)

We can see in this a version of the reader's interaction with a text in the course of reading and inevitable interpretation. It describes a dynamic process that proceeds in reaction to a text that also in turn influences the reading, partly accepting, partly resisting, partly diffusing and scattering attempts to determine meaning, but finally absorbing yet another reading or interpretation. On the other hand, the reader also plays the role of the boundary surface, unintentionally exercising all of those possible variations on acceptance and resistance, finally absorbing, in one way or another, the reader's own version of the text. The protagonist of this tale is a bundle of rays named *J* that — according to the particular system in which it is involved — is permitted entry or not, transferred or not, diffused or not, scattered or not, to a different degree in each case, and finally, after *J* has lost its central focus and identity and frittered away its integrity, it is absorbed into the system. In the case of Josef K., the absorption is violent and final.

If so many tales can be told by one narrative and shared by science and literature, then language itself has provided the order and the chaos, and the rich possibilities of telling the same tale in many equal discourses.

Planck also provides evidence for the problematic nature of representation. He challenges, by his practice, his own statement quoted above about the character of the description being inherent in the character of the described. We can examine a paradigmatic section of the *Lectures*. It follows one of Planck's important contributions to physical theory — his definition of entropy. He explains that there is no point in trying to provide rigorous (mathematical) proof of the definition, since probability (on which a definition of entropy depends) is still lacking a quantitative definition.

One could even perhaps suspect at first glance that for this reason the proposition has no definite physical meaning at all. It may, nevertheless, be shown by a simple deduction that — even without considering more closely the concept of the probability of a state — one is in a position just on the basis of the above proposition to determine quite generally the way in which entropy depends on probability.

[Man könnte sogar vielleicht auf den ersten Blick vermuten, daß er aus diesem Grunde überhaupt keinen bestimmten physikalischen Inhalt besitzt. Indessen läßt sich durch eine einfache Deduktion zeigen, daß man ohne noch auf den Begriff der Wahrscheinlichkeit eines Zustandes näher einzugehen auf Grund es obigen Satzes doch schon in der Lage ist, die Art der Abhängigkeit der Entropie von der Wahrscheinlichkeit ganz allgemein zu fixieren.] (116)

A translation that foregrounds the language of this segment produces an awkward English version. That is because of the necessity of conveying the many qualifications that carry this discourse multiple degrees of distance away from representation as Planck describes it. The passage begins with a subjunctive verb [könnte], setting up a contrary to fact situation. It continues with "even" [sogar], "perhaps" [vielleicht], and "at first glance" [auf den ersten Blick]. Adding the verb "suspect" [vermuten], the qualifiers "for this reason" [aus diesem Grunde] and "at all" [überhaupt], and the negative [keinen], gives us a sentence in which only seven out of twenty words do not reduce, limit, or qualify its meanings. The next sentence opens with yet another qualifier [indessen — "nevertheless" or "however"], then proceeds to interject at least eight layers of interference between the reader and that final, definitive verb "determine" [fixieren]. To arrive at determination, a reader must wade through the quicksand of the passive form "it may be shown," "the concept of the probability of a state," "without yet [or still — noch] considering more closely," "on the basis of," "the above proposition," "just [a rough English version of doch] already [schon] in a position," "the kind of dependence" [die Art der Abhängigkeit], and "quite [or completely] generally."[9] In other words, entropy's dependence on probability can be demonstrated by a simple deduction. My "In other words" is, itself, a key qualification, for the other words that take a shortcut around Planck's qualifiers and convey the ostensible message of direct representation also ignore a powerful, deeper meaning in the language of the original—that these theoretical propositions are a long way from representation in language, by corollary they may never be representable, by inference linguistic representation itself becomes questionable.

In writing, of course, as in life, representation is unavoidable. Making pictures, forming patterns, and interpreting them are essential to survival and belong to the biological capacity of all species. In this context, however, we are concerned only with representation in the sense of self-representation in a text. Representation, from this point of view, can be seen as a kind of internal dialogue. That dialogue may appear to be harmonious, as when Planck describes a perfect fit between description and described, or dissonant, as in his passage above on entropy and probability. Then again it may consist of yet a third possibility—reciprocal interaction, a dynamic relationship that follows a pattern like the chiasmus, an oscillation that is particularly intricate because the "voices" or the "moving" parts cannot be separated. Together, in their dialogue or interaction, they suggest knowledge beyond that of any fixed or single known.

Planck gives credit for the "reciprocity theorem" to his influential predecessor in Berlin, Hermann von Helmholtz. This theorem—whose definition Planck rephrases three times over the course of five pages—describes a mutuality, an equivalent coming and going of radiation rays:

---

9. Following Whorf (*Language*), we would have to consider here the peculiarities of German. Indeed, German grammar and syntax lend themselves to this sort of construction. There may be a connection between the origins of theoretical physics in the German-speaking culture, and the discourse of that science as it evolved. However, it is certain that Planck's texts are also made up of passages that do not operate in this manner.

. . . in the case of stationary radiation, for each ray striking the boundary surface and diffusely reflected from it on both sides, there is a corresponding ray at the same point, of the same intensity and opposite direction, produced by the inverse process at the same point on the boundary surface. . . . [10]

[. . . bei der stationären Strahlung jedem Strahl, der auf die Grenzfläche trifft und von dieser diffus nach beiden Seiten derselben zerstreut wird, an demselben Orte ein gleich intensiver gerade entgegengesetzt gerichteter entspricht, der durch den umgekehrten Vorgang an derselben Stelle der Grenzfläche . . . zustande kommt. . . .] (38–39)

There is no doubt that this theorem describes an order, but it is a peculiar order of equal processes heading toward each other in an act of mutual enhancement that creates the radiation state.

In his *Diaries*, Kafka can be seen as engaged in a continuing and essential dialogue with himself as his most critical reader. He writes: "I can carry on a dialogue with myself again and am no longer staring into such complete emptiness." ["Ich kann wieder ein Zweigespräch mit mir führen und starre nicht so in vollständige Leere"] (*Tagebücher*, 307). At one point this dialogue takes form like the reciprocity theorem, and then finds itself again in a passage of Planck's text that retells the story of Kafka's mirror dialogue. The three versions—from Helmholtz to Kafka to Planck—increase in complexity and in suggestiveness, with the last two being most closely related.

On December 12, 1911, Kafka wrote:

Just now I looked at myself closely in the mirror and seemed to me—of course only with evening lights and the source of light behind me so that actually only the fuzz on the edges of the ears was lit up—even under closer examination, to look better than I know I am. A clear, distinctly formed, almost beautifully delineated face. The blackness of the hair, the eyebrows, and the eye sockets breaks forth like life from the remaining

---

10. This translation is by Masius (*Theory of Heat Radiation*, 36). I only changed his "bounding" to the more current term "boundary."

waiting mass. The glance is not at all ravaged, not a trace of that, but it is also not childlike, rather—unbelievable as it seems—energetic, but perhaps it was only observing, since I was, after all, observing myself and wanted to frighten myself.

[Im Spiegel sah ich mich vorhin genau an und kam mir im Gesicht allerdings nur bei Abendbeleuchtung und der Lichtquelle hinter mir, so daß eigentlich nur der Flaum an den Rändern der Ohren beleuchtet war— auch bei genauer Untersuchung besser vor als ich nach eigener Kenntnis bin. Ein klares, übersichtlich gebildetes, fast schön begrenztes Gesicht. Das Schwarz der Haare, der Brauen und der Augenhöhlen dringt wie Leben aus der übrigen abwartenden Masse. Der Blick ist gar nicht verwüstet, davon ist keine Spur, er ist aber auch nicht kindlich, eher unglaublicherweise energisch, aber vielleicht war er nur beobachtend, da ich mich eben beobachtete und mir Angst machen wollte.] (250)

Reciprocity, of course, is intrinsic to a look in the mirror. Beyond that, Kafka's is also a reflection, like Helmholtz's and Planck's, on the workings of light. The location and intensity of the light (radiation) source provides the contrasts that result in a second to-and-fro. The primary to- and-fro operation that controls the passage is the glance that examines and is examined, that does not know, finally, whether it is observing or merely observed by the observing self. Back and forth, into the mirror, back to the face, into the reflection and back again with the addition of a motive and explanation—"wanted to frighten myself"—that deconstructs with humor the whole operation of self-redemption.

There is a to-and-fro between the notion of precision in examination allied with uncertainty as expressed in "seemed to me," and the qualifier "of course" [*allerdings*] that undercuts the above alliance and thus is allied with knowledge [*Kenntnis*]. The suggestion is made—but not pursued—that reflection might be more accurate than knowledge. Under close [*genau*] examination the self in the mirror looks better than it is according to its "own knowledge" [*nach eigener Kenntnis*]. (In the self-deprecation that is typical of Kafka, the superiority of the attractive mirror image over his "knowledge" is not finally granted, but is left open to question, and the face is not simply "beautiful," but "almost beautifully delineated.") There is a to-and-fro between the act of looking and the features that stand out, and between light and dark. It is only the lack of light ("evening lights") and its distance or indirectness, filtered by fuzz on the ears, that permits the "blackness" to issue forth as if it were "life" (despite Kafka's aversion to metaphors!). The separate foreground blacknesses are vital in contrast to the passive and featureless (because unlit) background. Paradoxes of light rays and blackness, blackness as clarity and vibrance, knowledge in league with qualification [*allerdings*] interacting with precise examination in league with "seems," the reciprocity of equal "glances" and their undecidability—bring us, as readers, as close as possible to Planck's work and texts. There is a taste in Planck's texts of all these paradoxes and, above all, in his writings on radiation in a black body.

In Planck's description, the operation of rays of radiation (or light) can cast out to the reader as many, or more, possible meanings as Kafka's mirror dialogue:

While the radiation that starts from a surface element and is directed toward the interior of the medium is in every respect equal to that emanating from any equally large parallel element of area in the interior, it nevertheless has a different prehistory. That is to say, since the surface of the medium was assumed to be impermeable to heat, it is produced only by reflection at the surface of radiation coming from the interior. In detail this can happen in very different ways, depending on whether the surface is assumed to be smooth, i.e., in this case reflecting, or rough, e.g., white (Sec. 10). In the first case there corresponds to each pencil that strikes the surface another perfectly definite pencil, symmetrically situated and having the same intensity, while in the second case every incident pencil is broken up into an infinite number of reflected pencils, each having a different direction, intensity, and polarization, however, always in such a way that the rays that strike a surface element from all different directions with the same intensity . . . also produce, collectively, uniform radiation of the same luminosity . . ., directed from the surface toward the interior of the medium.

[Während also die von einem Element der Oberfläche ausgehende, nach
dem Innern des Mediums gerichtete Strahlung in jeder Beziehung gleich
ist der von irgend einem gleichgroßen und gleichgerichteten im Innern
gelegenen Flächenelement ausgehenden Strahlung, so hat sie doch eine
andere Vorgeschichte als diese, sie rührt nämlich, da die Oberfläche des
Mediums als für Wärme undurchlässig vorausgesetzt ist, lediglich her
von der Reflexion der aus dem Innern kommenden Strahlung an der
Oberfläche. Im einzelnen kann dies in sehr verschiedener Weise gesche-
hen, je nachdem die Oberfläche als glatt, also in diesem Falle als spie-
gelnd, oder als rauh, etwa als weiß (§10) vorausgesetzt ist. Im ersteren
Falle entspricht jedem auf die Oberfläche auftreffenden Strahlenbündel
ein ganz bestimmtes symmetrisch dazu gelegenes von der nämlichen Intensität, im zweiten Falle aber zersplittert sich jedes einzelne auftreffende
Strahlenbündel in unendlich viele reflektierte Strahlenbündel von verschiedener Richtung, Intensität und Polarisation, doch immer so, daß die
von allen Seiten mit gleicher Intensität . . . auf ein Oberflächenelement
auftreffenden Bündel in ihrer Gesamtheit wieder eine gleichmäßige von
der Oberfläche in das Innere des Mediums gerichtete Strahlung von der
nämlichen Helligkeit . . . liefern.] (33)

Radiation from surface to interior, Planck's protagonist in this
"mirror dialogue" is distinguished from its opposite number and
from the protagonist of the Kafka mirror dialogue by its "prehistory," that is to say its origins (which do not enter the picture in
Kafka's passage) in a to-and-fro movement between outside and
inside. Kafka's protagonist is like Planck's, however, insofar as
both are exact duplicates of their reflected opposites. The unique
prehistory is the preoccupation of Planck's passage, as he defines
it in a motion of increasing bifurcation, finally splitting into "infinite" reflections, which, however, come together again in a harmonious uniformity directed from outside to inside. We find no
such concluding harmony in Kafka's mirror text, nor do we find
a historical narrative, but we do find in the undecidability of
reflection the suggestion of infinitude. Kafka's text is suspended
without resolution of the mutual reflections. It is closer, perhaps,
to the "rough," or "white" surface than to the simplicity and symmetry associated with the smooth reflecting surface. Kafka's dia-

logue moves from the narrative past, to a vivid present tense in the middle, as knowledge is introduced, to the past again with the notion of the observing/observed glance. Planck's text, despite its concentration on history, is entirely in the present tense, as is customary in scientific papers. In Planck's German text we find a regular, almost symmetrical alternation between the words *surface* and *interior*. It opens with surface and closes with interior. This distribution of terms imparts rhetorical force and literary rhythm to the to-and-fro movement. Planck's is a dramatic, action-packed narrative. Kafka's is a story of observation, examination, fear. They come together as mirror tales with their suggestion that the locus of light, thus (in)sight and interpretation, is the unending to-and-fro of reflection.

When light particles strike a reflecting body, or mirrored surface, that body moves according to the law of action and reaction. Its ensuing momentum is such that it is "equal and opposite to the change in momentum of all the light particles reflected from it in the same time interval" (57).[11] The *Lectures* are dominated in all categories by the notion of "equal and opposite" that describes the behavior of radiation. Like many of the concepts Planck treats, it is expressed as a law. In this segment of text the reference to law is straightforward and uncomplicated—just what we would expect: physical behavior is governed by certain laws.

There is, however, more to it than that. The notion of law, like the notion of definition, is compromised in Planck's text as it is in Kafka's. Since that assertion seems inappropriate to a scientific text, we need to examine the *Lectures* for some important variations on the idea of the law. That the "Stefan-Boltzmann radiation law can be used for an absolute definition of temperature independent of all substances" (63) describes the kind of absolutism we would expect. Law defines; the only unanswered question is what defines the law? Law itself is inevitably ungrounded, an a priori; we deduce on the assumption that there are laws of deduc-

---

11. Translation by Masius, *Theory of Heat Radiation.*

tion. This particular law, Planck explains in the preceding sentences, was initiated by Stefan, enhanced by Boltzmann, and confirmed by Lummer and Pringsheim, that is, a law has a history that implies that—like all histories—it could have evolved differently, and that it will continue to evolve.

Whether or not black bodies actually exist in nature is not relevant to the examination of black radiation. What *is* relevant is whether or not "their existence and their characteristics are at all compatible with the laws of electrodynamics and thermodynamics" (133). As in Josef K.'s predicament, what counts is not existence but compatibility with the law. By contrast, Planck writes: "taking advantage of the freedom guaranteed by this law . . . " (133). Freedom is not only compatible with, but dependent upon, the law. Yet law also means subjugation—Planck writes of processes that are "subjugated" (135) to the laws.

If we imagine, as Planck suggests, a system of ideal linear oscillators in a stationary radiation field, we need to have knowledge of the "dynamic elementary law" in order in make progress toward a theory. This law may not be the law prescribed by classical electrodynamics, but must rather be a "dynamic law" in which the "elementary quantum of action h plays a characteristic role" (147). The only acceptable dynamic law is one that takes account of "discrete values" (or discontinuity) in the emission of radiation by the oscillators. Thus, there is a conventional static law, and a superior, new, dynamic one associated with Planck's theory of radiation. Although there are hierarchical distinctions of value among laws, Planck is unwilling, in agreement with the politics of his science, to embrace the new wholeheartedly. In fact, he defines "rationality" as veering as little as possible from the classical laws: "In establishing the dynamic law we will proceed rationally in such a way that we presume the deviation from the laws of classical electrodynamics, which was recognized as necessary, as slight as possible" (148).

By contrast, agreeing with the law seems to mean no more than agreeing with the law in Planck's instructions on how to arrive at the laws: "and [we] inquire about the laws that the radiation processes . . . must obey if they are to be in agreement with the deduction from the second law of thermodynamics mentioned in the preceding paragraph" (24). Like defining knowledge in terms of knowledge, this is also an enclosed, self-referential proposition: our quest is to be for laws to obey if we want a law to be obeyed. There are yet further examples of the undermining of the notion of law as an absolute. "It is unnecessary now," writes Planck, "to add the definition [*die Fixierung*] of the law that states the probability, . . ." (149). Defining, it seems, will be sidestepped, at least when it comes to that indefinable probability that would predict when the full quantum of energy is reached that permits emission of radiation to take place. Another law, governing the "microscopic interaction of molecules," is "still completely unknown" (131). Yet other laws that describe the intervals in which the oscillator emits radiation energy are the "laws of chance" (155), to which Planck not infrequently makes reference.

"Law" is a slippery and undecided matter, even in a canonical (and in its time revered) scientific textbook. Like Kafka's "Stone Quarries," the *Lectures* can be read as destabilizing the imperatives of the law. They can be read as proferring "Talmudic" options of undecidability in addition to mathematical certainty and, thus, an oscillation between different types of knowledge. In *The Trial* the law is distinguished above all by its absence, in "Stone Quarries" by its erasure, and in the *Lectures* by its ambiguity. That situation, however, does not indicate lawlessness. On the contrary, a text has its own laws. Writing requires and realizes laws of grammar, rhetoric, and logic. Reading is law that embraces and imparts incompleteness, multiplicity, ambiguity, and disorder as well as order. Planck's text, when read accordingly, is without doubt a language game. The productive "chaos" of language is law encompassing oscillation in a dynamic order that includes the spectrum of options from literature to science.

Coda: The Sign of the Four

> The diagram upon it appears to be a plan of part of a large building with numerous halls, corridors, and passages. . . . In the left-hand corner is a curious hieroglyphic like four crosses in a line with their arms touching. Beside it is written, in very rough and coarse characters, "The sign of the four—. . . ." No, I confess that I do not see how this bears upon the matter. Yet it is evidently a document of importance.
>
> —Sherlock Holmes reading in "The Sign of the Four"

While no valorization of numerology is intended, it does seem as if four must be a significant number in this "diagram" of the "numerous halls, corridors, and passages" of discourse. The number four "bears upon the matter" insofar as the chiasmus has four arms that can represent the relationship between the four basic types of texts we have read: Kafka's technical and literary texts and Planck's essays and scientific papers. In a reductive sense we might also determine that we have been dealing with two Kafkas and two Plancks—in each case a "literary" type and a "scientific" type, connected by the play of linguistic possibilities in a kind of dialogue. That dialogue is carried on between four additional protagonists: Watson and Holmes, and Nietzsche in a literary-scientific exchange with his own text via Planck's essays. My readings have primarily followed four strategies: reading for textual logics, for rhetorics, for the story of *The Trial*, and for scientific or mathematical concepts. The four "crosses" are meant to be arranged so that "their arms [are] touching." Although the results of such a patterning are inevitably "very rough and coarse characters" off in a "left-hand corner," and much of the relations of lan-

---

Epigraph from Arthur Conan Doyle, "The Sign of the Four," *The Annotated Sherlock Holmes*, ed. William S. Baring-Gould (New York: Clarkson N. Potter, 1967), 1:621.

guage must remain as resistant to deciphering as a "curious hiero-glyphic," I hope that the readings have produced "a document of [at least some] importance" insofar as others may be stimulated to their own rereadings, or else to first readings of scientific texts by readers who may never before have considered them legiti-mate territory for investigation.

Having invested Holmes with the authority of a pundit, I would like to return to an irreverent reading of his comments as quoted at the beginning of chapter 1. Holmes's criticism of Wat-son's writing culminates in the accusation: "You have attempted to tinge it [the "exact science" of detection] with romanticism, which produces much the same effect as if you worked a love-story or an elopement into the fifth proposition of Euclid" (611). We have already looked, in chapter 1, at Holmes's intention and the self-undermining of his statement. Now I would like to point to a third and a fourth layer of meaning. *The Annotated Sherlock Holmes* contains notes and comments on the stories, obscure ori-gins, locations, and speculations about the biographies of Holmes and Watson. For those who are unfamiliar with the Holmes cult, it is necessary to explain that throughout the world there are clubs named after various Sherlock Holmes stories (or characters), whose members (along with other Holmes fans) attribute histori-cal existence to Holmes, Watson, and the other characters, and seek to fill the biographical gaps in the stories (whether tongue-in-cheek or not, I cannot say) by accumulating the "missing" bi-ographical data. Thus fiction laps over its banks onto the dry land of hard evidence. One such researcher is quoted on the subject of Holmes's remark on the "fifth proposition of Euclid":

"The Master here referred to the fifth proposition merely to illustrate his point," the late Dr. Ernest Bloomfield Zeisler wrote in "A Chronological *Study in Scarlet*," "for careful research has failed to reveal why any other proposition of Euclid would not have done as well." (611)

Yet the fifth proposition, or parallel axiom, of Euclid is notewor-thy as set apart from the other propositions of Euclidean geometry. As early as the time of ancient Greece, this axiom bothered mathematicians because it "could not be proven on the basis of the other nine Euclidean axioms; that is, it is independent of Euclid's other axioms."[1] Thus Euclidean geometry was revealed as requiring "some additional axiom about parallel lines" (Kline, *Mathematics*, 83), meaning that it became logically possible to think of alternative geometries. As a consequence, various non-Euclidean geometries were developed, culminating in the work of Georg Bernhard Riemann (1826–66). Together, these new geometries stimulated a momentous upheaval in the worldview of mathematicians (and lay persons schooled in mathematics) who had been absolutely certain that Euclid's propositions were the one and only geometry of physical space. "The mere fact that there can be alternative geometries was in itself a shock. But the greater shock was that one could no longer be sure which geometry was true or whether any one of them was true" (Kline, *Mathematics*, 88).

Thus Holmes, "the Master," has chosen for his paradigm of "exact science" the very proposition that led to the undermining of certainty and the prevailing standard of logical rigor in geometry. "Romanticism" or Watson's "facts" are built into the example Holmes chooses to refute them. We have added, then, the reading of another reader (quoted above), as well as a countertext to that reading and to the text ignorant of its wrong geometry that Conan Doyle has his character speak.

Models and paradigms will always have clay feet, just as logic itself does. Kline quotes from an anonymous source: "Logic is the art of going wrong with confidence" (*Mathematics*, 197). The tightest, most rigorous logical reasoning can have evolved from error. Logic begins with undefined axioms, "as any axiomatic theory must. . . . Some of these undefined ideas are the notion of an elementary proposition, the assertion of the truth of an elementary proposition, the negation of a proposition, the conjunction and the disjunction of two propositions, and the notion

---

1. Morris Kline, *Mathematics: The Loss of Certainty* (Oxford: Oxford University Press, 1980), 81.

of a propositional function" (*Mathematics*, 219). Thus there is a built-in contradiction in the "science" that depends upon "the principles of definition."[2]

Aristotle expressly founded logic on "the principles of reasoning used by the mathematicians" (Kline, *Mathematics*, 182), whence he borrowed "the law of contradiction (a proposition cannot be both true and false) and the law of excluded middle (a proposition must be either true or false)" (21). Thus we find at the origin of deductive logic enforcement of the apparently inherent human inclination toward binary thinking. In chapter 2 we saw that the wave/particle nature of light and Heisenberg's Uncertainty Principle challenge these logical certitudes, by demonstrating that the statements "this is a particle" and "this is not a particle" do not necessarily exclude one another.[3] The language of the texts we have read also engages in an assault upon such exclusionary demands. *The Trial* by itself is a monument to the denial of those very propositions of Aristotle.

As far as mathematical logic is concerned, since the eighteenth century mathematicians have sought without success to give it absolutely reliable foundations. In our time it was proved by Kurt Gödel that no mathematical system can be both consistent and complete.[4] That is, there are always statements that are true but not provable, or provable but not true. Kline provides an illustrative example in natural language of Gödel's theorem:

"This sentence is unprovable." Now if the statement is not provable, then what it says is true. If, on the other hand, the sentence is provable, it is

---

2. See *logic* in *Webster's Third New International Dictionary* (Springfield, Mass.: Merriam-Webster, 1961).

3. For a spirited defense of "classical logic" against "quantum logic," see chap. 7, "Critique of the Attempts to Correlate Quantum Mechanics with a New Logic," in Kurt Hübner, *Critique of Scientific Reason*, trans. Paul R. Dixon, Jr. and Hollis M. Dixon (Chicago: University of Chicago Press, 1983).

4. His paper, "On Formally Undecidable Propositions of *Principia Mathematica* and Related Systems" was published in 1931. The original is "Über Formal Unentscheidbare Sätze der *Principia Mathematica* und Verwandter Systeme, I," *Monatshefte für Mathematik und Physik* 38 (1931): 173–98. See also the treatment by Douglas

not true or, by standard logic, if true, it is not provable. Hence the sentence is true if and only if it is *not* provable. Thus the result is not a contradiction but a true statement which is unprovable or undecidable. (*Mathematics*, 262)

Many thinkers have questioned logic at its foundations and found it wanting. Whorf, for example, shows the logic of Aristotle to be built on the subject/predicate structure of Indo-European languages, and maintains that there are, in other language groups, ways of expressing relations that do not segment the world along those lines. Hayden White attends to logic as rhetorical troping:

. . . even the model of the syllogism itself displays clear evidence of troping. . . . The move from the major premise (All men are mortal) to the *choice* of the datum to serve as the minor (Socrates is a man) is itself a tropological move, a "swerve" from the universal to the particular which logic cannot preside over, since it is logic itself that is being served by this move. Every *applied* syllogism contains an enthymemic element, this element consisting of nothing but the *decision* to move from the plane of universal propositions (themselves extended synecdoches) to that of singular existential statements (these being extended metonymies).[5]

Margolis shows that multiple readings are possible of the "if . . . then" statements of propositional logic.[6] But the most impressive failure of logic to fulfill its own claims is its incapacity to meet the standard of those defenders who maintain that it distills or reflects cognitive processes. Anyone who has studied logic must be struck by its reductionism that eliminates all that is problematic and ambiguous, intricate and interesting, in other words, all that is characteristic of natural language and of thought.

R. Hofstadter in *Gödel, Escher, Bach: An Eternal Golden Braid* (New York: Vintage, 1980).

5. *Tropics of Discourse: Essays in Cultural Criticism* (Baltimore, Md.: Johns Hopkins University Press, 1978), 3.

6. Howard Margolis, *Patterns, Thinking, and Cognition: A Theory of Judgment* (Chicago: University of Chicago Press, 1987), 148.

For these reasons I have found it useful to make the distinction between standard logic and an alternative, or antilogic to be found in Kafka's and to a lesser extent occasionally in Planck's texts. One cannot deny the systematic rigor of Kafka's texts, whatever that rigor may be called. Thus there are alternative rigorous modes of reasoning that exist outside the conventions of logic. I contend that these modes transgress the limits of logic and multiply meanings in language. By this growth in complexity they enhance the knowledge that may be found in a text. At the same time such antilogic is subversive for it implies scepticism, even deep mistrust of naming and defining, of categorizing and reducing. With the conviction that naming is treacherous and, unavoidably, using language means lying, we return to Nietzsche as the godfather of such extralegal notions. Much of knowledge, nevertheless, depends upon categorizing, naming, and defining, and a written text inevitably also entails and proposes such knowledge.

There are, obviously, many kinds of knowing. For example, there is a felt association, a knowing that means recognition, even mutual recognition, such as "I know that tree." For this knowledge no words are required; as a knowledge shared by equals, it obviates mastery. There is a knowing that depends upon identification by selected, severed evidence and delivers mastery over the known: it is the knowing of science. Closely connected is the knowing demonstrated in definitions—a kind of knowing characterized by closure. There is also the knowing upon which the existence of the known in the mind of the individual knower depends. Most knowledge of events is late knowledge; until it arrives, these events did not exist for the knower. Speculatively, this condition can be connected to the epistemology of quantum mechanics, as we saw in chapter 2. These kinds of knowing can either be mutually exclusive, or they can overlap and be mutually enhancing. They may be subsumed in the kind of knowing described by Maturana and Varela as "autopoesis."[7] Living beings are characterized by an "autopoetic organization," which means

---

7. Humberto R. Maturana and Francisco J. Varela, *The Tree of Knowledge: The*

they are continually self-producing in a dynamic recursive process. In *The Trial*, Josef K. proposes his view of the autopoetic self: "like all living beings [he] could one day surprise with new capacities, however innocuous he might seem today" (212, uncompleted chapters).

According to Maturana and Varela, "a theory of knowledge ought to show how knowing generates the explanation of knowing. This situation is very different from what we usually find, where the phenomenon of explaining and the phenomenon explained belong to different domains" (*Tree of Knowledge*, 239). Recursiveness necessarily means that origins are hidden: "All we can do is generate explanations, through language, that reveal the mechanism of bringing forth a world" (*Tree of Knowledge*, 242). The authors conclude that "[t]he *knowledge of knowledge compels*. It compels us to adopt an attitude of permanent vigilance against the temptation of certainty. It compels us to recognize that certainty is not a proof of truth" (245). I believe that the reciprocity of language and meanings within and between Kafka's and Planck's texts suggest the very "knowledge of knowledge" that Maturana and Varela develop in an explanation of recursiveness beginning with the autopoetic molecular origins of life. It seems to me that a dialogic reading that foregrounds language can be an "autopoetic" process in which knowledge "generates the explanation of knowing," the explaining being engaged in a reciprocally generative process with the explained. In the view of Maturana and Varela, cognition, an interactive process by which the nervous system "brings forth a world" (169), has profound ethical implications for human behavior "since every human act has an ethical meaning because it is an act of constitution of the human world" (247). The ethical mandate, in their terms, of Kafka's texts is that we "adopt an attitude of permanent vigilance against the temptation of certainty," of Planck's texts that we "recognize that certainty is not proof of truth."

Biological Roots of Human Understanding, trans. Robert Paolucci (Boston: New Science Library, 1988).

Bibliography

For the sake of easier accessibility to readers, the bibliography is divided into two sections: (1) Kafka, language, logic, art, and literary criticism/theory; and (2) Planck, history and philosophy of science, scientific principles and concepts, and mathematics.

Kafka

Anderson, Wilda C. *Between the Library and the Laboratory: The Language of Chemistry in Eighteenth-Century France*. Baltimore, Md.: Johns Hopkins University Press, 1984.

Arnheim, Rudolf. *The Power of the Center: A Study of Composition in the Visual Arts*. Rev. ed. Berkeley: University of California Press, 1982.

Bakhtin, Mikhail. *The Dialogic Imagination: Four Essays by M. M. Bakhtin*. Edited by Michael Holquist. Translated by Caryl Emerson and Michael Holquist. Austin: University of Texas Press, 1981.

Bazerman, Charles. *Shaping Written Knowledge: The Genre and Activity of the Experimental Article in Science*. Madison: University of Wisconsin Press, 1988.

Beer, Gillian. *Darwin's Plots: Evolutionary Narrative in Darwin, George Eliot, and Nineteenth-Century Fiction*. London: Routledge and Kegan Paul, 1983.

——. "Problems of Description in the Language of Discovery." In *One Culture: Essays in Science and Literature*, edited by George Levine. Madison: University of Wisconsin Press, 1987.

Benjamin, Andrew E., Geoffrey N. Cantor, and John R. R. Christie, eds. *The Figural and the Literal: Problems of Language in the History of Science and Philosophy, 1630–1800*. Manchester: Manchester University Press, 1987.

Benjamin, Walter. *Illuminations*. Edited by Hannah Arendt. Translated by Harry Zohn. New York: Harcourt, Brace and World, 1968.

Binder, Hartmut, ed. *Kafka-Handbuch*. 2 vols. Stuttgart: Alfred Kröner, 1979.

Bloom, Harold. *The Anxiety of Influence*. New York: Oxford University Press, 1973.

———. *A Map of Misreading*. Oxford: Oxford University Press, 1975.

Bloomfield, Leonard. *Linguistic Aspects of Science*. International Encyclopedia of Unified Science, vol. 1, no. 4. Chicago: University of Chicago Press, 1939.

Brod, Max. *Franz Kafka: Eine Biographie*. New York: Schocken, 1946.

———. *Über Franz Kafka*. Frankfurt am Main: Fischer Bücherei, 1966.

Cassirer, Ernst. "The Influence of Language Upon the Development of Scientific Thought." *The Journal of Philosophy* 39 (January–December 1942): 309–27.

Christie, John R. R. "Introduction: Rhetoric and Writing in Early Modern Philosophy and Science." In *The Figural and the Literal*, edited by Andrew E. Benjamin, Geoffrey N. Cantor, and John R. R. Christie.

Conan Doyle, Arthur. *The Annotated Sherlock Holmes*. 2 vols. Edited by William S. Baring-Gould. New York: Clarkson N. Potter, 1967.

Corngold, Stanley. *Franz Kafka: The Necessity of Form*. Ithaca, N.Y.: Cornell University Press, 1988.

———. "Kafka's Other Metamorphosis." In *Kafka and the Contemporary Critical Performance*, edited by Alan Udoff.

———. "Metaphor and Chiasmus in Kafka." *Newsletter of the Kafka Society of America*, no. 2 (December 1981): 23–31.

Craige, Betty Jean. *Reconnection: Dualism to Holism in Literary Study*. Athens, Ga.: University of Georgia Press, 1988.

Curtis, James M. "Epistemological Historicism in the Arts and Sciences." In *Science and Literature*, edited by James M. Heath.

de Man, Paul. *Allegories of Reading: Figural Language in Rousseau, Nietzsche, Rilke, and Proust*. New Haven, Conn.: Yale University Press, 1979.

———. *Blindness and Insight: Essays in the Rhetoric of Contemporary Criticism*. Minneapolis: University of Minnesota Press, 1983.

———. *The Resistance to Theory*. Minneapolis: University of Minnesota Press, 1986.

———. *The Rhetoric of Romanticism*. New York: Columbia University Press, 1984.

Derrida, Jacques. "Devant la Loi." Translated by Avital Ronell. In *Kafka and the Contemporary Critical Performance*, edited by Alan Udoff.

———. *Of Grammatology*. Translated by Gayatri Chakravorty Spivak. Baltimore, Md.: Johns Hopkins University Press, 1976.

———. "White Mythology: Metaphor in the Text of Philosophy." Translated by F. C. T. Moore. *New Literary History* 6 (Autumn 1974): 5–74.

Eco, Umberto, and Thomas A. Sebeok, eds. *The Sign of Three: Dupin, Holmes, Peirce.* Bloomington, Ind.: Indiana University Press, 1983.

Elm, Theo. "Der Prozeß." In *Kafka-Handbuch*, edited by Hartmut Binder, vol. 2.

Facione, Peter A., and Donald Scherer. *Logic and Logical Thinking.* Reprint of 1978 edition. Woodbridge, Conn.: Oxbow, 1984.

Gilbert, Felix. "Einstein's Europe." In *Some Strangeness in the Proportion: A Centennial Symposium to Celebrate the Achievements of Albert Einstein*, edited by Harry Woolf.

Hayles, N. Katherine. "Chaos as Orderly Disorder: Shifting Ground in Contemporary Literature and Science." *New Literary History* 20 (Winter 1989): 305–22.

Heath, James M., ed. *Science and Literature.* Special issue of *Bucknell Review* 27, no. 2. Lewisburg, Pa.: Bucknell University Press, 1983.

Hermsdorf, Klaus, ed. *Franz Kafka: Amtliche Schriften.* Berlin: Akademie, 1984.

Jacobs, Louis. *Studies in Talmudic Logic and Methodology.* London: Vallentine, Mitchell, 1961.

———. *The Talmudic Argument: A Study in Talmudic Reasoning and Methodology.* Cambridge: Cambridge University Press, 1984.

Jacobson, Roman. "Linguistics and Communication Theory." In *Roman Jacobson: Selected Writings 2, Word and Language.* The Hague: Mouton, 1971.

Johnson, Barbara. *The Critical Difference.* Baltimore, Md.: Johns Hopkins University Press, 1980.

Kafka, Franz. *Briefe 1902–1924.* Edited by Max Brod. Frankfurt am Main: S. Fischer, 1958.

———. *Briefe an Felice.* Edited by Erich Heller and Jürgen Born. Frankfurt am Main: S. Fischer, 1967.

———. *Der Prozeß.* Edited by Max Brod. Frankfurt am Main: S. Fischer, 1986.

———. *Tagebücher 1910–1923.* Edited by Max Brod. Frankfurt am Main: S. Fischer, 1986.

Kepes, Gyorgy, ed. *Structure in Art and Science.* New York: Braziller, 1965.

Koelb, Clayton. *Kafka's Rhetoric: The Passion of Reading.* Ithaca, N. Y.: Cornell University Press, 1989.

Kuna, Franz, ed. *On Kafka: Semi-Centenary Perspectives.* New York: Barnes and Noble, 1976.

———. "Rage for Verification: Kafka and Einstein." In *On Kafka: Semi-Centenary Perspectives,* edited by Franz Kuna.

Lakoff, George, and Mark Johnson. *Metaphors We Live By.* Chicago: University of Chicago Press, 1980.

Levine, George. Introduction to *One Culture: Essays in Science and Literature,* edited by George Levine.

———, ed. *One Culture: Essays in Science and Literature.* Madison: University of Wisconsin Press, 1987.

Livingston, Paisley. *Literary Knowledge: Humanistic Inquiry and the Philosophy of Science.* Ithaca, N. Y.: Cornell University Press, 1988.

Margolis, Howard. *Patterns, Thinking, and Cognition.* Chicago: University of Chicago Press, 1987.

Markley, Robert M. "From Kant to Chaos: Physics, Metaphysics, and the Institutionalization of Knowledge." Paper presented at the seventh annual meeting of GRIP, "Disciplinarity: Formations, Rhetorics, Histories," Minneapolis, April 1989.

———. "Objectivity as Ideology: Boyle, Newton, and the Languages of Science." *Genre* 16 (Winter 1983): 355–72.

———. "(Re)constructing Theory in Literature and Science: Pragmatism, Newtonian Science, and the Fictions of Comprehensiveness." Paper presented at the annual convention of the South Atlantic Modern Language Association. Atlanta, November 1987.

Megill, Allan. *Prophets of Extremity: Nietzsche, Heidegger, Foucault, Derrida.* Berkeley: University of California Press, 1985.

Miller, J. Hillis. *The Ethics of Reading: Kant, de Man, Eliot, Trollope, James, and Benjamin.* New York: Columbia University Press, 1987.

Millikan, Ruth Garrett. *Language, Thought, and Other Biological Categories.* Cambridge, Mass.: MIT Press, 1984.

Mitchell, W. J. T., ed. *The Politics of Interpretation.* Chicago: University of Chicago Press, 1983.

Morot-Sir, Edouard. Review of *Between the Library and the Laboratory: The Language of Chemistry in Eighteenth-Century France,* by Wilda C. Anderson. *South Atlantic Review* 51 (May 1986): 125–29.

Neff, Kurt. "Kafkas Schatten: Eine Dokumentation zur Breitenwirkung." In *Kafka-Handbuch* edited by Hartmut Binder, vol. 2.

Neubauer, John. "Models for the History of Science and Literature." In *Science and Literature,* edited by James M. Heath.

Neusner, Jacob. "Why No Science in Judaism?" Lecture at Tulane University, New Orleans, La. Printed by Jewish Studies Program, Tulane University, 1987.

Nietzsche, Friedrich. *The Complete Works of Friedrich Nietzsche.* Vol. 2, *Early Greek Philosophy.* Edited by Oscar Levy. Translated by Maximillian A. Mügge. London: T. N. Foulis, 1911.

———. *Friedrich Nietzsche: Sämtliche Werke.* Kritische Studienausgabe in 15 Bänden. Edited by Giorgio Colli and Mazzino Montinari, vol. 1. Berlin: Deutscher Taschenbuch Verlag/de Gruyter, 1980.

Norris, Margot. *Beasts of the Modern Imagination: Darwin, Nietzsche, Kafka, Ernst and Lawrence.* Baltimore, Md.: Johns Hopkins University Press, 1985.

Paulson, William R. *The Noise of Culture: Literary Texts in a World of Information.* Ithaca, N. Y.: Cornell University Press, 1988.

Pawel, Ernst. *The Nightmare of Reason: A Life of Franz Kafka.* New York: Farrar Straus Giroux, 1984.

Perelman, Ch. *The New Rhetoric and the Humanities: Essays on Rhetoric and its Applications.* Dordrecht, Holland: Reidel, 1979.

Rolleston, James. Introduction to *Twentieth Century Interpretations of "The Trial": A Collection of Critical Essays.* Edited by James Rolleston. Englewood Cliffs, N. J.: Prentice-Hall, 1976.

———. "Kafka-Criticism: A Typological Perspective in the Centenary Year." In *Kafka's Contextuality,* edited by Alan Udoff. Baltimore, Md.: Gordian Press and Baltimore Hebrew College, 1986.

Rorty, Richard. *Philosophy and the Mirror of Nature.* Princeton, N.J.: Princeton University Press, 1979.

———. "Philosophy as a Kind of Writing: An Essay on Derrida." *New Literary History* 10 (Autumn 1978): 141–60.

———. "Text and Lumps." *New Literary History* 17 (Autumn 1985): 1–30.

Serrès, Michel. *Hermes: Literature, Science, Philosophy.* Edited by Josué V. Harari and David F. Bell. Baltimore, Md.: Johns Hopkins University Press, 1982.

Smith, Cyril Stanley. *A Search for Structure: Selected Essays on Science, Art, and History.* Cambridge, Mass.: MIT Press, 1981.

Sommers, Fred. *The Logic of Natural Language.* Oxford: Oxford University Press, 1982.

Speidel, Walter. *A Complete Contextual Concordance to Franz Kafka "Der Prozess."* Leeds, England: W. S. Maney and Son, 1978.

Spivak, Gyatri Chakravorty. Translator's Preface to *Of Grammatology*, by Jacques Derrida.

Stehr, Nico, and Volker Meja. *Society and Knowledge: Contemporary Perspectives in the Sociology of Knowledge*. New Brunswick, N. J.: Transaction Books, 1984.

Stepan, Nancy Leys. "Race and Gender: The Role of Analogy in Science." *ISIS* 77 (1986): 261–77.

Sussman, Henry. *Franz Kafka: Geometrician of Metaphor*. Madison, Wis.: Coda Press, 1979.

Thieberger, Richard. "Sprache." In *Kafka-Handbuch*, edited by Hartmut Binder, vol. 2.

Thorlby, Anthony. "Anti-Mimesis: Kafka and Wittgenstein." In *On Kafka: Semi-Centenary Perspectives*, edited by Franz Kuna.

Udoff, Alan. "Before the Question of the Laws: Kafkan Reflections." In *Kafka and the Contemporary Critical Performance*, edited by Alan Udoff.

———. Introduction to *Kafka and the Contemporary Critical Performance*.

———, ed. *Kafka and the Contemporary Critical Performance*. Bloomington, Ind.: Indiana University Press, 1987.

Wagenbach, Klaus. *Franz Kafka: Bilder aus seinem Leben*. Berlin: Wagenbach, 1983.

———. *Franz Kafka: Eine Biographie seiner Jugend, 1883–1912*. Bern: Francke, 1958.

White, Hayden. *Tropics of Discourse: Essays in Cultural Criticism*. Baltimore, Md.: Johns Hopkins University Press, 1978.

Whorf, Benjamin Lee. *Language, Thought, and Reality: Selected Writings of Benjamin Lee Whorf*. Edited by John B. Carroll, 1958. Reprint. Cambridge, Mass.: MIT Press, 1988.

Planck

Amsler, Mark, ed. *The Language of Creativity: Models, Problem-Solving, Discourse*. Studies in Science and Culture, vol. 2. Newark, Del.: University of Delaware Press, 1986.

Arbib, Michael A., and Mary B. Hesse. *The Construction of Reality*. Cambridge: Cambridge University Press, 1986.

Aspray, William, and Philip Kitcher, eds. *History and Philosophy of Modern Mathematics*. Minnesota Studies in the Philosophy of Science, vol. 11. Minneapolis: University of Minnesota Press, 1988.

Berge, Pierre, Yves Pomeau, and Christian Vidal. *Order within Chaos: Towards a Deterministic Approach to Turbulence*. New York: Wiley, 1984.

Bohr, Niels. "Discussion with Einstein on Epistemological Problems in Atomic Physics." In *Albert Einstein: Philosopher-Scientist*, edited by Paul Arthur Schilpp.

——. *Essays 1958–1962 on Atomic Physics and Human Knowledge*. New York: Interscience, 1963.

Boorse, Henry A., and Lloyd Motz, eds. *The World of the Atom*. 2 vols. New York: Basic Books, 1966.

Born, Max. "Max Karl Ernst Ludwig Planck." In *The World of the Atom*, edited by Henry A. Boorse and Lloyd Motz, vol. 1.

Brassard, Gilles, and Claude Crepeau. "Non-Transitive Transfer of Confidence: A *Perfect* Zero-Knowledge Interative Protocol for SAT and Beyond." In *Proceedings of the 27th Annual Symposium on Foundations of Computer Science*. Washington, D.C.: IEEE Publications, 1986, 188–95.

Brown, Harold I. *Perception, Theory and Commitment: The New Philosophy of Science*. Chicago: University of Chicago Press, 1979.

Bunge, Mario. *Causality and Modern Science*. 3d rev. ed. New York: Dover, 1979.

Čapek, Milič. *The Philosophical Impact of Contemporary Physics*. Princeton, N. J.: D. Van Nostrand, 1961.

Cassirer, Ernst. *Determinism and Indeterminism in Modern Physics*. Translated by O. Theodor Benfey. London: Oxford University Press, 1956.

Churchland, Paul M. "Karl Popper's Philosophy of Science." *Canadian Journal of Philosophy* 5 (September 1975): 145–56.

Cline, Barbara Lovett. *Men Who Made a New Physics*. 1965. Reprint. Chicago: University of Chicago Press, 1987.

Cohen, Robert S., and Thomas Schnelle, eds. *Cognition and Fact: Materials on Ludwik Fleck*. Dordrecht, Holland: Reidel, 1986.

——. Introduction to *Cognition and Fact: Materials on Ludwik Fleck*.

Cohen, Robert S., and Marx W. Wartofsky, eds. *Boston Studies in the Philosophy of Science*, vol. 3. Dordrecht, Holland: D. Reidel, 1967.

——, eds. *A Portrait of Twenty-five Years: Boston Colloquium for the Philosophy of Science 1960–1985*. Dordrecht, Holland: D. Reidel, 1985.

Dantzig, Tobias. *Number: The Language of Science*. 4th rev. ed. Garden City, N. Y.: Doubleday, 1954.

Einstein, Albert. "Max Planck als Forscher." *Die Naturwissenschaften* 1, no. 45 (7 November 1913): 1077–79.

——. *Relativity: The Special and the General Theory.* Translated by Robert W. Lawson. New York: Bonanza, 1961.

Elkana, Y. "The Historical Roots of Modern Physics." In *Proceedings of the International School of Physics "Enrico Fermi": History of Twentieth Century Physics,* edited by C. Weiner.

Eucken, Arnold. *Verhandlungen des Conseil Solvay 1911: Die Theorie der Strahlung und der Quanten.* Abhandlungen der Deutschen Bunsen-Gesellschaft für angewandte physikalische Chemie, no. 7. Halle: Wilhelm Knapp, 1914.

Feigenbaum, Mitchell J. "Universal Behavior in Nonlinear Systems." *Los Alamos Science* 1 (Summer 1980): 4–27.

Feyerabend, Paul K. "On the Improvement of the Sciences and the Arts, and the Possible Identity of the Two." In *Boston Studies in the Philosophy of Science,* edited by Robert S. Cohen and Marx W. Wartofsky, vol. 3.

Finocchiaro, Maurice A. *Galileo and the Art of Reasoning: Rhetorical Foundations of Logic and Scientific Method.* Dordrecht, Holland: Reidel, 1980.

Fleck, Ludwik. *Entstehung und Entwicklung einer wissenschaftlichen Tatsache: Einführung in die Lehre vom Denkstil und Denkkollektiv.* 1935. Reprint. Frankfurt am Main: Suhrkamp, 1980.

——. *Genesis and Development of a Scientific Fact.* 1935. Reprint. Translated by Fred Bradley and Thaddeus J. Trenn. Chicago: University of Chicago Press, 1979.

Flegg, Graham. *Numbers: Their History and Meaning.* New York: Schocken, 1983.

Forman, Paul. "*Kausalität, Anschaulichkeit,* and *Individualität,* or How Cultural Values Prescribed the Character and the Lessons Ascribed to Quantum Mechanics." In *Society and Knowledge: Contemporary Perspectives in the Sociology of Knowledge,* edited by Nico Stehr and Volker Meja.

——. "Scientific Internationalism and the Weimar Physicists: The Ideology and Its Manipulation in Germany after World War I." *ISIS* 64 (June 1973): 151–80.

——. "Weimar Culture, Causality, and Quantum Theory, 1918–1927: Adaptation by German Physicists and Mathematicians to a Hostile Intellectual Environment." *Historical Studies in the Physical Sciences* 3 (1971): 1–115.

Frank, Philipp. *Einstein: His Life and Times.* New York: Knopf, 1957.

——. *Foundations of Physics.* International Encyclopedia of Unified

Science. Vol. 1, no. 7. 1946. Reprint. Chicago: University of Chicago Press, 1969.

Frawley, William. "Science, Discourse, and Knowledge Representation: Toward a Computational Model of Science and Scientific Innovation." In *The Languages of Creativity: Models, Problem-Solving, Discourse*, edited by Mark Amsler.

Friedman, Michael. "Logical Truth and Analyticity in Carnap's 'Logical Syntax of Language.'" In *History and Philosophy of Modern Mathematics*, edited by William Aspray and Philip Kitcher.

Gillies, C. B. "Crossing-over (genetics)." *McGraw-Hill Encyclopedia of Science and Technology*. 6th ed. Vol. 4. New York: McGraw-Hill, 1987.

Gleick, James. *Chaos: Making a New Science*. New York: Viking, 1987.

Gödel, Kurt. *On Formally Undecidable Propositions of "Principia Mathematica" and Related Systems*. Translated by B. Meltzer. New York: Basic, 1962.

——. "Über formal untentscheidbare Sätze der *Principia Mathematica* und verwandter Systeme, I." *Monatshefte für Mathematik und Physik* 38 (1931): 173–98.

Goldberg, Stanley. "Max Planck's Philosophy of Nature and His Elaboration of the Special Theory of Relativity." *Historical Studies in the Physical Sciences* 7 (1976): 125–60.

Goldreich, Oded, Silvio Micali, and Avi Wigderson. "Proofs that Yield Nothing But their Validity and a Methodology of Cryptographic Protocol Design." In *Proceedings of the 27th Annual Symposium on Foundations of Computer Science*. Washington, D.C.: IEEE Publications, 1986, 174–87.

Gregory, Bruce. *Inventing Reality: Physics as Language*. New York: Wiley, 1988.

Hankins, Thomas L. "Triplets and Triads: Sir William Rowan Hamilton on the Metaphysics of Mathematics." *ISIS* 68 (1977): 175–93.

Hartmann, Hans. *Schöpfer des neuen Weltbildes: Grosse Physiker unserer Zeit*. Bonn: Athenäum, 1952.

Heilbron, J. L. *The Dilemmas of an Upright Man: Max Planck as Spokesman for German Science*. Berkeley: University of California Press, 1986.

——. "Lectures on the History of Atomic Physics 1900–1922." In *Proceedings of the International School of Physics "Enrico Fermi": History of Twentieth Century Physics*, edited by C. Weiner.

Heisenberg, Werner. *Physics and Philosophy*. New York: Harper and Row, 1958.

Hellman, Geoffrey. "How to Gödel a Frege-Russell: Gödel's Incompleteness Theorems and Logicism." *NOÛS* 15 (November 1981): 451–68.

Hermann, Armin. *The Genesis of Quantum Theory (1899–1913)*. Translated by Claude W. Nash. Cambridge, Mass.: MIT Press, 1971.

———. *Max Planck in Selbstzeugnissen und Bilddokumenten*. Reinbek bei Hamburg: Rowohlt, 1973.

Hesse, Mary. *Revolutions and Reconstructions in the Philosophy of Science*. Bloomington, Ind.: Indiana University Press, 1980.

Hiebert, Erwin N. *The Conception of Thermodynamics in the Scientific Thought of Mach and Planck*. Bericht Nr. 5/68. Freiburg im Breisgau: Ernst-Mach-Institut.

Hirosige, Tetu, and Sigeo Nisio. "Formation of Bohr's Theory of Atomic Constitution." *Japanese Studies in the History of Science* 3 (1964): 6–28.

Hofstadter, Douglas P. *Gödel, Escher, Bach: An Eternal Golden Braid*. New York: Vintage, 1980.

Holton, Gerald. *The Advancement of Science and its Burdens*. Cambridge: Cambridge University Press, 1986.

———. *Introduction to Concepts and Theories in Physical Science*. Cambridge, Mass.: Addison-Wesley, 1953.

———. *Thematic Origins of Scientific Thought: Kepler to Einstein*. Cambridge, Mass.: Harvard University Press, 1973.

Hübner, Kurt. *Critique of Scientific Reason*. Translated by Paul R. Dixon, Jr., and Hollis M. Dixon. Chicago: University of Chicago Press, 1983.

Hund, Friedrich. *The History of Quantum Theory*. Translated by Gordon Reece. New York: Harper and Row, 1974.

Jammer, Max. *The Conceptual Development of Quantum Mechanics*. New York: McGraw-Hill, 1966.

Jungnickel, Christa, and Russell McCormmach. *Intellectual Mastery of Nature: Theoretical Physics from Ohm to Einstein*. 2 vols. Chicago: University of Chicago Press, 1986.

Kangro, Hans. "Planck, Max Karl Ernst Ludwig." *Dictionary of Scientific Biography*, vol. 11. New York: Charles Scribner's Sons, 1975.

———, ed. *Planck's Original Papers in Quantum Physics*. German and English ed. Translated by D. ter Haar and Stephen G. Brush. London: Taylor and Francis, 1972.

Keller, Evelyn Fox. *A Feeling for the Organism: The Life and Work of Barbara McClintock*. New York: Freeman, 1983.

———. "Fractured Images of Science, Language, and Power: A Postmodern Optic, or Just Bad Eyesight?" Paper presented at the seventh annual GRIP Conference. Minneapolis, April 1989.

———. *Reflections on Gender and Science.* New Haven, Conn.: Yale University Press, 1985.

Kern, Leslie H., Herbert L. Mirels, and Virgil G. Hinshaw. "Scientists' Understanding of Propositional Logic: An Experimental Investigation." *Social Studies of Science* 13 (February 1983): 131–46.

King, Allen L. Foreword to *Planck's Original Papers in Quantum Physics*, edited by Hans Kangro.

Kitcher, Philip. "Mathematical Rigor—Who Needs It?" *NOÛS* 15 (November 1981): 469–93.

Klein, Martin J. "The Beginnings of Quantum Theory." In *Proceedings of the International School of Physics "Enrico Fermi": History of Twentieth Century Physics*, edited by C. Weiner.

———. "Max Planck and the Beginnings of the Quantum Theory." *Archive for History of the Exact Sciences* 1 (September 1960): 459–79.

———. "Mechanical Explanation at the End of the Nineteenth Century." *Centaurus* 17 (1973): 58–82.

———. "No Firm Foundation: Einstein and the Early Quantum Theory." In *Some Strangeness in the Proportion: A Centennial Symposium to Celebrate the Achievements of Albert Einstein*, edited by Harry Woolf.

———. "Planck, Entropy, and Quanta, 1901–1906." *The Natural Philosopher*, vol. 1. New York: Blaisdell, 1963.

———. "Thermodynamics and Quanta in Planck's Work." *Physics Today*, no. 11 (November 1966): 23–32.

Kline, Morris. *Mathematics: The Loss of Certainty.* Oxford: Oxford University Press, 1980.

Kuhn, Thomas S. *Black-Body Theory and the Quantum Discontinuity 1894–1912.* 1978. Reprint with new afterword. Chicago: University of Chicago Press, 1987.

———. "Einstein's Critique of Planck." In *Some Strangeness in the Proportion: A Centennial Symposium to Celebrate the Achievements of Albert Einstein*, edited by Harry Woolf.

———. *The Essential Tension: Selected Studies in Scientific Tradition and Change.* Chicago: University of Chicago Press, 1977.

———. "Metaphor in Science." In *Metaphor and Thought*, edited by Andrew Ortony. Cambridge: Cambridge University Press, 1979.

———. *The Structure of Scientific Revolutions.* 2d rev. ed. Chicago: University of Chicago Press, 1970.

Latour, Bruno. *Science in Action.* Cambridge, Mass.: Harvard University Press, 1987.

Maddy, Penelope. "Sets and Numbers." *NOÛS* 15 (November 1981): 495–511.

Mandelbrot, Benoit B. *The Fractal Geometry of Nature.* Rev. ed. San Francisco: W. H. Freeman, 1983.

Maturana, Humberto R., and Francisco J. Varela. *The Tree of Knowledge: The Biological Roots of Human Understanding.* Translated by Robert Paolucci. Boston: New Science Library, 1988.

McCormmach, Russell. "Editor's Foreword." *Historical Studies in the Physical Sciences* 3 (1971): ix–xxiv.

———. *Night Thoughts of a Classical Physicist.* New York: Avon, 1983.

Menninger, Karl. *Number Words and Number Symbols: A Cultural History of Numbers.* Translated by Paul Broneer from rev. German ed., 1958. Cambridge, Mass.: MIT Press, 1969.

Miller, Arthur I. *Albert Einstein's Special Theory of Relativity: Emergence (1905) and Early Interpretation (1905–1911).* Reading, Mass.: Addison-Wesley, 1981.

———. "Visualization Lost and Regained: The Genesis of the Quantum Theory in the Period 1913–27." In *On Aesthetics in Science,* edited by Judith Wechsler.

Morris, Desmond. *The Biology of Art: A Study of the Picture-Making Behavior of the Great Apes and Its Relationship to Human Art.* New York: Knopf, 1962.

O'Neill, R. V., D. L. DeAngelis, J. B. Waide, and T. F. H. Allen. *A Hierarchical Concept of Ecosystems.* Princeton, N.J.: Princeton University Press, 1986.

Pattee, H. H. "The Complementarity Principle in Biological and Social Structures." *Journal of Social and Biological Structures* 1 (April 1978): 191–200.

Peterson, Ivars. *The Mathematical Tourist.* New York: Freeman, 1988.

Planck, Max. *A Bibliography of his Non-technical Writings.* Berkeley Papers in the History of Science. Berkeley: Office of the History of Science and Technology, University of California, Berkeley, 1977.

———. "On Mach's Theory of Physical Knowledge." In *Physical Reality: Philosophical Essays on Twentieth-Century Physics,* edited by Stephen Toulmin.

———. *Physikalische Abhandlungen und Vorträge*. 3 vols. Braunschweig: Friedr. Vieweg und Sohn, 1958.

———. *Planck's Original Papers in Quantum Physics*. German and English ed. Edited by Hans Kangro. Translated by D. ter Haar and Stephen G. Brush. London: Taylor and Francis, 1972.

———. "Positivism and External Reality." *The International Forum* (January 1, 1931): 12–16 and (February 15, 1931): 14–19.

———. *A Survey of Physical Theory*. Translated by R. Jones and D. H. Williams. New York: Dover, 1960.

———. *The Theory of Heat Radiation*. Translated by Morton Masius. 1914. Reprint. New York: Dover, 1959.

———. "The Unity of the Physical World-Picture." In *Physical Reality: Philosophical Essays on Twentieth-Century Physics*, edited by Stephen Toulmin.

———. *Vorlesungen über die Theorie der Wärmestrahlung*. 2d rev. ed. Leipzig: Johann Ambrosius Barth, 1913.

———. *Vorträge und Erinnerungen*. 1949. Reprint. Darmstadt: Wissenschaftliche Buchgesellschaft, 1965.

———. *Where is Science Going?* Translated by James Murphy. 1933. Reprint. Woodbridge, Conn.: Oxbow, 1981.

Poincaré, Henri. *Mathematics and Science: Last Essays [Dernières Pensées]*. 1913. Translated by John W. Boldue. New York: Dover, 1963.

Poundstone, William. *The Recursive Universe: Cosmic Complexity and the Limits of Scientific Knowledge*. Chicago: Contemporary, 1985.

Prigogine, Ilya, and Isabelle Stengers. *Order Out of Chaos: Man's New Dialogue With Nature*. New York: Bantam, 1984.

Resnik, Michael. "Mathematical Knowledge and Pattern Recognition." *Canadian Journal of Philosophy* 5 (September 1975): 25–39.

———. "Mathematics as a Science of Patterns: Epistemology." *NOÛS* 16 (March 1982): 95–105.

———. "Mathematics as a Science of Patterns: Ontology and Reference." *NOÛS* 15 (November 1981): 529–50.

Schilpp, Paul Arthur, ed. *Albert Einstein: Philosopher-Scientist*. 3d ed. The Library of Living Philosophers, vol. 7. La Salle, Ill.: Open Court, 1970.

Schrödinger, Erwin. *Nature and the Greeks*. Cambridge: Cambridge University Press, 1954.

Stent, Gunther S., ed. *Morality as a Biological Phenomenon*. Berkeley: University of California Press, 1980.

Toulmin, Stephen. "The Construal of Reality: Criticism in Modern and Postmodern Science." In *The Politics of Interpretation*, edited by W. J. T. Mitchell.

——. "Ludwik Fleck and the Historical Interpretation of Science." In *Cognition and Fact: Materials on Ludwik Fleck*, edited by Robert S. Cohen and Thomas Schnelle.

——, ed. *Physical Reality: Philosophical Essays on Twentieth-Century Physics*. New York: Harper and Row, 1970.

Wayner, Peter. "Zero-Knowledge Proofs." *Byte* 12 (October 1987): 149–52.

Wechsler, Judith. *On Aesthetics in Science*. Cambridge, Mass.: MIT Press, 1978.

Weiner, C., ed. *Proceedings of the International School of Physics "Enrico Fermi": History of Twentieth Century Physics*. New York: Academic Press, 1977.

"When ignorance is bliss." *The Economist* (June 20, 1987): 93–94.

Whyte, Lancelot Law, Albert G. Wilson, and Donna Wilson, eds. *Hierarchical Structures*. New York: American Elsevier, 1969.

Willis, Jr., William D., and Robert G. Grossman. *Medical Neurobiology: Neuroanatomical and Neurophysiological Principles Basic to Clinical Neuroscience*. 3d ed. St. Louis: Mosby, 1981.

Wilson, E. O. *Biophilia*. Cambridge, Mass.: Harvard University Press, 1984.

——. *Sociobiology*. Abridged ed. Cambridge, Mass.: Belknap, 1980.

Woolf, Harry, ed. *Some Strangeness in the Proportion: A Centennial Symposium to Celebrate the Achievements of Albert Einstein*. Reading, Mass.: Addison-Wesley, 1980.

Index

Hesse, Mary B., 5, 25–27, 43, 135, 137

Hierarchy, 16, 18–20, 22–23, 38, 52, 58, 86, 101–2, 106, 108, 117, 128, 132, 157

Hofstadter, Douglas P., 5, 21, 44n.66

Holmes, Sherlock, 2, 9–14, 16, 28, 38, 197–99

Holton, Gerald, 62n.16

Insurance Institute. *See* Workers Accident Insurance Institute for the Kingdom of Bohemia in Prague

Irreversible systems and processes, 82, 133, 173, 180

Irreversibility, 91, 113, 180

Jacobs, Louis, 93n.9, 119n.30

Johnson, Barbara, 172

Johnson, Mark, 25

Josef K. (*The Trial*), 33, 36–38, 89–90, 108–16, 118–31, 147, 151, 154, 167–69, 185–86, 194, 203

Kafka, Franz, 1–2, 5–7, 9–11, 16–17, 20, 24, 26–28, 30, 34–36, 38–42, 47, 55, 73, 84–85, 88–102, 104, 106–7, 112, 114–16, 118–19, 121–23, 125, 127, 130–33, 139–40, 145–53, 155, 159–60, 170–71, 173–74, 176–78, 180–85, 189–93, 195, 197, 202–3

Kafkaesque, 28, 30–31, 135

Kant, Immanuel (Kantian), 49–50, 78, 85

Keller, Evelyn Fox, 3n.2, 86, 87

Klein, Martin J., 140–41, 143–44, 159

Kline, Morris, 199–200

Knowledge, 1, 25, 29, 35, 37, 42–43, 47–48, 60, 62–66, 72–73, 83, 88, 91, 93, 95, 97–98, 100–104, 106–8, 110, 114–15, 117–18, 120–21, 132–33, 135, 138–40, 156, 163, 170, 179, 180–84, 188, 190–91, 193–95, 202–3

Koelb, Clayton, 6n.6, 41n.64, 122n.32

Kuhn, Thomas S., 65n.22, 138, 140–44, 154, 159–60, 171–73

Lakoff, George, 25

Latour, Bruno, 165n.34

Law(s), 20, 22, 27, 31–32, 41–45, 51–52, 55, 57, 59–60, 73, 76, 79, 81–88, 91–93, 96–98, 102, 106, 114, 116–17, 119, 122, 124, 130, 132, 138, 143, 145, 159, 161–63, 165, 170, 172, 174–76, 193–95, 200

Lectures on the Theory of Thermal Radiation (Planck), 139, 142, 171–75, 177–80, 185–86, 193, 195

Light, 96, 120–22, 143, 147, 156–57, 164, 175–76, 189–91, 193; speed of, 28, 31–32, 69, 76, 79, 120; wave/particle nature of, 73, 74, 169, 200

Logic, 4–5, 12–14, 16–18, 20, 23–27, 31, 36, 38, 44–45, 47–48, 51, 57, 59, 61–63, 73–76, 78–79, 87, 91, 95, 100–101, 103–8, 110–13, 115–16, 125, 128–33,